Praise for

The Devil's Harvest

MARIE CLAIRE AND *OXYGEN*, "BEST TRUE CRIME BOOKS OF 2020"

"A killer who hides in plain sight, a justice system that fails its most vulnerable: with her deep dive into the life and many deaths of Jose Martinez, Jessica Garrison has tapped into a story that is as haunting as it is captivating. Meticulously researched and tightly woven, *The Devil's Harvest* is an important story because it tells us that if it can happen in one place, then it can happen in any place. And that's damn scary."
—**Michael Connelly**, *New York Times* **bestselling author of** *The Closers, The Lincoln Lawyer,* **and** *The Night Fire*

"Meticulously researched…a portrait of a place as much as it's a true-crime narrative." —*Los Angeles Times*

"[A] propulsive and incisive look at a hired killer who targeted those on the margins—often poor, undocumented immigrants living in the Central Valley—told with necessary compassion."
—*The Crime Lady*

"A spellbinding account." —*Zócalo Public Square*

"An urgent, highly readable work of crime swiftly committed and justice long delayed." —*Kirkus Reviews*

"This is a powerfully addictive read from start to finish, and a first-class true-crime narrative."   —*Booklist*

"Garrison's writing is enthrallingly thriller-esque while it sheds light on real-world horrors."   —*Shelf Awareness*

"Expertly researched...In a time of great frustration with law enforcement's role in the racial divide in America, Garrison's work shows another aspect of the social disparity in policing, namely that crimes against minorities are poorly investigated. This is essential reading for true crime buffs."   —*Publishers Weekly*

"Jessica Garrison is a writer to watch. Her ease with language and graceful storytelling make her a welcome new voice on the California literary scene. This book sheds light on the neglected history of American homicide and weak justice as it plays out in migrant farmworker communities and on the distinct challenges of rural policing, which are too often overlooked in the national conversation on violent crime."

—**Jill Leovy, *New York Times* bestselling author of *Ghettoside***

"The most enduring crime narratives zoom out past individual stories of senseless murder to larger issues of societal breakdown, cruel injustice, and ripple effects upon countless lives forever fractured. *The Devil's Harvest* brilliantly depicts not only the crimes of one decades-undetected hitman, but the lives of those he murdered—often poor, undocumented immigrants, overlooked and given little thought. Jessica Garrison demonstrates, with urgency and compassion, how necessary it is that we not look away and how much these lives count above all."

—**Sarah Weinman ("The Crime Lady"), author of *The Real Lolita* and editor of *Unspeakable Acts: True Tales of Crime, Murder, Deceit, and Obsession***

"Such a rich evocation of place is a rare find in a book about a killer and his crimes. The middle of California becomes another character, as richly drawn as the cunning murderer, the dedicated but often hapless detectives who chased him, and the people—poor and hardworking—trying to seek justice."

—**Mark Arax, award-winning journalist and author of** *The Dreamt Land: Chasing Water and Dust Across California*

"With great empathy and exhaustive research, Jessica Garrison weaves a compelling tale that is equal parts detective story and social commentary. *The Devil's Harvest* is a different and much-needed California story—trenchant and timely in an era of staggering inequality."

—**Miriam Pawel, author of** *The Browns of California*

The Devil's Harvest

A Ruthless Killer, a Terrorized
Community, and the Search for Justice
in California's Central Valley

Jessica Garrison

New York

Hachette Books
Hachette Book Group
1290 Avenue of the Americas
New York, NY 10104
HachetteBooks.com
Twitter.com/HachetteBooks
Instagram.com/HachetteBooks

First Trade Paperback Edition: August 2021

Hachette Books is a division of Hachette Book Group, Inc.

The Hachette Books name and logo are trademarks of Hachette Book Group, Inc.

The publisher is not responsible for websites (or their content) that are not owned by the publisher.

The Hachette Speakers Bureau provides a wide range of authors for speaking events. To find out more, go to www.hachettespeakersbureau.com or call (866) 376-6591.

Print book interior design by Marie Mundaca.

Library of Congress Cataloging-in-Publication Data
Names: Garrison, Jessica, author.
Title: The devil's harvest : a ruthless killer, a terrorized community, and the search for justice in California's Central Valley / Jessica Garrison.
Description: First edition. | New York : Hachette Books, [2020] | Includes bibliographical references.
Identifiers: LCCN 2019055804 | ISBN 9780316455688 (hardback) | ISBN 9780316455732 (ebook)
Subjects: LCSH: Martinez, Jose Manuel, 1962– | Murderers—California—Central Valley—Case studies. | Serial murders—California—Central Valley—Case studies. | Latin Americans—Crimes against—California—Central Valley—Case studies.
Classification: LCC HV6248.M4325 G37 2020 | DDC 364.152/32092 [B] —dc23
LC record available at https://lccn.loc.gov/2019055804

ISBNs: 978-0-316-45568-8 (hardcover), 978-0-316-45574-9 (trade paperback), 978-0-316-45573-2 (ebook)

Printed in the United States of America

LSC-C

Printing 1, 2021

For Michael
And in loving memory of
Courtney Everts Mykytyn

Contents

Part Three: El Mano Negra

Part Four: Catching a Killer

Part Five: The Death Penalty

Introduction

I first heard of Jose Manuel Martinez in the spring of 2014. The Associated Press reported that a man accused of murdering nine men over a span of three decades—and suspected of killing many more—was being extradited from Alabama to California. Police believed they had caught a professional hit man.

At the time, I was an editor for the *Los Angeles Times*, and I dispatched the paper's Fresno correspondent seventy miles south down Highway 99 to Tulare County—the heart of California's farm belt—to see what she could learn. After the report ran, I found I could not stop thinking about his case.

How could someone get away with murder after murder for more than thirty years while living in a sleepy, close-knit farmworker town where everyone knew everyone else?

Eventually, Martinez himself would explain it to me. He was "so damn good," he'd say. He left little evidence and few witnesses.

This was true but far from the whole story. Martinez, I learned, had been born and raised in California's vast Central Valley, which stretches about 450 miles down the interior of the state and is one of the richest farming regions in the world. He came from its stark and beautiful southern end, known as the San Joaquin Valley, where the peaks of the Sierra Nevada march upward toward their apex at Mount Whitney and where, down on the valley floor, any notion of California as a progressive, egalitarian land of opportunity disintegrates under the relentless, baking sun.[1]

Nearly half the fruits and nuts that Americans eat are grown here, in lavishly irrigated fields that roll out like a green carpet across the once-arid land.[2] In the cities and towns of the valley, meanwhile, something terrible has borne fruit: income disparity that is greater than anywhere else in California.[3] There are neighborhoods in Visalia and Exeter where those who have grown wealthy off the land live ensconced in homes with infinity pools, butler's pantries, and en suite bathrooms for every bedroom.[4] Just a few miles away, in the towns where the people who do the picking and planting live, homes are often crowded and dilapidated and the water that comes out of the taps is often not safe to drink.[5]

This is where John Steinbeck set his Depression-era classic *The Grapes of Wrath* and where, in the 1960s, Cesar Chavez launched his crusade to organize farmworkers, drawing the support of national politicians, activists, and celebrities. Yet even now, in the third decade of the twenty-first century, the Central Valley, particularly the San Joaquin Valley, remains a disturbing tableau of American inequality.

Growing up here to witness routine exploitation, shocking violence, and seemingly capricious police officers, Martinez assessed the circumstances and decided murder for hire was a reasonable way to make a living. And his greatest asset as a killer, it became clear to me, was that he had grasped a dark truth about the American justice system: if you kill the "right people"—people who are poor, who are not white, who may be presumed to be criminals themselves, and who don't have anyone to speak for them—you can get away with it. "El Mano Negra,"[6] the Black Hand, as Martinez was known, had found an ideal place to ply his trade.

Cecilia Camacho, a relative of one of Martinez's victims, knew this truth as well as Martinez. "There is no follow-through when the [victim] is from Mexico. We didn't have papers. We didn't have the means to speak up for ourselves."[7]

It was a familiar refrain. As I dug into the case, I tracked down other family members of Martinez's victims, their anguish and loss not lessened over the years or decades since their loved ones were killed. But I was struck most by how they had carried their suffering without public protest. Many say they were silenced not so much by fear of El Mano Negra as by the conviction that no one in power—not the police brass or the elected officials or the media—really cared what had happened to their fathers, brothers, husbands, and sons. Or to their communities.

Year after year, Martinez operated with impunity. In Tulare County, where he lived for decades, officials suspected him of murder after murder and yet never charged him. Next-door Kern County, where he also lived for a time and committed several murders, has one of the highest murder rates in California and one of the lowest murder-solve rates in the nation. Martinez's hometown of Earlimart—a tightly woven community where people knew each other's stories and watched out for each other's children—was also so violent, some nicknamed it "Murdermart." In other places, Martinez killed people in out-of-the-way areas and then vanished before anyone thought to look for him.

Eventually, after speaking with victims' family members and the police officers who investigated those cases, I reached out to Martinez himself. I addressed a letter to him, care of the jail where he was awaiting trial. I have written many such letters to prisons in my years as a reporter, and I knew better than to expect a response. But a few weeks later, my phone rang.

"How are you?" Martinez asked me. I was flustered, then stunned, as so many police officers had been before me, by how personable this cold-blooded killer sounded. "What do you want to know?"

At that point, I knew only the broad outlines of Martinez's story. I knew he had killed many people in a place where justice had always been in short supply. I also knew from police that he was a devoted father and grandfather who lived to make the children in his family laugh.

I told Martinez I was interested in why he had murdered so many people and how he had gotten away with it. I told him that I was curious, too, about how he could kill without remorse, sometimes, it seemed, even with relish, and at the same time be so generous toward his family.

He paused for a moment, and then he laughed ruefully. "It's a long story," he said.

From behind bars, he sat for numerous phone interviews and then arranged for me to review an astonishing document—a four-hundred-page memoir in his careful, round-lettered handwriting. It is by turns a sickening account of cold-blooded murder and a moving tale of family bonds. Martinez wants to be entertaining, and he often is. But he does not hide the fact that he is brutally, remorselessly violent.

His story also follows the sweep of nearly a half century of Central Valley history—the epic grape strikes of the 1960s and 1970s, the rise of drug cartels in the 1980s, the anti-immigrant sentiment of the 1990s, and the growing opportunities for political, economic, and social change of the 2000s.

As I read his account of his life and studied the police reports of his murders, as I sat with members of his family and the families of his victims, I came to believe that Martinez's improbable thirty-five-year run of murder and mayhem reflects a far more widespread injustice.

The Devil's Harvest is the tale of Jose Martinez's reign of terror. But it is also the story of a community and how the institutions that were supposed to protect that community failed again and again—as they do in many places across the United States.

Some lives count more than others, and nothing reveals this as starkly as death.

PART ONE

Murder for Hire

1980

Sgt. Christal Derington, Tulare County Sheriff's Department: *First of all, I hear you have a new one?*

Jose Martinez: *Yeah, I forgot about him.*

Derington: *What was his name?*

Martinez: *I don't know his name....I got that one when he was going to work. He was driving and he had five passengers. Good thing nobody else got hurt. I shot him in the head with a .22.*

—Partial transcript of police interrogation,
June 19, 2013, 9:07 a.m.

Chapter One

J ose Martinez woke up on June 13, 1980, intent on transporting himself from the crime and poverty of his childhood into a new and noble future. It was his eighteenth birthday, and he was going to mark it by joining the US Marines.

Martinez had dreamed of being a soldier since he was a little boy, idolizing his uncles who had fought for the United States overseas. The discipline and brotherhood of the armed forces appealed to him, not to mention the status and security of being part of the greatest military in the world. To shoot and kill for country and glory—what could be better?[1]

He'd spent countless hours practicing for it. Roaming the banks of the Deer Creek ditch near his stepfather's ranch, he blasted targets, rabbits, and raccoons with the gun his stepdad had given him. He was an excellent shot. He was also a fierce and brutal fighter. Martinez had a gentle, joking disposition, with a mischievous smile that flashed easily and often across his face, lighting up his brown eyes. But his temper was vicious, especially if he felt disrespected. All this, he figured, would make him a perfect marine.

"You should come with me," Martinez said to his wife. She

agreed, as he knew she would.[2] They'd been together since he was fifteen years old, around the time he had dropped out of school to take a larger role in his stepfather's smuggling operations running heroin across the Mexican border and up through California. Their courtship had begun—according to him; his first wife has not provided her account—when she came from Mexico to work for his mother. They dated for a while, and then "one day I told her, if she really loves me, she must elope with me." He put her in his car and refused to let her out. Then he took her to Disneyland for their honeymoon. His wife made him feel secure and happy. He wanted her—and their toddler son—to witness this important moment. After all, the whole family was embarking on this adventure.

When his son had been born, Martinez had held the tiny boy up, marveling at this creature he had created, and kissed him over and over again. "Son, don't be proud of me," he whispered. "I'm a real criminal and a drug dealer."

But becoming a marine was noble.

Martinez and his family piled into his brand-new black Ford LTD—he'd paid for it in cash because the drug business was that good—and drove forty-five minutes south from their home in Tulare County to the US Marine recruitment center in Bakersfield.

Martinez walked in and found a recruiter. "I'm here to sign up," he said, as his wife stood beside him with their son in her arms. "I know how to shoot real good."

He neglected to mention something else that he thought would make him a good marine: he knew he had the nerve to kill when necessary. He had already done it once. When Martinez was sixteen, his older half sister had been raped and murdered, her body dumped on the banks of the Salton Sea, an inland desert lake in Southern California. A few weeks after the funeral, Martinez left his wife and the rest of his extended family, all reeling from grief, and drove four hours south. He brought with him a friend and an M1 carbine with a thirty-round clip and soon found the house where his sister had last been seen. Three men were inside, laughing and playing cards. "All 3 motherfuckers die," he wrote in his memoir. It was one of his proudest moments. He had taken the powerlessness and rage of his grief and—bang-bang-bang— squeezing the trigger made him feel magically better: powerful, able to protect his family. "It feels good to take vengeance," he explained. "It feels good to kill and the heart relaxes a bit."

Obviously, he couldn't tell the recruiter about this. Instead, he said he was sure he had what it took.

Martinez had thought about what life in the marines would be like. Ronald Reagan, California's former governor, was just weeks away from clinching the Republican nomination for president in a campaign staked in part on restoring glory to the armed forces. In the farmworker communities of the San Joaquin Valley where Martinez had grown up, some people still bitterly recalled how Reagan had sided with growers against farmworkers during the grape strike. But Martinez didn't pay much attention to politics. He wanted to be a fighter. Invulnerable. Fearsome. Respected. All the things farmworkers were not allowed to be. Maybe he would join the Special Forces. He might even be stationed at Camp Pendleton, the marine base near San Diego. That would be nice for his family, to live by the beach while he was overseas fighting for his country.

It would be a real change from where they were living at the moment: Earlimart, with a population of about forty-five hundred that could swell during the harvest, was one of the poorest of the poor farmworker communities that dotted this southern end of the valley.

Martinez's grandmother had been the first in the family to settle here, leaving Mexico after her husband was shot dead in a dispute over a card game in the mountains of Durango. Working in the fields, she met and married a Filipino American farmworker, which enabled her and her Mexican-born children to become legal US residents and eventually citizens. Citizenship offered some small protections. You could not be deported if you complained about not being paid, for example. But farmwork was still backbreaking, often exploitive work, as sixteen-year-old Loreto, Martinez's mother, learned when she joined his grandmother in the fields in 1959. Farmworkers were excluded from virtually all health, safety, and labor laws. They were paid as little as the market allowed, and they could be fired at will. There were no bathrooms and no clean drinking water in the fields. The bosses often treated the workers with contempt, like just another easily replaceable farm implement.[3]

It had always been this way, no matter who picked the crops. Before Mexicans became the dominant workers in the fields, there had been waves of Chinese, Japanese, and Filipino farmworkers. Only when many farmworkers had been white, during the Great Depression, when hundreds of thousands of "Okies" fled the Dust Bowl, did their plight garner national attention.[4]

Martinez's mother married a man from her home village, a relative on her mother's side who already had two girls from a first marriage. In short order, Loreto and her much older husband built a family. Martinez had an older sister born in 1960. He came along in 1962, and two more brothers and two more sisters followed.

Sometimes, farmworkers sent their American-born children to Mexico to be cared for by relatives while they worked in the fields. When Jose Martinez was about six, he and four siblings were installed in Cosalá, Sinaloa, a cobblestoned town of pastel buildings and mango trees high in the Sierra Madre, where his parents had family. The children landed there just as the area was becoming a center of the drug world. By the mid-1970s, about 90 percent of the heroin sold in the United States came from Mexico's Sierra Madre.[5] The Martinez children had a front-row seat as the business—and its attendant violence and corruption— began to boom.[6]

By the time the siblings returned to California around 1972, their parents were on the verge of divorce. Their mother, Loreto, soon after married a man named Pedro Fernandez. Their new stepfather was much better off than their father: he was not a farmworker; he was a farm labor contractor, hiring crews for farmers who needed crops planted, tended, or picked. He was also a drug smuggler, one of the biggest in the San Joaquin Valley. The family's new home, on a ranch on the outskirts of Earlimart, was the center of Fernandez's massive smuggling operation, frequented by many who would go on to play prominent roles in the drug trade on both sides of the border for years to come.

Meanwhile, in the vineyards that rolled out in every direction just beyond the ranch, another larger-than-life story was taking shape. Cesar Chavez and Dolores Huerta were leading farmworkers in one of the greatest civil rights movements of the twentieth century: the epic battle to organize a farmworkers union. Chavez lived and worked out of a house in Delano just a few miles down the road from Earlimart. Born in Arizona to Mexican immigrants, he had worked the migrant farmworker circuit as a child after his family lost their land. After a decade as a community organizer, Chavez had moved to the valley in 1962, just a few years after Martinez's mother, and he and Huerta had set out to show its poorest workers they could take on its most powerful industry. In 1965, when Filipino grape workers like Martinez's step-grandfather went on strike, the fledgling union of Mexican Americans joined the battle. Over the next few years, the United Farm Workers transformed the strike from a local labor dispute into a global cause. Political icons like Robert Kennedy, celebrities like Joan Baez, and legions of other volunteers streamed down Highway 99, through Earlimart into Delano, to support and cover *la causa*. In 1965, before the strike, farmworkers earned, on average, less than $1.50 an hour. After a five-year strike and boycott, Chavez's movement brought increased pay, job protections, and—just as crucial—a sense of dignity and power to Mexicans and Mexican Americans across the valley and beyond.[7]

The change was not always easy, or always peaceful. Growers, threatened by the demands that were upending the economic and social order, used every available power to quash the rebellion, including their influence with law enforcement. With little or no provocation, the Tulare and Kern County Sheriff's Departments marched into the fields with their batons drawn and squared off against workers in brutal clashes.[8]

Martinez saw Chavez around Delano as a child and admired him. He was offended by the violence the police had unleashed on the farmworkers, most of whom, he knew, worked from dawn to dusk to put food on the table. But whatever their sympathies, the Fernandez-Martinez clan did not join Chavez's United Farm Workers of America. After all, they were running a criminal enterprise—smuggling not just drugs but also undocumented immigrants across the border. They tried to stay out of the fray.

Eventually, the law caught up with them anyway. One morning in the summer of 1977, a drug task force descended. Police officers emerged from the grape vineyards and invaded the property with their guns drawn. Before long they had found several stashed guns and three kilos of heroin, worth approximately $2.5 million in 1977 dollars, hidden in a bag of dog food. This raid—prompted, some said, by a tip from a person with ties to a rival drug operation—resulted in one of the largest heroin seizures to date in Central Valley history.[9] Martinez's stepfather wound up at Lompoc federal prison, and Martinez, then fifteen, wound up with a larger role in the family business.

Obviously, Martinez wasn't going to mention this to the military recruiter either.

But it turned out the recruiter had a few questions in a

different, equally unwelcome arena. To start: Did Martinez have a high school diploma?

He did not. Martinez's mother—whose own chance at an education had been derailed by pregnancy at a young age—considered schooling one of America's greatest gifts. Some of Martinez's younger siblings excelled in school. But Martinez had moved so many times in his childhood, from school in Mexico and then back to a four-room schoolhouse that sat in the fields not far from Earlimart, that his education had been disrupted. On top of all the skipped days and switching back and forth between English and Spanish, he often had to miss school to make drug runs for his stepfather. He missed his middle school graduation to pick up his very first heroin shipment at a Greyhound bus station.

There was also the not insignificant matter of his temper. He fought. On the school bus. On campus. Defending his sisters' honor or because someone pissed him off. Eventually he got suspended, then dropped out. He was only fourteen or fifteen, too young to drive legally. But far from urging him to complete his education, his stepfather gave him a 1969 Ford Galaxy and a job delivering drugs.

Sitting there in the recruitment center in Bakersfield, Martinez told the recruiter the truth: I didn't get past ninth grade, he admitted.

The recruiter delivered a crushing piece of news: he'd need a high school diploma or a GED before he could enlist. The recruiter might as well have said Martinez needed a graduate degree in astrophysics. With his stepfather locked up, his entire family was depending on him to keep the drug business going. Protecting and caring for his family was what Martinez had always done, from watching out for his younger siblings in Mexico to hunting down and killing those he believed responsible for his half sister's death. Reality hit: he could never put that aside to study for some giant test he might not even pass so that he could join the military and leave his family.

Martinez registered for the marines anyway. "Just in case you need me," he said. Then, he and his family drove straight to Sears, where he bought a book that the recruiter had mentioned about how to be a marine. Martinez read it so often that forty years later, he could still vividly recall bits of its instruction, such as the purpose and mechanics of simple bridge building.

Even so, he felt his dream of becoming a marine dying inside him. As he drove home, the flat monotony of the fields stretched out in every direction, and the disappointment pushed down on him. He and his wife had a second child fast on the way. He needed a new plan.

A few months later an opportunity presented itself. Martinez had a baby girl now, along with his little boy, and he was at home on the night of October 20, 1980, when a friend dropped by. Fall was finally coming. The grape harvest was winding down, the olives were coming in, and while the days were still hot, the nights brought a hint that winter would soon arrive.

While his wife and children slept in the bedroom, Martinez and his friend smoked a joint, and the friend confided his problem.

Back in Mexico, a man had raped his little sister. He needed help getting revenge. And he was willing to pay good money for it. Martinez said he didn't ask any questions. Not who the alleged rapist was or how the friend could be so sure he was the one. Certainly not whether vigilante murder was the appropriate response. He thought of his own dead sister. He felt the rage rise up in him. And the possibilities.

Chapter Two

A hint of light was just beginning to glow behind the mighty wall of the Sierra Nevada mountains in the east on the morning of October 21, 1980, but sunrise was still a way off. The roads were dark and peaceful at this time of day, and in the back of the car Cecilia Camacho's brother-in-law and cousin grabbed a little more sleep before a long day picking olives.

In the front passenger seat, Cecilia was awake. Her husband, David Bedolla, was driving, and she was keeping him company. She was twenty-one, and he was twenty-three. They were poor and undocumented, but they had big dreams and a young son back home with her parents in Mexico who was depending on them to work hard in the fields of California to build a better life for him.

They were chatting quietly in their dark car, when suddenly they were blinded by bright headlights behind them. Then there was the roar of an engine as a vehicle sped up beside them.

Cecilia heard loud popping noises.

The driver's side window shattered, and sparks flew up at them from the other car. Her husband slumped sideways onto her lap.[1]

Their car careened off the road and plowed into a vineyard, hurtling through rows of vines before finally shuddering to a stop.

It took Cecilia a moment to understand what was going on. Someone had shot at them. There were two bullets lodged in the windshield.

Two more had hit her husband in the head. He was bleeding and gasping for air.

Shocked and frantic, Cecilia and her husband's brother got David out of the driver's seat and into the backseat. Her husband's brother, panting, started the car. They had to get David home. Or to a hospital. They had to get him somewhere.

Then, their misfortune compounded. Their car engine sputtered out. Damaged by its off-road venture, it refused to start again.

Desperate, Cecilia stood on the side of the road and tried to flag someone down.

Nearly four decades later, sitting at her dining room table recounting the events of that morning, Cecilia stared into the middle distance, oblivious of her grandchildren scampering and laughing around her. She was trying to be careful, precise, to get every detail right. At times, she looked across the table, past the shrine to the Virgin, and out the window of the house she shared with her second husband and her family. Her home was comfortable and well kept—clearly the reward of decades of hard work. And yet, beyond the beautifully tended front yard, it seemed as if the shooting and its horrible aftermath were still in plain view.

After a few long moments on the side of the road, as her husband lay gasping in the backseat, Cecilia managed to get a car to pull over. It was a couple heading to Los Angeles.

"My husband is hurt," Cecilia cried. "Please help us take him home."

Their good Samaritans assessed the situation and mentally rearranged their plans for the day. "I think you need to go to the hospital," the man said.[2]

They reached Lindsay District Hospital at about 6:30 a.m., but the small facility could not treat David. Doctors almost immediately transferred him to the Kaweah Delta Hospital in Exeter, one of the wealthiest towns in Tulare County, home to many of the farmers who owned the orange orchards that rolled across the hills.

Cecilia found a seat in the waiting room. She was shaking. Her beautiful husband. The father of her child. Why would anyone shoot at him?

After eighteen months of hard labor picking oranges and olives, she and David had saved nearly enough money to build a proper house back in Mexico. She couldn't wait to go home and be reunited with her baby.

Cecilia was from one of the poorest families in a place where everyone knew poverty: La Excusa, Puruandiro, in the state of Michoacán. Her family was so poor that she'd had to leave school after the second grade just to help her parents put food on the table.

As she grew into her teens, she fell for green-eyed David Bedolla, two years her senior and also working the fields to help support his eleven siblings. He was handsome, but it wasn't just that. Whereas she was serious, he was always smiling. But he had a certain gravity to him. He too knew what it was like to have to quit school to help your family, and he too wanted more than their little town could provide.

They became a couple when she was fifteen and got married just before her nineteenth birthday, with a son already on the way. But well-paying work was hard to find. David concluded that if he wanted to make enough money to support his growing family, he would have to leave. He had family up in California, in Tulare County, in a town called Lindsay tucked into the base of scrubby foothills that rose higher and higher into the peaks of the southern Sierra Nevada mountains. Even when it was so hot down in the valley that you could burn your skin on the pavement, the tops of those mountains glinted with ice and snow.

David set out to work there but was soon deported. Cecilia wasn't sure of the circumstances—the important thing was he was back by her side in time for the birth of their son.

The next time he went north, Cecilia went with him, leaving their son with her parents. They could make more money working together. Back then, the border did not present much of an obstacle. Mexican workers had been crossing for fieldwork in California and Arizona for decades. Often, they came legally, through guest-worker programs that allowed agricultural workers to enter the United States for temporary or seasonal jobs.[3] But others crossed without authorization, often walking through the desert in the company of a coyote, or smuggler, or slipping through a hole cut in the chain-link border fence.

Even if caught, the workers usually weren't charged with a crime. The Border Patrol merely returned them to the other side of the line, where, often, they would try again. In 1977, the year Cecilia's husband was returned to Mexico, nearly one million other people were too.[4]

Cecilia and David didn't know the finer points of US immigration policy, but they knew this: they could get across. If not on the first try, then on the second or the third. After all, David's parents, along with several of his brothers and cousins, were already in California, as were Cecilia's sister and at least one of her cousins. David and Cecilia knew something else: when they did get across, farmers would be only too happy to hire them and wouldn't be asking any questions about whether they had legal permission to work.

In January 1979, Cecilia and David made their way north, then paid a coyote $200 each to take them across "the line," through the desert near San Luis Río Colorado, Mexico, and Yuma, Arizona. They made the run when darkness fell, racing through high grasses wet with dew. It took them a full night to walk from the Mexican side to the place where their coyote had arranged for them to be picked up. Cecilia felt anxious. Would they make it? What if everything she'd heard about crossing was wrong? Would her husband be in more trouble if he were caught again? And if they did make it across, what then? What would life in the United States be like?

Thankfully, the crossing went smoothly. They reached the pickup spot, scrambled into the coyote's car, and drove north out of the desert, up into the mountains, and down into the San Joaquin Valley to Lindsay.

David had arranged for them to move into a boarding house where some relatives also rented rooms. By American standards, it was a study in poverty and deprivation. But Cecilia noticed that everything was made of wood—a step up from the rock-and-mud dwellings at home.

They went to work harvesting oranges almost immediately. Cecilia had worked in the fields in Mexico since she was a child, but the work here was harder and so much more monotonous. You had to climb up a ladder with a fifty-pound sack around your neck and balance precariously as you pulled oranges off the branches, trying and failing not to get poked and scratched by the sharp citrus thorns. When the sack was full, you climbed down and dumped the fruit into a box. It took twelve full sacks to fill one box. And for each box the farmer paid a mere $5.

After the oranges were done, the grapes came in. Grapes were even harder, because they ripened in summer, when the temperature in the valley often climbed up above one hundred degrees. The olive harvest followed the grapes: better weather but the same hard work. California's landmark Agricultural Labor Relations Act of 1975 had been designed to protect field hands, establishing a right to unionize. There were also procedures for reporting abuse, such as bosses who didn't pay what they were supposed to or tried to exploit their workers. But for people like Cecilia and David, it made little difference. If they were mistreated, whom could they tell? They were not members of Cesar Chavez's United Farm Workers. And government inspectors certainly weren't hanging around trying to improve working conditions. Quite the opposite: the local governments tended to side with the farmers, and everyone knew it.

It had been this way for a long time. In 1949, historian Carey McWilliams had surveyed conditions in the Central Valley and observed, "The farm labor problem is the cancer which lies beneath the beauty, richness and fertility of the valleys of California." The farmworker, he added, is "often disenfranchised, consistently unrepresented, and on many occasions, brutally repressed."[5] Seventy-five years before that, McWilliams pointed out, journalists from San Francisco's *Morning Chronicle* had found conditions so deplorable that they observed, "In many respects…it is even worse than old time slavery."[6]

Cecilia and David were not about to agitate for change. They were undocumented. They kept a low profile. In the wider world, the national media was increasingly using words like "crisis," "flood," and even "invasion" to describe the arrival of immigrants from Mexico.[7] Even in Tulare County, whose entire agricultural economy depended on immigrants, anti-immigrant sentiment sometimes bubbled up into open hostility—and violence. On the last Sunday afternoon in August 1980, two months before David Bedolla's murder, an angry crowd of people had attacked two young men with branches, bottles, and knives in a park not far from where Cecilia and David lived—because they were undocumented workers, according to the local newspaper.[8]

Still, Cecilia and David had no other option but to work as much as they could. They labored side by side, each dumping what they picked into the same box and then turning the boxes in at the end of the day for wages. Together, they earned about $200 per week: some went to rent and food, some they sent back home for their son, and some they saved for their future house.

By October 1980, they had worked through two seasons of

oranges and two seasons of grapes. They were almost done with their second season of olives, and then they would go home, build their house, and be with their son.

Except Cecilia began to perceive that something strange and menacing was going on. One morning as she and David left for work at 4:45 a.m., Cecilia noticed an unfamiliar car parked across the street. "It's just the neighbor's new car," David said. She didn't believe him.

Around this time, one of her husband's brothers—impulsive, maybe violent; fond of alcohol, maybe drugs—showed up at the boarding house without warning. Cecilia had some inkling that the brother was involved in bad things, maybe even in the drug trade. But she didn't ask questions—it seemed safer not to know. The brother seemed almost panicked, whispering to his parents about something urgent, then stopping the moment Cecilia walked in.

At one point, three strangers showed up looking for David's brother. Cecilia's mother-in-law, not a woman to be trifled with, sent them away.

A little while later, on the way to her sister's house, a car again seemed to be following Cecilia and David. David stayed outside while Cecilia went in for a visit; when she returned, she found him slumped in his seat as though in despair.

"Take care of our son," he said. "I feel like I'm going somewhere, but I don't know where." He wouldn't tell her what he meant.

Only a few days later, on the way to work in the predawn gray, the end came at last. Now, Cecilia sat in the hospital waiting room, reeling from shock.

After what seemed like hours but may have been only a few minutes, a police officer came to find her. Speaking perfect Spanish and wearing an intimidating frown, he introduced himself as Detective Ralph Diaz of the Tulare County Sheriff's Department.

Forty years later, Cecilia still can't believe what he said to her.

Your husband has been shot, he said. Why aren't you crying?

Chapter Three

The call came into the Tulare County Sheriff's Department at 6:56 a.m. It was flagged as "a 217," California penal code for assault with a deadly weapon, "believed at any time to turn into a 187"—murder. David Bedolla was the victim, and he was not expected to live much longer.

By 7:20 a.m., Detective Sergeant Robert Byrd and Detective Ralph Diaz arrived at Kaweah Delta Hospital. Bedolla lay on a table, his naked torso studded with an IV and heart-monitor tabs, bleeding from his head while a nurse performed CPR. On his left arm, which was muscled from work in the fields, Byrd saw a single tattoo of the letter *B* in blue ink.

The doctor on duty bustled by, made a quick examination, and told Byrd that nothing could be done. No surgery could save Bedolla. He was going to die.

Byrd took the time to write a few notes about Bedolla and his possessions—he wore two black work boots, two white socks, and one pair of blue trousers, with one nickel in the right front pocket. Then he and Diaz went to find Cecilia.

The first order of business was to correct an earlier

misunderstanding. Not speaking Spanish, the officers who initially interviewed Cecilia's brother-in-law had misunderstood the location of the shooting, thinking it was where the car had sputtered to a stop during the frantic drive to find help. So Diaz piled Cecilia into the car to find out where the bullets had actually been fired.

They drove along country highways past the fruit stand and the gas station, until they spotted where the tire tracks ran off the road. Diaz got out of his car and took in the shattered glass littering the roadway and petering off like a trail of dusty diamonds onto the dirt shoulder. He traced the Bedolla car's path into the vineyard, weaving through the bent and broken grapevines. Finally, Diaz spotted a baseball cap with blood on it.

Martinez was back home by then. That morning, before the shooting, he and his friend had parked outside the boarding house where Cecilia and David lived and watched as they headed to work. When their car pulled out, Martinez and his friend followed them.

Martinez watched his bullets flash into Bedolla's car, smiling as the wounded man's vehicle hurtled off the road into vines. He felt a surge of exhilaration. He and his friend continued north on County Road 65, "driving normal like nothing ever happened," he would later write.

He said a prayer that Bedolla—although he wouldn't learn his name for decades—was dead or dying. "Or else I won't get paid," he later wrote. He also noted, with a small amount of satisfaction, that his bullets hadn't hit anyone else in the car.

But what he really cared about, he said, was that he had helped his friend achieve vengeance. Avenging rape, Martinez insisted, was the reason he had so readily agreed to the job in the first place. The rape of a sister. It was intolerable. He thought of his own sister. Maybe his friend had known that he would.

His older half sister had been like a second mother to him,

loving and protective. When she had asked him for a ride to visit a friend in Southern California, he had happily taken her there. She had been killed. He had been devastated.

At his sister's funeral, Martinez had stood next to his father. He had not seen him in some time.

"I'm going to get those motherfuckers," the son said.

His father's answer: "Son, let God take care of them."

Martinez shook his head. "Dad, God ain't gonna do shit."

Before he was a killer, before he was even a drug dealer, he was—above all else—a protector of women and children, most of all those in his family.

It had always been this way. When he and his siblings had been sent to live in Mexico, he stole food for them when there wasn't enough. And when punishments were doled out, Jose stepped up and took the beatings meant for his siblings to spare them the pain. Martinez didn't like to recall this—he didn't like to dwell on the unhappy stories of his childhood—but his siblings never forgot it, and they never stopped feeling gratitude.[1]

The protection continued when they returned to California, to their stepfather's ranch. His parents' divorce—which from the children's perspective came suddenly—was confusing. Nothing was explained to them. One of Martinez's younger sisters thought for years that Pedro Fernandez was actually her biological father, not her stepfather. Although her parents and her older siblings knew the truth, for whatever reason no one told her. The older children learned, at some point much later, an even more startling fact: their mother and father were not just husband and wife but also related. By some accounts, their mother had been all but forced into marriage before she was sixteen years old.[2]

Their mother's new relationship, while much happier, held its own confusions. In some ways, life on the ranch with Pedro Fernandez was a huge improvement, with more money and fantastic gifts like guns and motorcycles. But there was also the danger of

Fernandez's associates. Somewhere between thirty and sixty men worked for Martinez's stepfather in various capacities, from picking grapes on his work crews to helping with his drug-smuggling and coyote businesses. Many lived on the ranch, in the stables and the barn. They liked to party. There was always drinking. Martinez's sisters were dispatched to sell beer to the men. As the men drank, some of them would grab at the young girls. Sometimes they did more than grab.

Finally, one of Martinez's middle sisters could take no more. She, much more than her older siblings, had found a world outside the ranch and her family's various criminal enterprises. She had fallen in love with reading and had a teacher who took an interest in her studies and her future. But the contrast between her school life and the near-weekly terror of assault by drunk men got to be too much. In despair and feeling trapped, one weekend she cut her own wrists.

Her brother Antonio saw the marks, demanded to know what had happened, and went straight to their older brother. After that, "the molestations stopped," the sister said.[3] She didn't know exactly what Martinez had done, only that the offending ranch hands left.

His protective instinct was deep-seated. But according to Martinez, his sister's murder flipped a switch in him.

"I was a nice man until they killed my sister," he said in one of my first conversations with him. He gave the same explanation to detective after detective. "When they raped my sister, they left her in the middle of the desert. It's something that God doesn't want to happen."

So, on that night in the fall of 1980, Martinez said, when his friend offered him the chance to kill another alleged rapist and get *paid* for it, he saw no need to hesitate, to ask more questions, to demand proof, or even to think too hard about it.

The Tulare County Sheriff's Department officials said they have no record that Bedolla ever committed sexual assault.

*   *   *

As the sun rose higher on the morning of Bedolla's shooting, Detective Diaz summoned officers to process the crime scene and other officers to take Cecilia to the sheriff's substation in Porterville to sit for a more formal interview.

Then he got in his car and went off to interview Bedolla's family.

The case was shaping up to be a tricky one: bullets fired into a dark car on a deserted road by an unknown assailant didn't yield a lot of physical evidence. The crime scene likely would not tell them who had done it. Figuring that out would require understanding the victim and why someone might want him dead. Diaz hoped the victim's family would be able to shed some light.

Diaz had some distinct advantages as he pointed his car toward the town of Lindsay and the boarding house where the family lived. Not only did he speak Spanish, which many detectives did not, but he also knew farmworker communities intimately. He had grown up in one. Born in Tulare County to Mexican American parents, he had spent part of his childhood in the old labor camp run by the Redbanks Packing Company, amid orchards of peaches and almonds stretching out like a great green blanket north of the Tulare County town of Woodlake. His parents and his elder siblings worked in the orchards or in the packinghouse or both.

After high school, Diaz had served in Vietnam, where he was awarded a Bronze Star for meritorious service. After a stint in the Woodlake Police Department, he landed in the Tulare County Sheriff's Department in 1977.[4]

Detective Diaz was part of the first great wave of Latino law enforcement officers in the valley.[5] This integration was happening in departments up and down California, pushed by a federal mandate. In Tulare, the new Mexican American officers had been greeted with words like "wetback" and told that Mexicans were stupid.

Detective Diaz never let on, at least not widely among his colleagues and bosses, if he was bothered by racism or disturbed when people called Mexicans stupid or wetbacks. He did, however, serve as a founding member of the Tulare County Latino Peace Officers Association, an organization that advocated for more recruitment and better treatment of Latino officers.

As a police officer, former colleagues remembered, Diaz went above and beyond. He got to work early, always meticulously dressed—first in his uniform and, once he made detective, in a three-piece suit with the snake-skin cowboy boots favored by all members of the sheriff's department, Anglos and Mexicans. On long nights at murder scenes, he came prepared with burritos he made at home, then wrapped in foil and packed under the hood of his car next to the engine to keep warm. A cigarette almost always dangled from his lips.

His talents were obvious from the start and included an astonishing memory. For faces. For places. For the little details in people's stories that shifted over time and provided clues about what they might be hiding.

And because he was short, skinny, and unassuming, he developed a way of slipping into rooms and conversations, quietly watching until he gained his listeners' trust or they forgot he was there and revealed more than they intended.

The interview with the Bedolla family was no exception. Diaz left it bursting with new information.

Cecilia was in the bathroom when Diaz returned to the Porterville substation. She hadn't even come out before she realized that something had changed.

Are you trying to escape? Detective Diaz was shouting and banging hard on the door. Open this door! Let me in![6]

Escape? What was he talking about? "Can you please wait?" Cecilia asked. "I'm using the restroom."

When she came out, she saw that his face was contorted with anger.

Do you see your dead husband? Diaz asked her. Don't you want to cry?

"I don't want to cry," she answered. The enormity of what she felt was too much for mere tears.

Do you know what just happened to your husband? he demanded. Did your lover do it?

Cecilia started in astonishment. Her lover? She didn't have a lover.

Diaz told her that he had talked to her mother-in-law. And her mother-in-law had told Diaz that her son had no enemies; therefore, the only possible motive could be that Cecilia had a boyfriend and was trying to get her husband out of the way.

Diaz was likely floating a balloon. With little physical evidence and no clear reason why anyone would want Bedolla dead, the detective was pushing on every lead he could get, however unlikely. But Cecilia didn't know this. Waves of anxiety pulsed through her, breaking against the numb shell she had formed around her. Her mother-in-law had never liked her, had at times seemed almost jealous of her, but to suggest she had been unfaithful? And that she and some fanciful lover had conspired to kill David?

She fought for breath. Her husband had been murdered in front of her eyes. She was twenty-one years old. She was stuck in this violent, terrifying country all by herself now. She had a toddler son at home in Mexico and no way to provide for him. And now, all of a sudden, this angry police officer was accusing her of an unspeakable crime. What was she going to do?

Cecilia took a breath and collected herself. "I had nothing to do with this," she told the officer. "As God is my witness."

And then, though she was a frightened, grief-stricken young woman in the country without permission, she mustered the ferocious courage that had allowed her to come to California to build a better life for her son and would allow her to keep going now that her husband was dead. She told the detective, "Your theory makes no sense. If I did have a lover, would I really tell him to shoot my husband while he was driving a car that I was a passenger in?"

Diaz, she said, had no answer to that. Finally, he let her go home.

Chapter Four

Cecilia returned to Mexico with her husband's body. A hearse met them at the airport, and they set out, first across highways, then roads, and finally bumpy dirt tracks.

She had dreamed of a joyful and triumphant return with her husband at her side and enough money to build their own house. Instead, she was coming to tell her son that there would be no house and that he no longer had a father.

She settled into her parents' home. It was grim. Depressed and poor, she took in other people's washing, but it was never enough, and she went to bed each night and woke up each morning anxious that she would not be able to feed her son. It felt like her future had been stolen from her. Who had killed her husband? And why?

Her husband's family had also returned after the murder, and a few months after she arrived home, she was at her mother-in-law's house. One of her husband's brothers was also there, talking to a friend.

"I am the one who should be dead," she heard him say. His friend responded that the brother should be ashamed of himself.

This brother, who had been sitting in the back of the car during the shooting. This brother, whose sudden appearance at Cecilia and David's home a week before the murder had seemed to presage the terror and anxiety that consumed them. This brother, who, Cecilia suspected, might have been involved with drugs and who, just before the murder, had been visited by strange, angry men.

Cecilia froze. She didn't know what it meant, but it didn't sound good. Still, she didn't ask any questions or even reveal that she had overheard the conversation. She was afraid.

At some point, she got in touch with Diaz by phone and reported what she had heard.

What Diaz thought about the information, she never found out. She didn't speak to him again for more than thirty years.

Back in Tulare County, Detective Diaz already had more leads than anyone might know what to do with.

There had been a second car-to-car shooting the same day Bedolla was murdered. Was that significant?

What about the fact that Bedolla had gotten into a fight a couple of weeks before his death?

And then there was this: two of Bedolla's cousins—or maybe they were second cousins—had been arrested in yet another murder in Tulare County in 1978. Surely that had to be relevant?

On November 10, about three weeks after the murder, Diaz got a strange phone call relating yet another lead, yet more suspects, yet more brutal violence. The caller said that the car Bedolla had been driving at the time of his death had recently belonged to someone else—a cousin, a brawler who had recently stabbed a man over a card game. The bullet had been intended for the cousin, not Bedolla.

Diaz made a note in the file that he planned to meet the tipster that night to get more information. Whether the meeting happened, the police file does not say—presumably it did not. The file contains nothing more about it, except the name by which the tipster identified himself: Jose Martinez. (Martinez adamantly denies that he made any such phone call.)

Soon the investigation into who killed David Bedolla—despite its plethora of leads—went cold. And aside from Bedolla's grief-stricken family, no one seemed to care or even notice.

The local paper, the *Tulare Advance Register*, chronicled events in the area in such minute detail that it devoted column inches to things like wedding gift registries and the theft of irrigation pipe. But the early-morning murder of a twenty-three-year-old farm-worker as he drove to work in a car with his wife in the passenger seat was mentioned exactly once, in a three-paragraph news brief buried on an inside page. And only then because Diaz had issued a press release asking anyone with any information to please get in touch.

Diaz moved on to other murders. There were more than enough to keep him busy. But the Bedolla case nagged at him. So much so, he told Cecilia years later, that when he left the sheriff's department for a job at the district attorney's office, he took a copy of the file with him.

PART TWO

Mr. X

1981–1992

Jose Martinez: We killed that guy because he killed four guys in Mexico....

Santa Barbara County Sheriff's Detective: We know the law enforcement world, but you are in a different world, so it's intriguing.... You were not the only person who did this type of stuff—Did a lot of you guys know each other? Were you kind of friends?

Jose Martinez: You just meet people. For example, I do a job for you, and a few months later…

Santa Barbara County Sheriff's Detective: It sounds like you were a pretty popular person…you were kind of one of the grandees, right?

Jose Martinez: I was.

—Partial transcript of police interrogation, June 26, 2013, 10:25 a.m.

Chapter Five

In late 1981, a man from the Mexican state of Durango with a gift for working with horses and a dangerous secret crossed the border into California and took refuge in one of the safest places imaginable: the horse ranch of a rich, powerful white woman in Santa Barbara County. His new boss.

The man, Silvestre Ayon, never told his boss he was hiding. It wasn't the kind of thing you would talk about with a boss, particularly not one like Susan Davidge, or Sue, as everyone called her.

The Davidge family was among the most prominent in the Santa Ynez Valley, a hidden pastoral paradise on the bluffs north of Santa Barbara. The family owned acre after rolling acre of ranch lands and vineyards, and its members were frequently featured in the society pages of the local newspaper. The family had been among the first to cultivate pinot noir grapes in the Santa Ynez Valley, a seemingly quixotic choice that eventually turned out to have been yet another brilliant business decision.[1] But Sue Davidge's passion was not wine; it was horses. Dressage horses, specifically—stately animals trained to perform intricate choreographed steps and seem to be dancing. Davidge had been instrumental in bringing dressage to the West Coast, hosting many events at her property.

Her ranch was on Refugio Road, in the misty blue-gray hills of chaparral that rise above the Pacific Ocean. President Ronald Reagan's ranch, known as the Western White House and visited by Queen Elizabeth II, Mikhail Gorbachev, and Margaret Thatcher, was just up the hill. Down the road sat a piece of property that, a few years later, would become Michael Jackson's Neverland Ranch.

Ayon had found work at the Davidge ranch the old-fashioned way: he walked up the road one day and asked the ranch manager, Jean Charles Sarri, if he needed a hired hand. Sarri, who was French but had come to America after marrying a ballet dancer he met in Cannes, had since picked up enough Spanish to get by as a ranch manager.

Sarri asked if Ayon knew horses.[2]

Yes, Ayon said.

Sarri and Davidge decided to try him out. He impressed them immediately with his competence and dedication. A short time later, Ayon's wife and children moved to the ranch as well, staying in one of the cabins reserved for workers. Sarri worked with Ayon a lot. He got to know his wife a little bit too and appreciated the way she would bring her husband and the other workers fresh-baked pastries with their coffee during the 9 a.m. work break. He thought they both seemed like warmhearted, hardworking people.

But Sarri didn't get to know them very well. He didn't know where they were from or precisely how old their children were— and he certainly had no idea that by the time thirty-one-year-old Ayon arrived at the ranch, he had survived a shotgun blast to the chest before fleeing Mexico with a price on his head.

People had been trying to kill Ayon since a party in a small town up in the Sierra Madre in Durango in the summer of 1979. Maybe a dispute had broken out over who was dancing with whom; maybe rival drug factions were trying to kill each other in a battle over market share; maybe both. Numerous people had whipped out guns, which many men carried in that rough highland community. At the end of the night, seven people had been shot, and four or five were dead. The fatal shots had come from at least three different guns.[3]

Ayon had been at the party, gun in hand, and relatives of the dead had blamed him and two other men for the killings. They had vowed to kill him. They had very nearly succeeded in the ambush with the shotgun carried out soon after the deadly party.

Ayon protested his innocence and headed to California. He had brothers near Earlimart, but that area didn't seem safe—the people who were hunting him had family there too.

So he and his wife and children moved to the Santa Ynez Valley. There were farmworkers from Mexico in the Santa Ynez Valley, just as there were farmworkers from Mexico almost everywhere food was grown in California. But the Santa Ynez Valley wasn't like the San Joaquin Valley. It wasn't as brutal. A man could, for example, find a job and a place to live on the same estate as one of the area's most prominent citizens and share pastries with her as she walked by in the mornings. His children could go to school in classrooms that weren't as segregated and grow up in a community that wasn't as riven with conflict and violence and exploitation.

For many months, it seemed like Ayon had done the impossible: he had traded his life on the run for a refuge in this gorgeous land of ocean breezes, wine, and horses.

But in the late summer of 1982, Ayon began to get nervous. Maybe he heard people were asking questions about him. Or maybe he saw someone in the little nearby town of Los Olivos looking at him too closely. Whatever it was, other workers at the ranch noticed that he had become preoccupied. Although he never mentioned anything to his bosses, he did confide in his fellow ranch workers about the failed ambush against him in Mexico.

One day, Ayon even lifted up his shirt and showed them the scars from the shotgun pellets that pocked his stomach and chest.

Around the same time, he confided to his wife that he was afraid the people who had been after him in Mexico would somehow find him here, in this bucolic pocket of American privilege.

The little community of La Cofradia, nestled deep in the mountains that form the border between the Mexican states of Sinaloa and Durango, was almost unimaginably remote in the late 1970s. There were few paved roads. Few phones. Even fewer institutions of government or civic life. People got around on horseback. And they largely made their own laws and took care of their own justice.

Nevertheless, the shootout at the party there in June 1979—the shootout for which people blamed Ayon—quickly became the talk not just of La Cofradia but also of Earlimart, twelve hundred miles to the north. The victims and the alleged perpetrators all had family living across the border and picking grapes. Or smuggling drugs. Or both. What happened in La Cofradia was in many ways more immediate and more important to many of the people in Earlimart than what happened in Sacramento or Los Angeles.

Two of the victims of that fatal shooting were related to Pedro Fernandez, the ranch-running, drug-smuggling stepfather of Jose Martinez. Two more were related to Fernandez's powerful drug-smuggling friends.

After Martinez's stepfather was released from federal prison, Martinez and other family members went to pick him up. He was so happy to see them. He was also excited about all the drug-business contacts he had made while behind bars. (Prison, it turned out, was like Harvard Business School for drug dealers, in terms of the powerful connections that could be forged there.) And then he heard the news that his relatives had been killed. The family watched Pedro Fernandez's face crumble.

Martinez wanted in on the revenge.

In his stepfather's absence, he had taken a prominent place in his business—as best he could anyway.

But that was business. And this, well, this was personal to many of the powerful people in Martinez's life. Helping them with such an important family matter would be great for his secret ambitions to be an enforcer.

But in the first months after the dance hall ambush, there wasn't much to do. Ayon was in the wind. People had tried to shoot him in Mexico, and he had somehow managed to survive and then disappear.

Martinez had plenty of other things to keep him busy.

He moved again. He feared he was becoming too well-known in Tulare County for smuggling and selling drugs. Law enforcement had begun stepping up its efforts against the heroin flowing through the valley. In August 1980 the Tulare County Sheriff's Department launched a massive undercover operation targeting dealers in Earlimart. One of the dealers Martinez supplied, Raul Gonzalez, was arrested in the sting.[4]

Sheriff Bob Wiley invited the media to watch the raids unfold. Reporters were welcomed with donuts down at the station as teams of deputies fanned out across Earlimart to arrest people and then came back to the station, crowing about how many they had caught.

The sheriff did not publicize, however, that some of the local officers had been frustrated in these efforts.

Drugs were flooding into the valley. Smugglers had realized that the area's vast fields—and the dirt roads that crisscrossed them—made perfect clandestine landing strips. A small plane loaded with drugs could fly from Sinaloa in five or six hours, and the valley was full of experienced crop duster pilots, some of whom were happy to make the trip and earn in one flight what they might earn in a month of spraying pesticides and fertilizer across fields.[5]

Meanwhile, many police departments refused to authorize their undercover officers to spend more than a few hundred dollars on drug buys. That meant police could rarely move up the chain to the bigger suppliers, so they were forever busting the low-level dealers, like Gonzalez. Occasionally, as when they had arrested Martinez's stepfather, Pedro Fernandez, in 1977, they got a big fish. But that happened only when they had a good informant with an ax to grind and a lot of luck.

Some, including the editors of the *Tulare Advance Register*, suggested such raids, scooping up small fry, were cynical election gambits. An "election-year-drug raid, the one that seems to happen with regularity every four years," the paper grumbled in a 1986 editorial about another such action. The article went on to add that the suspects arrested always seemed to "involve Hispanics" and that "minority suspects make for politically safe arrests in the heat of an election season."[6]

Martinez wasn't really worried about being caught up in such raids. Still, he noticed that the sheriff's deputy who worked the area seemed to have developed an interest in him, often pulling him over and searching his car.

So he moved his wife and children to a small house in the little town of McFarland. One of his godfathers—who was also involved in his drug business—moved in with them. In the interconnected way of life in Earlimart, the godfather's wife was also Martinez's cousin.

Staying on the move, even within a relatively small area, is one tried-and-true tactic of a successful drug dealer. If the police can't watch you and can't find you, they can't arrest you. Plus, Martinez believed most police were lazy. If you made it just a little hard for them, they often moved on to someone else.

McFarland was a farm town incorporated in 1957, known over the decades, like Earlimart, for its close-knit community and for its poverty and environmental degradation amid the bounty of the valley's fields and orchards. About ten miles south of Earlimart, McFarland was also slightly more difficult for the Tulare County Sheriff's Department to police because it was in Kern County. McFarland did have its own police department, but Martinez wasn't worried about it.

Martinez and his wife and children quickly settled in. He continued his drug business, working with men, some loosely related, many from the same mountainous region on the border between the Mexican states of Sinaloa and Durango. He coordinated marijuana and heroin shipments across the border and delivered to buyers around the valley or in other parts of California. When he took his children and wife to visit relatives in Cosalá, Martinez made trips to Culiacan, the capital of Sinaloa, to meet with traffickers. He said he also invested in buying his own crop of opium in the region.

During this period, men from the highlands of Sinaloa and Durango, some with ties to Martinez's family home in Cosalá, were forming what law enforcement would eventually come to know as the Guadalajara Cartel, a highly sophisticated transnational drug-trafficking organization and precursor to the infamous Sinaloa Cartel.

The leader of the Guadalajara Cartel, Miguel Angel Felix Gallardo, had been a bodyguard for the governor of Sinaloa, Leopoldo Sanchez Celis, who was from Cosalá. Felix Gallardo had been smuggling heroin and marijuana out of the highlands of Sinaloa for years before he had an inspiration: he could also use his smuggling routes—the passage eased by corrupt Mexican officials—to transport vast amounts of cocaine from Colombia through Sinaloa and into the United States. Colombian traffickers were looking for new routes because the US Drug Enforcement Administration had made it more difficult and expensive to smuggle drugs through Miami.[7]

But before Sinaloa became a drug smuggler's paradise, it had been, for decades, a poverty-stricken rural area that sent thousands of workers to California's fields to eke out an existence there. As a result, many of the newly powerful figures in the Mexican drug world—overnight millionaires, willing to defend their fortunes with canny brutality—had familial ties to the San Joaquin Valley. Police acknowledge that they have never fully understood these networks and certainly did not in the 1980s.

Martinez came of age in the middle of this. He abhorred the idea of farmwork. Not just the low pay and backbreaking labor but the contempt with which farmworkers were treated. Drug smuggling meant easy money. But it also meant, in his circles anyway, respect.

By 1981, Martinez had already committed four murders— the three people he killed to avenge his sister's death and David Bedolla. But according to both Martinez and his family, in this era, his primary focus was his business and taking care of his wife, children, and siblings. He was a joyful presence in their lives— when he was around anyway. He professed to adore his wife. His children made him burst with happiness. To his nieces and nephews, especially the children of his murdered sister, he was the "fun uncle," desperate to make them laugh, to make them happy. To his sisters, he was a constant protector, checking on them to make sure they were safe and that their husbands were caring for them properly.[8]

Now that he had money, he was determined to give his children the kind of gifts and experiences he had never had. His younger siblings too. He took them to San Francisco and Yosemite. They rode the roller coasters at Disneyland and Knott's Berry Farm.

Nearly four decades later, one of his younger sisters said she could still vividly recall how those trips opened up her world. "Disneyland. Magic Mountain. Fisherman's Wharf," she said, memory softening her face into a smile even though she was under stress, sitting in a witness box in a Florida courtroom. On those trips with her brother, she remembered, she felt "like royalty. They got," she said, "red carpet treatment."

Martinez also took his wife on a second honeymoon, hitting theme parks, a beach near Santa Barbara, and Las Vegas. While there, he took her on a detour to the old gunslinger town of Tombstone, Arizona. Martinez wanted to pay homage to the outlaw ethos.

It seemed possible, at this point in his life anyway, that the horrific violence he had engaged in as a teenager might have faded as he matured. He might have become a person with a criminal past, determined to go straight and grab a piece of the American dream, watching over his children to make sure homework got done, that college applications were filled out. That, indeed, was the trajectory of some members of Martinez's family who may have engaged in smuggling but were not violent.

But then in September 1981, when Martinez was nineteen, rumors swept Earlimart that Ayon had resurfaced and was in central California looking for work.

Martinez jumped into the task of hunting him down. He began making inquiries among his networks in all the little towns where farmworkers from Durango and Sinaloa followed the grapes. He went to Indio, in the Coachella Valley, where the harvest started, and to Arvin, in Kern County, where they ripened next. Then he headed farther north to Huron, one of the poorest places in California, nicknamed "Knife Fight City" because farmworkers armed with lettuce cutters streamed out of its bars on weekends and sometimes used their farm implements in fights.[9] And finally he went to Mendota, a rural farming community in Fresno County so under the control of criminal gangs that, it emerged eventually, even police officers were terrified for their lives. But Martinez got nowhere. "It's hard to look for a person when you don't even know them, or how they look," he wrote.

He even tried offering a reward, putting it out that he would pay $300 for information leading to Ayon. This also yielded nothing.

Never did it occur to him not to hunt the man down. It was a particular feature of his personality that once he decided someone deserved to die, dissuading him was nearly impossible. Even the words he used spoke to this: he called his jobs "missions."

Then, in September 1982, a powerful man in the drug world came to Martinez's house in McFarland with some new information.

To protect this man's identity, Martinez has been scrupulously careful to reveal almost nothing about him. He insists on calling him "Mr. X"—as though he were a figure in a spy film. He has said that Mr. X is rich. That he has ties to Sinaloa and spends time in Culiacan, its capital. That he also has ties to Modesto, a small Central Valley city about 150 miles north of Tulare County, and to Los Angeles. And, needless to say, Mr. X is deeply involved in drug smuggling. Mr. X also appears to be a courteous, family-oriented person, eschewing violence when he can. Of course, in his business, that is not always possible. Which is where his relationship with Martinez comes in.

Chapter Six

—

Martinez and Mr. X drank beer in the backyard of the little house in McFarland. They talked for hours until Mr. X eventually landed on the reason for his visit. "We may have found Silvestre," Mr. X said, referring to Ayon. "He's near Santa Ynez. Turn every rock upside down" in your search.

After Mr. X left his house, Martinez thought about the job he had been given. "It's very, very important that I kill Silvestre," he thought. "If I do this job right, a lot of doors are going to open up for me."[1]

The next morning, Martinez resupplied his lower-level dealers with heroin as usual. Then he hit the road. He headed south on the 99 and cut west on State Route 166, over the Sierra Madre Mountains and onto the famed coastal highway US 101. His destination was Los Olivos, a small farm town in the Santa Ynez Valley. These days, Los Olivos is gentrified, full of bistros and people up from Los Angeles tasting wines and spending money. But in 1982, it was still very much a California farm town whose little stores catered to farmers and farmworkers.

One of Martinez's godfathers lived there. And his godfather

was from the same region of Durango as Ayon, so Martinez figured there was a chance he might know something.

His godfather wasn't home. Martinez waited all afternoon outside the trailer where he lived, then turned around and made the three-hour drive back to the valley. He didn't leave a note. He'd been trying to learn about police procedures in order to evade law enforcement and decided that it would be best not to leave physical evidence that he'd been in the area.

A week later, when he figured he might catch his godfather at home, Martinez returned. This time, he had success. His godfather knew exactly where Ayon was working. Martinez and the man had a barbecue and smoked some pot, and the next morning his godfather showed him Sue Davidge's stately property, which was so fancy it even had a name: the Etcetera Ranch.

Martinez drove back to McFarland ebullient. He picked up his family, and by 9 p.m. he was at Mr. X's house in Modesto. They stayed up all night making their plans.

Martinez said nothing to his wife about the purpose of their visit to Mr. X. She was not completely ignorant. She had come to the United States from Cosalá, Sinaloa, at about the age of fifteen. She had landed at Pedro Fernandez's ranch, in the milieu of smugglers. She was close to Martinez's sisters, but unlike them she did not leave the ranch to go to school and did not learn English. She was a hard worker, and when she became a mother while still a teenager, she loved her children fiercely.

"My wife knew I was a drug dealer," Martinez wrote. "But she never knew I was a serious killer, or that I *liked* to kill people."[2]

She also knew better than to ask too many questions about his business.

On the appointed day, October 1, 1982, Martinez, Mr. X, and two other men set off in three cars from McFarland at 3 a.m. and drove straight to Santa Ynez.

They had done their scouting work. They parked at a little country market, and three of the men—Martinez and two others—got into a gray AMC Gremlin and set out. Mr. X stayed at the market.

When they arrived at the ranch, they parked and waited. It was 6:45 a.m. and not yet fully light. They knew from their reconnaissance that Ayon usually came past at around 7 a.m. in a tractor with hay for Sue Davidge's horses.

And indeed, as the clock ticked past the hour, they first heard and then saw the little tractor, pulling a wagon full of hay.

Martinez, in the driver's seat of the Gremlin, had two guns ready, one in each hand.

But first, he had to know: Was it Silvestre Ayon? Martinez had never laid eyes on the man.

Martinez pulled up next to the tractor and asked for directions, as if he were a farmworker looking for the day's jobsite. With his friendly face and courteous tone, nothing about this alarmed Ayon at all. As Ayon told them where to go, one of Martinez's associates in the passenger seat confirmed their target's identity.

Martinez opened fire, blasting away with his 9mm handgun. He hit Ayon numerous times and watched his body collapse.

Then, an unexpected development: Ayon was not the only person in the tractor. A seventeen-year-old high school student had been hidden in the wagon in the back, helping distribute the hay. Martinez fired one shot at him, striking him in the stomach but not killing him. The boy tumbled or jumped off the tractor and ran behind it. Martinez decided it wasn't necessary to finish him off. He couldn't have seen them, and even if he had, he couldn't recognize them.

Martinez threw the Gremlin in reverse and hit the accelerator. They sped backward down the driveway into a skidding U-turn, then shot forward and flew onto Refugio Road.

Within minutes they were back at the country market, where Mr. X was waiting for them. They tore the license plates off the Gremlin, hopped into the other two cars, and scattered, one car heading north and the other south. They left the Gremlin behind. They weren't worried about anyone linking it to them—they'd left no fingerprints because they'd been wearing gloves.

Jean Charles Sarri, the ranch foreman, heard the shots come one after another after another: *pow pow pow pow, pow pow pow.*

He didn't think much of it. Probably one of the nearby farmers had decided to scare off birds eating grapes in the vineyards.

But a few minutes later, there was a commotion right outside his house on the ranch. People screaming—something about Silvestre being shot.

Sarri jumped in his car and sped across Refugio Road to the other half of the ranch.

When he got there, he saw Ayon's lifeless body slumped in the tractor. Good-humored, hardworking Silvestre. Dead. Almost worse was the sight of the teenaged boy, still alive and lying on the ground, a piece of his jacket somehow driven inside his body by the force of the bullet to his stomach.

Murder was comparatively rare in Santa Barbara County. And a murder at a fancy ranch owned by some of the county's most prominent citizens, a ranch that was just a few miles from President Reagan's Western White House—well, that was unheard of.

The sheriff's department responded within minutes and in force.

Santa Barbara sheriff's deputy Art Knight was among the first officers to arrive. Lights and sirens blaring, he raced up the long driveway of the ranch.

A worker flagged him down and pointed to the tractor where Ayon's bullet-ridden body was still slumped in the driver's seat. Then, before Knight could head over there, the worker pointed to the teenaged boy, who was somehow now standing up beside the tractor. "He's been shot too," the worker said. On cue, the boy raised his shirt to reveal a bullet wound.

Knight knew the boy a little bit. He was a high school student whose family lived in the area. He stared at the hole in the boy's stomach. It was gaping, as though the injury must be very serious, and yet the boy was running to and fro around the tractor in a state of agitation.[3] Knight tried to get him to calm down. He urged him to get into his police car, where he could rest until paramedics arrived, but thankfully just then an ambulance pulled up.

As the paramedics loaded the boy into the vehicle, the other worker came to talk to Knight. "I think I know what happened," he said, telling Knight how Ayon had feared that people from his home in Mexico were out to get him.

Another detective heard the same thing from another worker when he arrived at the ranch. And another officer heard it from the teenaged boy himself just before 9 a.m., as he stood over the boy as he lay on a gurney in the emergency room at the Santa Ynez hospital, peppering the young man with questions as doctors prepared to wheel him off to surgery.

By the time the lead detectives arrived on scene, numerous responding officers from the Santa Barbara County Sheriff's Department were buzzing about tips they'd heard about a wild shootout at a party three years earlier in a place most of them had never heard of and couldn't pronounce, deep in the Sierra Madre of Mexico.

It was just the kind of setup Detective Bruce Correll and his partner, Leo Ortega, were good at sorting out.

Correll and Ortega were two of the department's most celebrated detectives, known for solving hard cases and going to great lengths to do so.[4] They'd joined the department at the same time, in the spring of 1969, and despite their vast differences in background and temperament, the two had become lifelong friends.

Correll was tall, with a commanding presence that intimidated people into talking and a fierce intelligence for taking in what they said. Ortega, shorter and slighter, had been born on the Gila River Indian Reservation in Arizona and grown up partly as a migrant farm kid before landing in Stockton for high school. He'd come to law enforcement from the air force, which he'd joined after he was caught, drunk, throwing beer cans at ducks in a park; a judge had told him to join the military or face criminal charges. Ortega had a raucous sense of humor and an effortless charm that put almost everyone at ease, from traumatized children to seasoned criminals.

He was also a native Spanish speaker and handled all the Spanish interviews. Correll understood a bit of Spanish but didn't speak it well. Still, he learned to recognize the moment when Ortega concluded a long sentence with a distinctive "Eh?" That meant whomever Ortega was talking to was going to start telling him everything the detectives wanted to know.

As different as the two detectives were, Correll said they had something else in common: "We were hunters," he said. "That's all we were." They lived for the thrill of the chase, of painstakingly and patiently following the evidence, wherever it led. Someone was dead, and they would not stop until they had figured out who had done it.

Most murders, when you got right down to it, were not that difficult to solve. The perpetrator was an enraged acquaintance, usually drunk. Or a violent husband or boyfriend. Clues were often everywhere. And if that wasn't enough, you'd be surprised by how many people simply confessed.

But this—the murder of a hardworking and beloved employee fleeing a secret violent past, at the estate of one of the wealthiest families in the county—had all the makings of a great hunt.

Unlike the detectives in Tulare, Correll and Ortega had some key advantages. Powerful people would want this crime solved.

What's more, the Santa Barbara County Sheriff's Department, drawing on its rich tax base of fancy mansions and old money, had resources. Most importantly, Correll and Ortega weren't overwhelmed with murders the way their counterparts on the other side of the hills were. And their department didn't have the terrible weight of a history against farmworkers pressing down on it whenever its officers tried to talk to anyone.

The hunt was on.

Chapter Seven

By 9 a.m., as Ayon lay dead in the tractor and the teenaged victim was being wheeled into surgery, Martinez and Mr. X were comfortably seated in a plush vinyl booth at Denny's in Santa Maria, digging into breakfast.

They were very hungry.

Don't worry about the guy we left alive, Martinez told Mr. X. He was very young, and I don't think he saw our faces.

"Plus," Martinez added with a smile, "it's not like we're going to come back for the funeral to give him another chance to ID us."[1]

After breakfast, the pair cut east away from the soft ocean mist and back into the bright, harsh heat of early fall in Tulare County. Martinez realized this was his fifth killing. He was twenty years old. "Every crime I do, I love it more and more," he would later write.

They arrived back at Martinez's house in McFarland by noon. Mr. X told Martinez he could keep all the guns used in the shooting as a gift. He also gave him $2,500. Martinez tried to turn down the money, insisting the killing had been personal for him too because his stepfather's relatives had died in the dance hall shooting, but Mr. X told him to keep it. And, Mr. X continued, as an added bonus, from now on he would try to see to it that Martinez got a better price for his wholesale drugs.

But Martinez wanted something else too. "Spread the word about me," he told Mr. X. "Tell all your people what I'm capable of doing. Tell them, whenever they have a problem, they should think about me. I can take care of the problem."

Mr. X promised he would. Martinez was happy to hear it.

He vowed then and there that he would begin the hunt for the other man that Mr. X and his associates claimed was responsible for the dance hall shooting back in La Cofradia. With that, Mr. X headed back to Modesto.

Martinez had been up all night, but he was exhilarated. He decided to drive up to Earlimart to see if word of Ayon's death had reached the town. Ayon, after all, had two brothers who lived there.

He wasn't disappointed.

Though it had been less than a day, the whole town knew of Ayon's death—or at least everyone in Martinez's circles. Everyone was talking about it. Some people said he had been shot more than fifty times, others that he had been shot with a machine gun. Martinez didn't say a word, of course. But he felt very proud.

Police officers investigating drug- and gang-related crimes often complain that witnesses and family members of victims refuse to share what they know, either out of fear or because they want to "handle it themselves."

That was not the case with Silvestre Ayon's relatives.

By 3 p.m. on the afternoon of the murder, when detectives Correll and Ortega caught up with one of Ayon's relatives at the Santa Maria sheriff's substation, the young woman had decided she knew exactly who had killed her relative and why. And she was prepared to share her theory with any police officer who would listen.

The young woman repeated, yet again, the story that detectives had been hearing snippets of all morning: Ayon had been shot because powerful families in Durango blamed him for a shootout at a dance in Mexico in 1979. When Detective Correll asked her if she had any idea who, specifically, might have been behind the murder, she did not hesitate: Yes, she did. A man named Tacho Chaidez.

Chaidez, she explained, was from the same mountainous region of small ranchos in Durango as her family but had more recently resided in Tulare County and in Los Angeles. Two of his brothers had been killed in the infamous dance shootout, and he had made a public vow of vengeance. He was not the kind of man, she noted, to make such a vow lightly.

She told detectives a bit about her own life too, including that she had immigrated to California in the mid-1970s. But she left out one important detail—perhaps because she didn't think it was relevant or perhaps out of a sense of caution. She didn't tell the detectives where she spent time when she first arrived in the United States: at a ranch outside Earlimart. A ranch that belonged to Pedro Fernandez, Martinez's stepfather.

Earlimart.

Correll had never heard of this place, but he soon learned that it was a tiny town over the hills in Tulare County.

He'd never been there. He knew little, really, of the San Joaquin Valley, aside from what everyone knew: It was where most of the food came from. It was flat. It was hot in the summer and cold and foggy in the winter. Cesar Chavez, the leader of the farmworkers' movement, still had his base there. Correll's partner, Ortega, had actually met Chavez. But that was the end of Correll's knowledge.

And yet, now people would not stop talking about this town with the strange name. Family and friends of Ayon were literally walking into the department's substation in Santa Maria and advising them to go look in Earlimart. Sometimes they talked of Earlimart and drugs. Sometimes they talked of Earlimart and family members from Durango. But always they talked of Earlimart.

Earlimart wasn't even really a town at all. It had never incorporated and relied on the county for whatever paltry services it received. There was not a single sizeable playground, police station, or other major recreational or civic amenity. This was not an accident; few with any power thought its farmworker residents deserved any better. In fact, county officials had, in 1971, declared that Earlimart and other unincorporated towns were "nonviable communities" that had "little or no authentic future." Public services should be withheld, officials advised, to encourage people to leave.[2]

They did not. Earlimart's dilapidated, sun-faded houses, apartments, and trailers sat amid a vast expanse of vineyards and almond orchards, hunched down at the bottom end of Tulare County like an island in the middle of an ocean of fields. As poor as it was, as violent as it sometimes was, it was also a close community. People knew each other intimately—who was suffering from health problems, whose child had defied the odds and gotten into medical school, whose child was overseas fighting for the US military, whose child was locked up. Despite Tulare County officials' plans, instead of withering, Earlimart grew.

Earlimart had once been destined for greater things. An 1888 real estate ad dubbed the land "Alila, the Arcadia of the San Joaquin Valley." The town's founding came at a moment of transformation. As the gold rush wound down, the ingenuity that had been directed at damming California's rivers to extract gold from the foothills of its mountains was applied to diverting water to grow crops down on the floor of its massive Central Valley. From 1900 to 1920, the number of irrigated acres in California tripled.[3] Trees and vines brimming with peaches, plums, grapes, oranges, lemons, and grapefruits spread across the landscape.

Eventually, Alila turned into Earlimart, so named, its early boosters claimed, because produce grown there would be "early to market." But another characteristic less celebrated by advertising copywriters also emerged: a penchant for attracting gangsters. The town had its first brush with notoriety in 1890 when it was the site of a brazen train robbery by an infamous band of criminal brothers.[4]

Detective Correll figured they might have to go to Earlimart eventually. But first, they had physical evidence to process.

Victims' families couldn't always be trusted. Their stories could be full of half-truths and either deliberate or incidental misdirection, misinformation, or plain falsehoods. Physical evidence, on the other hand, didn't lie.

Late on the evening of the murder, detectives found a 1975 AMC Gremlin matching the description of the car that sped off shortly after the shooting. It had been abandoned in the parking lot of the El Rancho Market just a few miles away from the crime scene. Two shell casings from a .32 revolver were stuck in the crevice of the hood, and a handgun cartridge casing lay on the driver's seat. The car had recently been painted white—but not very well. It was a fast, sloppy spray job over the original green.

Whoever thought pulling off the license plates and spray painting the car would prevent detectives from figuring out who owned it had been laughably wrong. The car's VIN number was visible through the front windshield.

In no time at all, Correll had the car's original plate number and the name of its registered owner, along with the PO box in the Santa Barbara farm town of Los Alamos where the California Department of Motor Vehicles (DMV) had sent the owner his registration and stickers.

By 2 a.m. that night, Correll had woken up a judge and gotten a warrant to search not just the car but also the PO box.

The following morning, he had the names of people who received mail at the box. One of them was Chaidez. Just as the victim's relative had predicted. Maybe the hunt wouldn't be so fierce this time. But first they had to find Chaidez. And the PO box itself wasn't much help.

Police fell back on DMV records. They looked for other cars belonging to the Gremlin's owner or the Chaidez family and pulled addresses where those cars were registered. Then they took a breath. Boy, did these people have a lot of cars. And they appeared to like to register them seemingly at random around the state of California.

There were addresses in Long Beach and Compton and South Gate and Paramount, cities spanning the blue-collar industrial belt of Los Angeles County. And there were more addresses up north in Fresno and the rural communities around it.

The detectives hit the road, driving hours south to LA and then hours more back up the state to Fresno. Still, they came up mostly empty-handed. They ran into many people at some of those addresses who seemed tied to drug trafficking in one way or another. But there was no sign of Chaidez.

Finally, another detective called the Tulare County Sheriff's Department to see if detectives there could provide any leads.

You've got to talk to Ralph Diaz, Tulare officials told him. He speaks Spanish. He knows Earlimart.

They got Diaz on the phone.

Let me see what I can find out, Diaz said.

By this point, Earlimart was well-known to the Tulare County Sheriff's Department as a locus of drugs and the attendant violence. Good detectives always had at least a few informants who traded information for a few bucks or a promise to go light on them the next time they got caught. Diaz didn't tell the Santa Barbara detectives who his informants were or how he knew them.

But when he called back twenty-four hours later, he was a font of information.

In just a few hours, he had heard all about the original dance hall shooting—although the version he was told differed a bit from the one told to Santa Barbara detectives. In Diaz's version, Ayon hadn't shot anyone at all. He had just been in the wrong place when the shooting broke out. One of the Chaidez brothers allegedly asked him to "pick up a gun and back him up," which he did. But though he hadn't killed anyone, according to the version Diaz heard, other members of the family had seen Ayon holding a gun and assumed he was to blame for their relatives' deaths.

Lastly Diaz told the Santa Barbara detectives something they had already heard before: the talk of Earlimart was that Tacho Chaidez was the killer.

Everything the Santa Barbara detectives heard made their heads spin a little more. Diaz fleshed out details of the complicated relationships between the Ayon family, the Chaidez family, and a few others.

Many of the suspects seemed to be somehow related to the victim or to members of Ayon's family in a complicated tangle of first cousins and second cousins, nieces and nephews, wives and sisters. The detectives' notebooks began to look like complicated genealogy worksheets, as they tried to piece together who was related to whom, who had been married to whom, and what it all might mean. Many of the Santa Barbara detectives were also flummoxed by Spanish naming conventions, in which people take both their mother's and father's last names.

Not to mention that many of those involved in the feud seemed to move constantly. From Earlimart to Durango to Sinaloa to Santa Barbara to Los Angeles and back.

As they tried to puzzle it out, Detective Diaz called again.

There had been more murders in Earlimart, and it appeared that people connected to Silvestre Ayon were involved.[5]

Chapter Eight

On the morning of October 21, 1982, a rancher driving across the rolling hills of eastern Tulare County to feed her cattle found the body of a young man.

By 11 a.m. Detective Diaz was standing on a dirt embankment next to a barbed-wire fence, staring down at a man's body that was wearing a brown bathrobe. The man was dead and had been for a while, and he was covered in stab wounds. He'd also been shot, although the bullets clearly weren't what had killed him.

Diaz quickly determined that the man had likely been killed elsewhere and then, as the police file noted, "taken out of a trunk of a vehicle and dragged over and thrown across a barbed wire fence at this location."

By the time Diaz cleared the scene and got back to the sheriff's department around 2:30 p.m., he had a good idea of who his victim was. A local drug dealer, car upholsterer, and beloved father, brother, and son, Raul Gonzalez of Earlimart, had been reported missing by his family a day earlier.

Gonzalez was well-known to police. They had arrested him at least twice in the last two years on drug charges. But despite his run-ins with the law, Gonzalez's wife had called the police in a panic to report that her husband had been forced to leave their home around 9 p.m. on the night of October 19, after a friend of his insisted that he come outside to talk.

That friend was no stranger to police either. He was the nephew of Pedro Fernandez, Jose Martinez's stepfather. He was also—as Diaz noted—some kind of cousin to Silvestre Ayon.

Raul Gonzalez's wife told police that after the friend showed up at her home, her husband walked outside in his bathrobe, and then she heard a car trunk close, followed by one car door and then another, and finally the sound of a car driving away from their Earlimart home.

As Diaz wrote in his report, "This was the last she saw of her husband."

At 3 a.m., when her husband still had not returned, Raul's wife woke up his brothers and his father.

Worried, Raul's family began canvassing the streets of Earlimart, looking for him or the friend who had taken him away or anyone else who might know anything. Worrying about Raul—who had a sweet nature and a real talent for upholstering cars—was something the family did. They hated his heroin addiction and the way it had driven him to sell drugs. If only he could be free from its grip.

Diaz reviewed the story from Gonzalez's wife. After running Gonzalez's name, he realized he needed to speak to one of his colleagues on the narcotics desk.

Diaz's colleague held another disturbing piece of the puzzle. Gonzalez, he said, had been arrested on drug charges on October 9, as part of the Tulare County sheriff's push against heroin dealers, and was subsequently locked up in county jail. Ten days later, on October 19, Gonzalez had flagged the narcotics detective down while in custody and offered to work as an informant in exchange for reduced charges. The narcotics detective told Diaz that Gonzalez had promised to "do in his heroin connection."

Informants who could help the police build evidence against higher-level dealers were worth their weight in gold. Most people were too terrified to cut such deals. The narcotics detective agreed to Gonzalez's plan, but his report on the encounter ended ominously: "I think prisoners inside the holding tank might have overheard Raul's conversation." If the narcotics detective did anything to protect Gonzalez after that, he didn't note it in the file. Immediately after the deal was struck, Gonzalez was released to begin working as an informant.

That very night, he was kidnapped and killed.

Diaz didn't hesitate. Within just a few hours of hearing how Gonzalez had been taken from his home by a friend who was related to a well-known drug smuggler on the very same day he had agreed to become an informant, the Tulare County Sheriff's Department, at 4:05 p.m. on October 21, issued an all-points bulletin for the friend who had come to Raul Gonzalez's house. Then Diaz and his partner, Jay Salazar, hit the streets of Earlimart to try to find Pedro Fernandez's nephew themselves.

First, they went to the friend's family home on Lane Street in Earlimart and talked to his wife, who was also Jose Martinez's cousin.

She informed them that her husband had gone out on the night of October 19 and had not been home since. Diaz and Salazar asked about the friend's uncle, Pedro Fernandez, and learned he was out of federal prison and could be found at his new home at the old Sierra Vista Labor Camp, in the southern part of the county. The friend's wife also explained that she and her husband actually had two addresses and were living most of the time in McFarland, at 344 Industrial Avenue. The other occupants of that house: Jose Martinez and his family.

By 6:30 p.m. detectives were at Martinez's house in McFarland, where they confiscated several items, including an address book, a Luger pistol, ammunition, and the nephew's Mexican passport, which showed that he had been born in Cosalá, Sinaloa, the same town in the heart of drug cartel territory where the Martinez children had spent some of their childhood. If Martinez was present at the house, and if detectives talked to him, it isn't reflected in their police report.

The detectives didn't stay at Martinez's house for long. A tip came in—from an informant—that the car used to kidnap Gonzalez had been spotted at the Sierra Vista Labor Camp. The detectives sped off to the camp.

Sierra Vista, a ratty assemblage of cabins and converted railroad boxcars tucked into the bottom of the county, could easily have been the model for one of the labor camps in John Steinbeck's *The Grapes of Wrath*. It had been built in the 1940s by the DiGiorgio Corporation, the largest grape grower in California. The company had housed its workers in segregated camps around the valley. Filipinos in one place, Mexicans in another, Anglos, who were fewer and fewer in number as the years went on, in still another.

By that night in the fall of 1982, when the detectives thundered into the camp, there were almost no Anglo farmworkers left in the valley. And the DiGiorgio vineyards were long gone too. In response to demands for higher pay and better working conditions from Cesar Chavez and the United Farm Workers in the 1960s, the company had pulled its vines out of the ground and left.[1] Eventually, a Bakersfield man named Robert Maloy, a slumlord in the classic mold, bought the camp and collected rent while steadfastly refusing to make repairs.[2]

The camp was well-known as a hotbed of drug trafficking and other kinds of illegal activity, including cockfighting and the occasional knife fight. But rent was relatively cheap, between $100 and $200 a month. And if you looked past the collapsing ceilings, broken heaters, and myriad other health and safety hazards, parts of it were actually quite pleasant. Giant old oak trees shaded some of the property, vegetable gardens burst with corn and tomatoes, and everyone knew everyone else.

Many members of the Martinez family had wound up at Sierra Vista after Pedro Fernandez had been packed off to federal prison, and when he got out, he moved there too.

As Diaz and his partner moved through the camp, they didn't find the car they were looking for, but they did run into Fernandez. They seized the opportunity to question him. He was, after all, an infamous drug smuggler and the uncle of their suspect. Fernandez, no stranger to sparring with police, denied knowing his own nephew. This was irritating and typical. But the detectives had nothing on Fernandez—this time anyway. They left the camp. They had to find Raul Gonzalez's erstwhile friend, who was now a murder suspect.

By 9 p.m. they had another tack. They went looking for the friend's cousin. Some sources said they had been together that night. They found the cousin's wife (incidentally, another of Martinez's cousins), who confirmed that her husband had been drinking beer with the murder suspect on the night in question. But the cousin had been home by 1 a.m., she said. He certainly had not been involved in any kind of murder.

Where was her husband now? He had fled, she said. Not because he was guilty of anything but rather because Raul Gonzalez's brother had come and threatened him, and he feared for his life. She had taken him to the bus station in Delano and had no idea where he had gone from there.

The trail was cold. The friend and his cousin were in the wind.

And with the suspects safely in hiding, people began to change their stories.

On October 25, detectives went back to the Sierra Vista Labor Camp to talk to Pedro Fernandez again. This time, Fernandez admitted that the murder suspect was his nephew, and he admitted that he had lied. He informed police that both his nephew and his nephew's cousin had left the country and were now in Mexico.

Then the investigation took a surprising turn.

On November 4, more than two weeks after the murder, three of the cousin's relatives came forward to try to clear his name.

The cousin had wanted nothing to do with this murder, they claimed. His only crime was that he had been hanging out with Pedro Fernandez's nephew when the man abruptly decided to kidnap Raul and then shot and stabbed him. The poor cousin had just been in the car, scared out of his mind but forced to help drag the body into the trunk and then back out so they could dump it, the relatives said.

The first two relatives told basically the same story when questioned separately by Diaz.

But the third relative, a teenaged girl, offered a strange variation on the murder scene.

The friend "ran after Raul. And then [the friend] started to hit him I think with the scissors but Raul was screaming away over there," she said.

"What was the deceased saying?" Diaz asked.

The young woman answered that he was screaming, "Jose, let me go. Jose, let me go."

Diaz asked the obvious question: "Why did he call [the friend] Jose?"

The girl thought about that for a second. Her answer made no sense. "To him, it was easier to call him Jose."

Diaz didn't seem satisfied. "To the deceased it seemed easier to call [him] Jose?"

The young woman's answer, according to the transcript, was, "Ahem."

*   *   *

The murder of Raul Gonzalez, according to Martinez, was "not planned" but rather a spur of the moment act. "I got mad because he said a bad word to me," he said.

Gonzalez was a regular client. He bought heroin from Martinez and sold it on the streets of Earlimart both to make money and to support his own drug habit. Martinez said he didn't usually mess around with such small buyers, but they had known each other for years. He was from Earlimart, and their families moved in some of the same circles.

His beef, he said, was that Gonzalez owed him $2,000. Gonzalez had plenty of customers. He should have had no problem coming up with the money. But he hadn't paid up. Martinez had been after him for a while. Raul kept saying, "Tomorrow. I got your money. Tomorrow."

But then when tomorrow came, no money. Even so, he wanted more drugs.

"Who the fuck do you think you're talking to," Martinez wondered, according to his memoir. Did Gonzalez think he could punk him, look down on him, just because Martinez was younger than him? He told Raul, "When you pay me, you get more drugs."[3]

Raul started ducking him. In fact, he disappeared for several days. As it turns out, he'd been locked up in county jail on drug charges—but Martinez said he hadn't known that.

On October 19, Martinez took his wife shopping in Delano. Main Street was the place to see and be seen. It was lively and full of fun. There were restaurants, clothing and hardware stores, bakeries, taquerias, Filipino food. He and his wife strolled down the storefronts, window shopping and taking it all in.

They were in the car headed home when Martinez saw Raul. He was at a bank—taking money out of an ATM machine, no less. The nerve of that. How disrespectful. Rage bubbled up inside Martinez. He looked for a parking space so he could run after

Raul, but parking was often impossible on busy Main Street. By the time Martinez found a spot, Raul was gone.

Still, Raul couldn't evade him for long. That night, some friends of Martinez's—he takes care never to name them—somehow got Raul in their car. Martinez met up with them at a Chevron station and jumped in the backseat with Raul.

"You got my money now?" he asked. "Because I saw you taking money out of an ATM machine today."

Raul told him he was "a big liar." And then he insulted Martinez, which was the last straw.

"Drive out of town," Martinez ordered. And as soon as they rolled onto a dark, abandoned country road, Martinez whipped out his gun and shot Raul in the stomach, right there in the car. His friend stopped the car. Raul took off running through an almond orchard. Martinez jumped out of the car and tried to shoot him again, but the gun jammed. Raul kept running.

Martinez grabbed pruning shears from the floor of the car—many fieldworkers kept such tools in their vehicles—and began to chase Raul.

When he caught him, he stabbed him again and again.

Then he put his body in the trunk and got back in the car.

According to Martinez, his friend "didn't say a word." He didn't even ask why Martinez had done it. They just drove to an isolated field and together they dumped the body. Then his friend went to Mexicali.

Martinez does not name the friends who were with him that night or say if they were the same people Detective Diaz connected to the crime. As for the fact that Gonzalez had agreed to become a police informant on the very night he was killed—Martinez said he knew nothing about that.

Chapter Nine

The police car appeared in Martinez's rearview mirror as he was driving home from the Sierra Vista Labor Camp. He pulled over. He wasn't worried—he was in a "clean" car. No drugs. No weapons. Just a young man visiting his mother.

The officer walked to his window and identified himself as Detective Ralph Diaz.

This gave Martinez a little jolt. He knew Diaz was the homicide detective on the murder of Gonzalez.

Still, he wasn't particularly worried. He knew the cops didn't know anything. He knew they kept coming to Sierra Vista, where everyone gave them the runaround. He knew they had come to his house. Well, they could keep coming. His friends were safely in Mexico.

As he always was with police officers, Martinez was courteous and calm. Cheerful even.

Diaz made a show of checking Martinez's car carefully, looking for guns or drugs. He found nothing. But it soon became clear that the detective really wanted to talk about the murder of Raul Gonzalez.

Diaz mentioned Martinez's friend and his cousin. Martinez knew them, he said. Did he know where they were?

Yes, Martinez said, but he wasn't going to say. "It's not my job to tell cops where my friends go."[1]

Well then, Diaz countered, had Martinez known Raul Gonzalez?

"Everybody knew that punk," Martinez replied.

This got Diaz's attention. Why are you calling him a punk? he asked.

"Because he was a punk," Martinez said. "Are you done searching my car? I have a wife and two kids waiting for me at home and I have to take my wife shopping for food."

Diaz let him go. There was a lot of evidence in the case, and it mostly pointed straight at the friend who had kidnapped Raul from his home and to the friend's cousin. On November 5, 1982, Detective Diaz officially "closed" the Gonzalez case. The district attorney filed murder charges against the two men. The clearance form indicated that both suspects were in Mexico, out of reach of US law enforcement.

Even though they knew their suspects had fled to Mexico, Diaz and his partner, Jay Salazar, continued to look for them, on the off chance that they were foolish or arrogant enough to come back. But the detectives were also very busy with other murders. Some kind of turf war was clearly ripping the streets of Earlimart apart.

On October 19—the same day Raul Gonzalez was murdered and two days before his body was found—there was another drug-related killing: Javier Vega was shot to death in a trailer park at about 11:30 p.m. in what police determined was an argument over drugs.[2]

Ten days after that, on Halloween, Quentin Ayon—a cousin of Silvestre Ayon—was shot to death in Earlimart. The suspect was a friend of none other than Tacho Chaidez, the man Santa Barbara

County detectives were so interested in finding in the Ayon murder.[3] A week later, on November 7, Jesse Salazar was stabbed to death outside a party in Earlimart.

All those murders, sheriff's detectives determined, were likely drug related.[4] And on top of that, there were two more killings in October in Earlimart that detectives said were prompted by fights.

If police had any indication that at least some of those deaths in Earlimart could be traced directly back to major drug-trafficking organizations in Mexico, they made no mention of it to the newspapers.

Earlimart had a population of about forty-five hundred at that time, giving it one of the highest murder rates in the United States. The violence was so extreme that even the *Tulare Advance Register*, which usually ignored such events or confined them to short crime briefs on the inside pages, took notice: "Murder in Earlimart Becoming Routine" was the blaring headline across the front page on November 10, 1982.

The story listed death after violent death. It did not quote any Earlimart residents or provide any information about the town's history, population, economics, or demographics. Instead, it quoted sheriff's department officials, some of whom essentially blamed immigrants for the problems. The paper made little attempt to address the fact that most of the people who lived in the town were hardworking, and law-abiding, and terrorized by a small group of violent drug traffickers.

"We're getting more and more of the younger generation of illegal aliens coming into this area," one sergeant told the paper. "They're used to dealing with situations in a more violent manner. Their society is tough and they're bringing it here with them." He added that police were unable to bring the perpetrators to justice because "we have a lot of our suspects disappearing to Mexico. It's extremely difficult to get them back."[5]

Another sheriff's official told the reporter that some Earlimart residents were so terrified of the violence on their streets that there was a feeling of "paranoia." But he added that among some residents "this type of activity is not looked upon as unusual."

In one sense, this official was correct: folks in Earlimart were more accustomed to violence than, say, folks in wealthy Exeter—forty minutes or five planets away. But that didn't mean people in Earlimart found it acceptable. If the reporter had managed to track down Raul Gonzalez's relatives, he might have learned that the family was reeling. Gonzalez's widow was so distressed that she tried to hurt herself; his mother sat at the kitchen table every night and simply wept for hour after hour.

Martinez—the American-born son of an American citizen—was not a regular reader of the *Tulare Advance Register*. But his family did know the Gonzalez family, and he likely would have heard about their anguish. If this caused him guilt or remorse, he never talked about it.

Instead, Martinez came to his own conclusions about the police response to the murder. As he wrote in his memoir, "Raul Gonzalez was not a very important person for the community of Earlimart, because after a few weeks of his death, they stopped asking questions."

And indeed, so did the newspaper.

Chapter Ten

The detectives in Santa Barbara had a lighter caseload. They could afford to remain focused on who had killed Silvestre Ayon while he went about caring for the horses of one of the most prominent citizens in their county.

As they drilled down on the case, they could not believe what they were learning about Earlimart. It was nothing short of crazy that in just a few short weeks after Silvestre Ayon was murdered, three of his relatives had been involved in other homicides there, as either victims or suspects. Quentin Ayon, killed in Earlimart on October 31, was Silvestre Ayon's cousin. The two men now wanted for the murder of Raul Gonzalez were also distantly related.

The town didn't even have a stoplight!

Soon the Santa Barbara detectives learned about another Earlimart character, a figure with such an outsize legend he sounded almost mythic, right down to his moniker: "El Abuelo," or "The Grandfather."

El Abuelo was known to be a coyote, and such a skilled one that he had not only transported untold numbers of people and drugs over the border but had also managed to escape from the custody of the US federal government when he finally got caught.

He was also reputed to be a "highwayman" wanted for numerous murders in Mexico. The detectives heard differing figures on how many, although the number was never less than a dozen. El Abuelo had also reputedly committed murders in the United States too, maybe in Oregon and Crescent City, California. And he had a connection to their case.

Detectives heard word that two of El Abuelo's brothers had been killed in the infamous dance hall shootout in La Cofradia, Durango. Did El Abuelo know the Chaidez family? Yes, he did. Also, in the complicated web they had come to expect from Earlimart, El Abuelo was also a distant cousin of Silvestre Ayon.

All this seemed so outlandishly colorful that it was hard to imagine it could be true. And yet, source after source told officers, often in a whisper, that El Abuelo had to be involved. They often added a plea not to mention their names, lest harm come to them or their families.

As usual, when Santa Barbara detectives called Ralph Diaz for help, his knowledge was encyclopedic.

Why yes, El Abuelo was a real person. His real name was Manuel Ayon Nunez. He was about forty years old. And in fact, he had been spotted in Earlimart—at the Sierra Vista Labor Camp—in mid-October, shortly after the murder.

On November 14, 1982, Santa Barbara detectives decided it was time to see this place for themselves. They drove over the hills and down into the valley. They met up with Diaz that afternoon and talked through the cases with him for nine hours, finally breaking up about midnight.

Detective Correll cannot recall many of the specifics of this long session. He does remember that much of the conversation took place in Spanish. And he remembers the shock of it all. He was a seasoned homicide detective. He had seen a lot of violence and criminal behavior. But he was floored by the world of drug smuggling and murder Diaz was telling them about, here in this little town just over the hills from his own county.

What's more, it seemed to Correll and Ortega that Diaz and his partner were somehow dealing with this almost all by themselves. Many of the Tulare County detectives and other officers they met "didn't seem to care much about Mexicans getting murdered," he said. But Diaz clearly did. "He was like the Lone Ranger," Correll marveled. "He was unrelenting, and he didn't have much help."

Correll wasn't well versed in Tulare County history, but he had something right: the department where Diaz worked did not have a great reputation for achieving justice in farmworker communities.

The sheriff at the time, Bob Wiley, had been elected in 1966, the year after the United Farm Workers (UFW) launched the grape strike. Wiley, then twenty-nine, had almost no background in law enforcement. He'd been a rodeo champion and, before that, a high school football star, two qualities much appreciated by the electorate even though they didn't necessarily have much to do with policing. As the grape strike evolved into a national civil rights struggle, Wiley's Tulare County Sheriff's Department acquired a reputation not just for taking the side of growers over farmworkers but for doing so with savage brutality. "It's been going on for a long time and a lot of hatred has built up," a Tulare County sheriff's deputy matter-of-factly told the writer John Gregory Dunne in the summer of 1966 when he came down to the valley to research his masterful book *Delano: The Story of the California Grape Strike*.[1] Cesar Chavez said the Tulare County Sheriff's Department was the worst he'd ever dealt with. "We've been in many, many strikes, and we've been in places like Florida and Texas, and I'd be willing to say that even though the Texas Rangers were extremely brutal to us, we haven't seen anything anywhere as bad as the Tulare County sheriff against our people,"

Chavez told the California State Assembly.[2] Wiley, who led the charge on hiring more Mexican Americans into government jobs in Tulare County, insisted this was an unfair characterization. And he compared the farmworkers' movement to a "revolution" of the leftist kind overthrowing regimes across Latin America. "My officers never push people around," Wiley said. "These farm workers that cause violence have to be expected to be arrested. We just can't tolerate this kind of revolution, and that's what this is, a revolution in our country."[3]

Supporters of Chavez were appalled by Wiley and his department, with some using the word "gestapo." But Wiley, who was also frequently featured in the local newspaper for swashbuckling hijinks like personally engaging suspects in car chases and shootouts, was reelected by large margins. Tulare's electorate, then as now, represents only a portion of the county's population since so many residents aren't citizens and can't vote.

Diaz had been in Vietnam during the height of the violence between the sheriff's department and the UFW and so hadn't seen it firsthand. In any event, his colleagues do not recall him as especially political, and he and Wiley, by many accounts, got along. What Diaz was, they said, was a ferocious detective, determined to solve his cases.

This much Correll could see: "Ralphie cared about these folks....He was from there. He wanted to see justice done." Correll gave him the ultimate seal of approval. Diaz, he decided, was "a master hunter."[4]

After their marathon meeting with Diaz, the detectives grabbed a few hours of sleep at a local motel and were back with Diaz by 8 a.m. the next morning. As the sun climbed over the mountains, Diaz took them hopscotching across southern Tulare County. They visited small, rundown houses and trailers and grim-looking apartment buildings, all to meet with a host of locals who had known Silvestre Ayon or who knew El Abuelo.

Some of them wanted to help.

Some of them clearly did not.

Almost every conversation was in Spanish. Correll listened for the words he knew, tried to read people's body language and tone of voice, and translated as best he could. He heard new stories about El Abuelo's alleged perfidy. They sat with a woman who had known both Silvestre Ayon and El Abuelo. She told police that El Abuelo had shot and killed her mother in Durango in 1977.

The level of violence was incomprehensible.

But what was worse was the fear that these people were obviously harboring. The detectives would show up at someone's home and knock on the door, and if they were allowed in, the resident would immediately draw the blinds so no one could see inside. "Don't tell anyone I've been talking with the police," they pleaded. "Or they will come and kill me next."

By 2:45 p.m., Diaz had led them to the Sierra Vista Labor Camp to speak to a man whose name they never got, but the exchange turned out to be a bust. The man, far from being helpful, "appeared to be very nervous and evasive in his answers."

After they left the labor camp where so many of Martinez's family members lived, Diaz took them to an address in a little town just south of the Tulare County line, in McFarland. Number 344 Industrial Avenue was a stucco bungalow behind a chain-link fence. Diaz wanted them to speak with an immigrant from Durango who was related to Silvestre Ayon.

Diaz had visited that house on numerous occasions. It kept coming up in his cases. He knew by this time that the house had another resident, although detectives in their police reports never noted the importance of this fact. That resident, of course, was Jose Martinez.

Santa Barbara detectives didn't talk to Martinez or take heed that he lived there.

They came up empty and went back home.

The case stayed cold.

The day after the Santa Barbara detectives returned home, there was yet another murder in Earlimart. A fifteen-year-old girl was charged with stabbing and then running over a twenty-four-year-old man. She claimed self-defense.

That killing was the last straw. Earlimart residents, as inured to violence and as fearful as many of them were, had had enough. People took to the streets in the kind of protest they had rarely staged since the height of the farmworker movement more than a decade earlier. A group of about 150 held a peace march on the night of Friday, December 3, 1982, holding candles and signs that read "Stop Mothers from Crying" and "Peace."

The local newspaper sent a reporter out to cover the event, and as he moved through the crowd, a teacher tried to call his attention to the lack of municipal services in Earlimart. "I'm feeling sad, but at the same time I'm feeling a little angry," the teacher said, explaining that while she was marching through town she was taking note of "the lack of things."[5]

The marchers' demands were modest. They wanted the sheriff's department to increase its patrols in Earlimart to take the streets back from the drug traffickers. And they wanted the county to build a sheriff's substation in town, to have a permanent police presence in the area.

But the substation was never built.

Earlimart and the little towns around it collectively had lots of residents but few voters. And sheriffs are elected, meaning they tend to be more responsive to the voters' concerns than are police chiefs, who are appointed by mayors or city councils. More than 80 percent of American counties have an elected sheriff. Broadly speaking, police departments handle law enforcement in cities, and sheriffs take care of it in small towns and rural areas. But the purview of a sheriff is wider than that of a police department. Sheriffs can also be coroners, jailers, and sometimes paramedics. Because sheriffs are politicians as well as law enforcement figures, they can be more receptive to the priorities of voters—and big campaign donors. But the converse can also be true: areas without voters and big campaign donors may find their concerns do not get as much attention.

In Earlimart, some people were disappointed by law enforcement's lack of response to their marches and demands. But some, even some law-abiding people who desperately wanted safer streets, were also somewhat relieved. Some in town had someone—a cousin, a nephew, an uncle—who dabbled in the drug trade. A much larger number had someone in the family who was in the country without papers. If officers started knocking on doors, there was no telling who might get caught up in the dragnet. And no one trusted the sheriff's department to target only the big, violent dealers who were causing all the problems. There was too much history to the contrary for anyone to believe that.

Then some community members had a better idea. If the county and the sheriff's department wouldn't help them, they would help themselves. It was obvious what was needed: youth programs to keep kids off the street, give them something productive to do, and show them there was a wider world than backbreaking farmwork or drug smuggling.

In short order, several residents and teachers founded a non-profit organization, the Earlimart Youth Foundation. Led by the school music teacher, Bruce Boaz, the group also included another teacher, Lorenzo Morales, who had grown up in Earlimart, gone off to Idaho on a baseball scholarship, and then come home to raise his family and teach in the schools where he had once been a student.

A decade earlier, county officials, in their long-term plans, had decided to "starve" communities like Earlimart of municipal resources in an effort to get people to move away and abandon their towns. But in just eighteen months, the foundation showed how motivated residents were not just to have their town survive—but to thrive. They managed to raise money for a dizzying array of programs. They scraped together funds to build a baseball diamond for Little League games. They built a tiny park. They even organized a "swim bus" to take kids to the public pool in Delano to cool off in the scorching heat of summer.

But they were dreaming even bigger. Morales and Boaz and other members of the foundation wanted the kids in Earlimart to have their own public pool. While they were at it, they wanted a running track, and a gymnasium, and more classrooms so kids didn't have to sit on top of each other while they were trying to learn.

The town didn't have any money, obviously. So Boaz and others spent weekends hunched over kitchen tables, writing grant proposals and filling out loan documents so detailed Boaz complained they were the size of telephone books. By 1985 they had come up with an unusual bond program, which Earlimart voters approved in 1986, to tax themselves to make the community better for their children.

"We're going to have a pool if we have to dig it ourselves," Boaz told the *Tulare Advance Register.*[6]

Lorenzo Morales's daughter, Melissa, was twelve the year the pool opened. All summer long, she and her friends swam until their skin gave off the scent of chlorine, staring in awe up at the towering high dive but not yet brave enough to jump off it.

The important part of the story for Melissa was not the violence that had shattered her town's streets or the lackluster response from county officials. It was the way her community had come together and, despite its limited resources, built something beautiful. It was a lesson she would carry with her throughout her life: her hometown, despite its problems, was a place where people moved mountains to help children when it seemed like no one else would.[7]

Chapter Eleven

Sometime after the murder of Silvestre Ayon, Mr. X rewarded Martinez with a pager.

A pager! Doctors and firefighters and other important people had had them for years, but pagers, also known as beepers, had only recently become available to the general population. These devices, about the size of a bar of soap, would buzz or beep and deliver the number of whoever had phoned. The pager made Martinez feel important, and a few days later, when it chirped, he rushed to return the call.

Whenever someone summoned him on the pager—whether for a kill or a kidnapping or to collect a debt—Martinez would refer to them as having "a little problem" they needed his assistance to solve.

Martinez's first page was from Mr. X, who, Martinez wrote, "was having a little problem with a man who owed him $95,000."

By midnight, Martinez was in his car, speeding north on Highway 99 through orange and almond orchards, past the lights of Fresno that glow yellow through the valley haze. When he arrived in the city of Modesto, he found a cheap motel and slept for a few hours.

As the sun rose, Martinez was up again.

He followed the plan he had discussed with Mr. X. He went to the debtor's house, kidnapped him at gunpoint, and took him to an associate's ranch near Fresno.

According to Martinez, this was the first time he collected on a drug debt. It went off without a hitch.

Martinez said he deposited the man in a chair inside a garage and sat down opposite him.

"Listen really good to what I'm going to tell you," Martinez told him, "because I really don't like to talk too much."[1]

Then he laid it out: "I'm still getting paid if I get the money or not. It's up to you, how you want to get back home. You have two fucking hours."

The captive wasted no time in thinking it over. He asked to use the phone and called his wife.

"*Mujer*, in the hallway closet, there's a black backpack," Martinez heard him say.

To Martinez, he said, "My wife has the money."

Martinez replied that Mr. X would be by shortly to pick it up.

Then it was Martinez's turn to use the phone. He called Mr. X and told him to retrieve the backpack and send him a message on the beeper if the money was there.

An hour later, the beeper sounded with the good news. Martinez loaded his captive into his car and dropped him off at the Greyhound bus station in Fresno. Next, he drove north to meet Mr. X.

"You didn't kill him, did you?" Mr. X asked.

Martinez shook his head. "No, Mr. X, you told me no violence. I don't want you to have problems."

Mr. X gave him $30,000 for his troubles.

Thirty thousand dollars! Martinez was exultant. He hadn't had to torture anyone. He hadn't even used a gun. He'd merely scared an "old fucking man." It was beautiful.

He got on the 99 freeway, headed to his new house. He had recently moved again—twice.

Earlimart was overrun with drugs and violence. Martinez had played starring roles in the production of both—but that didn't mean he wanted his family around them.

It was also becoming clear that the problems in both Earlimart and McFarland, the two places he had been raising his children, went far beyond the violence of the drug trade. Year after year, Earlimart had some of the highest unemployment figures in the valley, which tended to have the highest unemployment figures in California. At times, unemployment in Earlimart approached 50 percent of the population.

Even more disturbing: children were getting cancer in mysteriously high numbers.

Community members and doctors first flagged a higher incidence of childhood cancer in McFarland, where the Martinez family was living in 1981 and 1982. By the late 1980s, officials had identified thirteen children with cancer in the town of six thousand people. This rate, health officials said, was three to four times higher than expected in a town that size.

By the late 1980s, the entire town buzzed with anxiety. The school nurse reported that children were running to her in terror at the slightest symptom.[2]

Some years later, health officials identified another unexplained cluster of childhood cancers in nearby Earlimart. Mothers in both towns were experiencing high rates of miscarriage. People searched for an explanation. Had the water supply been contaminated? Had agricultural pesticides that farmers sprayed on their crops been swept up by the wind and drifted over homes, sending poison into people's lungs?

The unexplained sickness of the children cast a pall of worry and dread over the area. It was so horrific, in fact, that it brought rare outside attention to the cares and concerns of people living in Earlimart and McFarland. The Reverend Jesse Jackson made a stop in McFarland during his 1988 run for president, trying to call attention to the plight of farmworkers. Art Torres, a member of the state legislature from Los Angeles, sponsored a bill with Trice Harvey, a Republican from Bakersfield, the biggest city in Kern County, to set aside $500,000 for cancer screens for children and clinical services in the area. Jack Pandol, a prominent grape grower, signaled his support. Even so, Governor George Deukmejian, a Republican with close ties to farmers, vetoed the bill.

"I am truly sympathetic to the unfortunate situation that has caused much fear and anxiety," the governor wrote in his veto message.[3] However, he added, the state was already studying the cancer cluster, and screenings were already available.

Once again, the power structure had decided these towns didn't deserve much.

Some Earlimart residents, meanwhile, told newspaper reporters they were afraid to even speak out about the children with cancer, for fear that powerful employers would punish them for complaining about pesticides. "If you are seen as a troublemaker," a local barbershop owner told the *Los Angeles Times*, "then you show up the next day and your boss tells you your job is gone."

Martinez did not follow these details. But he moved his family away from Earlimart and McFarland to Porterville, a slightly larger community east of Earlimart near the citrus belt. Porterville wasn't exactly Beverly Hills, but it was a little better off economically, and it definitely seemed better for children in some ways. It had parks, for one thing. And a high school. There was a big lake five miles east of town and mountains nearby for camping. It was also a much larger town—with a population of about fifty thousand and even its own newspaper—making it an easier place to get lost in. Martinez rented a two-bedroom house in front of the sheriff's substation and enjoyed the thought that the officers going in and out had no idea that a contract killer was living just across the street.

A year after that, he moved again, to Delano, to be closer to his extended family.

It took Martinez about three hours to make the drive from where he had left Mr. X near Fresno to his new house. He walked in the door with a huge, bright smile, holding up the $30,000 in cash Mr. X had given him.

"Help me count your money," he called to his wife.[4]

She happily did—according to him.

The next day, Martinez drove his family to the mall in Bakersfield and told them to go nuts.

And shortly after that, he took them on a celebratory vacation to San Francisco. Cable cars! Fisherman's Wharf! Even Alcatraz, the former island penitentiary that is now a museum. Martinez said he combined the tourist outing with a meeting about sourcing cocaine.

While Martinez and his family were living lavishly off the proceeds of the drug world, there were days when Cecilia Camacho, the wife of Martinez's first murder-for-hire victim, David Bedolla, did not have enough money to feed her son. The two were living in her parents' home in Puruandiro. In the nearly two years since she had returned to her village with her husband's body, she had been washing clothes and linens for money. But it often wasn't enough.

One day in the summer of 1982, her son asked if, as a special treat, they could have a drink of soda.

Cecilia felt like sobbing. She couldn't even buy her son a soda. That day, a neighbor brought over extra wash. Her son stood up, all two feet of him. "I'll help you," he said. "I'll help you wash the clothes, so you can get money quick, so we can buy a soda."

Though he was only about four years old, her son stayed by

her side as she scrubbed the clothes and then hung them to dry. He checked them constantly. Were they dry yet? How about now? Now were they dry?

Finally, the answer was yes. They gave the clothes back to their neighbor, who, in an act of grace, gave them an extra hundred pesos. Cecilia bought her son a piece of bread. And to go with it, a soda!

Watching him drink the sweet, fizzy liquid, she realized she might have to leave him again. She had to return to the United States. It was the only way she could think of to give her son a better life. He had already lost his father. She couldn't watch him go hungry.

In August 1982, she again left her son with her parents and took a bus with her siblings from Michoacán to San Luis Río Colorado, near Yuma, and hired a coyote. As he led them across the desert, Cecilia felt loneliness rise up in her. She remembered the last time she had made this crossing. Her husband had been by her side.

"You have to keep going," she told herself. "You have to make a better life for your son. It's all up to you now."[5]

The town of Lindsay was just as she had left it nearly two years before. She went right back to the same old boarding house. She found the same crew leader that she and her husband had worked for, and she went back to work. At night, she returned to the very same room she and her husband had once lived in. Even the bed was still there, the same bed they had once shared. Except now he was dead. And she was alone.

Chapter Twelve

On Valentine's Day in 1983, Martinez gave his wife a dozen red roses. She had a better gift for him: she was pregnant with their third child.

Life was perfect. But it was not without complications. Not only did Martinez have to keep from his wife that he was a murderer. Now he also had to hide a mistress. A pregnant mistress.

It had started, he said, innocently enough, with a favor for his brother. Antonio needed help: his wife's sister wanted to come to the United States, but she didn't have papers, and so someone needed to get her across the border.

"Bro, I'm a drug dealer, not a coyote," Martinez said. But he quickly relented. "We can go to Mexico and try. You know I can't say no to you."[1]

The brothers went to collect the young woman at the bus station in Mexicali, a Mexican city directly across from Calexico in the southeastern corner of California. When Martinez saw her, his heart began to pound. "I am in love," he wrote in his memoir.

He got her across the border. It was easy. They simply walked.

The young woman was living with his brother and sister-in-law, which meant Martinez could visit as often as it took to seduce her. He even convinced her to go on a trip with him, including a few days at the beach. Soon, she was pregnant.

Martinez said he explained to her that he couldn't marry her because he was already married, but he promised to support her. "I'm a very responsible man," he told her.

Clearly, Mr. X thought Martinez was responsible as well. Mr. X was giving him job after job.

He dispatched Martinez to Twin Falls, Idaho, to kill a man, allegedly in part for raping a young woman in or near the San Joaquin Valley town of Madera, California. Martinez wasn't exactly sure. He didn't ask too many questions.

He set out east, stopping in Vegas to stretch his legs and play the tables, and then in St. George, Utah, to see the famous Mormon temple. He marveled at its beauty and couldn't help but notice the strange looks he was getting. *I guess they don't like Mexican people*, he thought to himself. In Salt Lake City he gazed at the mighty Rocky Mountains rising above the bustling downtown and thought about sightseeing some more, then reminded himself there was still a mission at hand. He continued north to Twin Falls, where, he said, he found his victim, stabbed him, and left his body in the woods.

Martinez was never caught or charged. Records from the Twin Falls County Sheriff's Office do confirm the unsolved homicide of a Mexican adult male around this time. In the spring of 1985, a pair of teenaged Boy Scouts came upon what they initially thought was a cow skeleton in the town of Buhl, outside Twin Falls. It turned out to be the skeleton of a man police later said had likely been stabbed to death. Authorities determined the victim was likely male and Mexican or Mexican American. After talking to local farmers, they concluded that the body may have been dumped there in the summer of 1984.

Police received a handful of confusing tips—among them, that the crime involved farmworkers, that it involved the Mexican Mafia, that the motive was to avenge a rape, that the motive was to punish someone who had stolen cocaine, and that it had all stemmed from a fight at a labor camp. But there was nothing substantive. The case went cold.[2]

For other crimes that Martinez claims to have committed during this era—which include murders across the country—there is only his word, with no other documentation.

Back home, Martinez's complicated romantic life became more so. His girlfriend's pregnancy became apparent, and her brothers, who were also living in the area, were furious. Martinez talked them down, but it was the end of his relationship with the young woman.

Martinez said he was "happy and sad at the same time. Happy for having another baby, sad because I won't be seeing [the woman]. But that's OK, I can find another girl."

In August 1984, the Martinez-Fernandez family received some unexpected news: the other alleged assailant in the dance hall shooting—the other object of the vendetta—had been spotted in the farm town of Shafter, which sits in the middle of Kern County, about ten miles south of McFarland. Rumor had it that the man had found work in the fields harvesting grapes.

Martinez called Mr. X, who came down from the Fresno area.

Not for one minute did they consider the idea of letting the man live. The pain of losing their loved ones persisted inside Mr. X and the others who had suffered a loss.

Martinez and Mr. X found a woman who knew what their target looked like and arranged to pay her $500 to point the man out to them. On the appointed day, the men donned ski masks, loaded their guns, and picked up the woman from her home. At around noon they parked and began to walk through the vineyards, past row after row of vines, looking for their target.

Finally, they spotted three men working next to a tractor. "That's him, the one standing up," the woman whispered. She ran back to the car.

Martinez took his gun from his waistband and shot the man two or three times. Then they too ran back to the car, leaving the man dead in the field.

The woman, Martinez noticed, spent the car ride home crying. "But when she saw the $500, she stopped crying."

They drove back to Martinez's house, which was not far from where Cesar Chavez had launched the United Farm Workers, and when they got there, Mr. X gave Martinez $5,000 in cash. Martinez was thrilled. Yet again, he had avenged his family's honor and been paid for doing it.

The next day, Martinez and Mr. X learned they had made a mistake. The man they had shot to death was not their target at all; it was his brother.

Chagrined, Martinez called Mr. X and offered to return the $5,000. Mr. X told him to keep it and added that he wasn't sorry for what they had done. Now their target would know the pain of losing a brother.

In early 1985, Mr. X again summoned Martinez up north. Martinez brought his family with him, but he and Mr. X still found some time alone to chat. Mr. X said he needed Martinez to take a man from Modesto to Mexicali. The wrinkle: the man didn't want to go.

Have you ever crossed a person to Mexico while they were in handcuffs, Mr. X asked nonchalantly.

Martinez said he had not. But, he said, he had a plan. He drove his family back home after a quick visit to Yosemite National Park. Then he put his plan into action.

He asked a woman he knew—he had once helped her cross the border too—if she wanted to earn a few hundred dollars going on a long car trip. By 10:45 a.m. the next morning, the two pulled into Mr. X's garage. Martinez walked into the living room, where he found Mr. X and several other men standing while a man in handcuffs sat on the couch.

"Is this my package?" Martinez asked.

Mr. X replied that it was.

Martinez said he would call Mr. X when the package was delivered. "When I started out in this business, the packages were small," he joked. "Now they are big."

Martinez and his accomplice put the man in the backseat of their car, handcuffed and under strict orders not to make trouble at the border crossing, or there would be consequences. The delivery went off without incident. With the proceeds, Martinez bought a new truck—a burgundy Nissan, paid for in cash—and put one hundred thousand miles on it in one year, mostly delivering drugs.

By now, the Martinez family business involved not just getting drugs into the United States and around California but also running them to Chicago.

But unbeknownst to his family, Martinez was also becoming firmly established as a go-to hit man. In 1985, he did a job for Mr. X in Washington State, which went off—as usual—without a hitch.

But if his professional life was under control, his personal life was heading into stormy waters. When he returned from the job in Washington, he said he was confronted by an angry wife. She had heard rumors that he had had a child with another woman. Was it true?

She demanded to know when, where, and how many times he had had sex with the other woman.

He answered that he didn't like to give explanations of what he did with his life. This, also, failed to satisfy.

His wife responded that she needed time alone to figure out

what to do. "Months passed with silence in our bedroom. No more good-bye kisses. No more 'I love you.' No more good morning. No more hot coffee. My breakfast was always cold," Martinez wrote in his memoir. What's more, according to Martinez, every time he left to do a drug deal, his wife assumed he was spending time with the other woman.

Finally, his wife said she was going to visit her mother in Sinaloa and asked for a ride to Tijuana, where she could pick up the express bus home. She took the children with her.

Martinez went home to "an empty, lonely house." He had a bad feeling, but he hoped his wife would come back. He continued with his drug business and delivered another kidnapping victim to Tijuana. When he got back from that trip, he cleaned the house so it would be sparkling for his wife's return.

His family worried that his wife's departure had unmoored him. Since she had come to his stepfather's ranch when he was a teenager, she had been a calm, loving presence in his life—in the whole family's life. They all adored her. Though he took pains to hide it from them, family members also worried that Martinez's drug use spiked around this time.[3] He had long been a recreational user of marijuana, but some family members worried that it was becoming excessive. Martinez did not share their concerns and says his drug use was never excessive or a problem.

With Thanksgiving approaching, Martinez sent a telegram to his wife's mother, asking his wife to call him. Instead, his mother-in-law phoned to say that his wife had left Cosalá, but she was not coming home.

"She is very, very upset with you," his mother-in-law told him.

Martinez spent Thanksgiving with his mother, siblings, nieces, and nephews. He told himself he didn't need his wife. "Fuck," he remembers telling himself, according to his memoir. "I can get any woman I want. I got thousands of ways to get a woman's panties down."[4]

But he missed her and his children. Desperately. Family was the most important thing in his life—even if he wasn't always the most faithful of husbands or ever-present of fathers. Without them, he felt lost.

After Christmas in 1986, Martinez called Mr. X and asked for a favor. He was coming to Sinaloa to find his wife, and he needed to borrow a car.

Of course, Mr. X said. Anything you need. Mr. X was a huge proponent of Martinez's reconciling with his family.

From Culiacan, Martinez drove to Cosalá. He tracked down his mother-in-law and convinced her to reveal that his wife was staying with her aunt in a small town near San Luis Río Colorado, on the border. He traveled all the way there before realizing that he didn't know where his wife's aunt lived. He went door-to-door in that town, asking for the aunt. It took hours, knocking on doors, asking for the woman, walking to the next house.

Finally, he found the aunt. She let him in. His wife wasn't there. But his children were.

When he asked when his wife would be home, he got shocking news: his wife was working in Yuma, Arizona, and returning to her children on weekends.

Martinez couldn't believe it. His wife had never worked a day since he'd taken her as his girlfriend more than a decade before. He told his wife's aunt that he was going to take the two oldest children with him. "You can stay with the small one, because he still shits on the diapers," he said. When his wife came back, Martinez continued, the woman should tell her that he had taken what was his, and if she had any problems, he was still in the same house where she had left him.

Other Martinez family members offer a slightly different version of this story. According to them, Martinez had gone with one of his sisters and another family member specifically to rescue the children after hearing they weren't being well cared for while their mother worked in the fields.[5]

In the family members' version, only the daughter was brought home to Delano. In both versions, the family lavished loved on the girl.

A short time later, according to Martinez, his wife showed up at his house "ready for battle." She said she didn't want to talk to him. She just wanted to take her child and her car and go.

"I love you," he told her. "You have been the love of my life since the first day I saw you. I'm not going to give up. I'm going to fight to win your love back."

She refused to give in and replied that she was leaving because he had cheated on her.

"I didn't cheat on you," he protested. "I just don't say what I do in life."

This logic failed to persuade her. What's more, she had heard "bad things" about him, "real ugly things."

"Everyone does ugly things in life," Martinez answered.

In response, his wife gave him an address near Yuma. And with that, she left.

Martinez stayed in his valley, where the streets petered out into fields and neat rows of almond and orange orchards and vineyards marched all the way to the hills and the mountains. Beyond them, his family was gone.

Chapter Thirteen

On March 1, 1991—eight and a half years after the murder of Silvestre Ayon—Tacho Chaidez finally resurfaced.

Police officers in the Los Angeles suburb of South Gate pulled him over while he was driving through the city with his brother and a friend.

The reason for that original traffic stop is unclear, but when police searched the car, a late-model Ford Taurus, they found pagers galore and even a cell phone—a rare luxury item in 1991. In the trunk, they also found $35,000 in cash in a paper bag.

The men were arrested on suspicion of being drug traffickers, but that was the least of Tacho's problems. Because when police ran his name, they found an outstanding murder warrant from Santa Barbara County dating back to January 1983.

Detectives Bruce Correll and Leo Ortega had convinced their district attorney to issue the warrant after their trips to Earlimart and because they had finally managed to trace the Gremlin car used in the shooting back to someone close to Chaidez.

Tacho was delivered to the county jail in Santa Maria, a city in the northern part of Santa Barbara County, and on March 6, detectives showed up to interview him.

Though he had been in the United States for years, he claimed not to speak English. So Detective Ortega spoke to him in Spanish. It was a short conversation. Despite his alleged lack of English, Tacho knew how the American legal system worked, and he knew just what to do. He confirmed his identity, then asked for his lawyer. No more questions.

Three days later, Correll and Ortega were back in Los Angeles, serving search warrants on all the various addresses associated with Tacho Chaidez and his brothers, hoping to gather evidence that might link them to the murder of Silvestre Ayon. They were particularly interested in Tacho's brother Domingo, who was also rumored to have been involved.

It was a very different trip from the first time the two old friends had bounced from address to address around the small cities on LA's southern swath. Correll had begun his rise up the ranks in the department—he was now a patrol sergeant. And Ortega had changed too. He was no longer hitting the town at night when the work was done. It meant they got an earlier start in the morning.

But a few things remained the same: A lot of addresses. A lot of dead ends.

They started at the address listed on Tacho's driver's license, in Carson, another small city south of Los Angeles. Yet, when they knocked on the door, the woman who answered told them she had never heard of Tacho Chaidez. She added that her own husband had left her for another woman a year earlier and shortly after that had been arrested for drug trafficking. The Drug Enforcement Administration (DEA) had already searched her house once, she said.

The detectives decided to search Tacho's brother's house in the nearby suburb of Downey, on the theory that Tacho might be living there. To avoid a repeat of their less-than-fruitful morning in Carson, they went door-to-door around the neighborhood first, showing residents a picture of Tacho and asking if he lived there. Ortega was worried that Correll, because he was a six-foot-tall white dude, might frighten people off. So he told Correll to stand back and look small while Ortega did all the talking. And if anyone asked who Correll was, Ortega told them, "This is my friend, El Dufo."

Amazingly, this was not a total wash. They found one man who said he had seen Tacho around a lot lately and added that he wasn't very friendly. "A lot of expensive new cars come to the house at all hours of the day and night," the man noted.

A confidential informant also told detectives that both Tacho and Domingo were living in the Downey house. The person added that both brothers were cocaine dealers and reportedly threatened to kill anyone who cooperated with law enforcement.

At 10:25 that night, the detectives, armed with a search warrant, went back to Domingo Chaidez's house. When no one answered the door, they busted in.

Then, they gaped in surprise.

From the outside, the house looked like any other nice, middle-class bungalow in a neighborhood full of them. But inside, it was a palace. Marble floors. Marble countertops. New everything. Expensive furniture. Giant TV screens. And signs that the occupants had left in a big hurry.

The detectives found closets full of brand-new designer clothing, "many pairs of expensive men's cowboy boots in exotic hides," and "several expensive Stetson 'El Patron' cowboy hats in boxes," according to their police reports.[1] They found receipts for Rolex watches. And they also found more than one hundred rounds of AK-47 assault rifle ammunition, as well as ammunition for .45s, .357 Magnums, .30 carbines, and .22 rifles. In short: an elaborate display of high-end narco-culture.

Once again, the detectives realized, they weren't in Santa Barbara anymore.

Despite the plentiful evidence of wealth in the home, the detectives also found a 1989 federal tax return for a business called Mingo's Lawn Service reporting less than $10,000 in income.

Ha, they thought. Unlike their counterparts in the Los Angeles County Sheriff's Department and even the Tulare County Sheriff's Department, the Santa Barbara detectives didn't routinely interact with drug traffickers. There were drugs in Santa Barbara, of course. It was a playground for the rich and famous and also home to one of the nation's most flamboyant party schools, UC Santa Barbara. But Santa Barbara wasn't a major transit point for drugs and money like Los Angeles or the San Joaquin Valley. Still, the detectives knew signs of money laundering when they saw them. And an all-cash business like a lawn service, showing less than $10,000 in income in a house cluttered with Rolex watches, fit the bill.

They also found paperwork for trailers registered to yet another address, in the San Joaquin Valley city of Clovis. Four days later, the detectives had made the two-hundred-mile drive north and teamed up with their Fresno County counterparts. They all headed to a mobile home park in the Fresno suburb of Fowler, arriving about 6:45 p.m.

As they drove up, they saw people running from the home. One man was hiding in the cab of his truck. When police pulled him out, they found almost two kilograms of cocaine and a bag containing $10,000 in cash.

Inside the house, they found a wife of one of the residents. She claimed to know nothing about a murder in Santa Barbara County or about any drug trafficking. "I'm just a piece of furniture he's kept around for ten years," she told Detective Ortega bitterly.

If that was so, Ortega asked her, then what about that guy hiding in his truck outside with a lot of cocaine and all that cash?

The woman looked away, with tears in her eyes, and said she didn't know anything about that either.

When police searched her bedroom, they found a Beretta .380-caliber handgun. In another bedroom, they found two more guns and some heroin.

Fresno police packed everyone off to jail to face charges on the guns and the drugs.

After their days-long odyssey through drug stash houses across California, the Santa Barbara detectives could only shake their heads. "We had never experienced people like this before," Correll said. "We were learning more and more about the network of drug smugglers out of Mexico, and how they had infiltrated California, and all the things that were going on with that."[2] The detectives had seized tens of thousands of dollars, numerous guns, and a lot of ammunition. And they had left their colleagues in various departments with multiple big narcotics arrests.

As for their own murder case, though, they drove home empty-handed, with nothing more to connect Tacho Chaidez or his brother to the Santa Barbara murder.

A few weeks later, there was another setback: They brought the teenager who had been shot alongside Silvestre Ayon at the ranch down to the station to view a live lineup, hoping he would identify Tacho Chaidez. After the shooting, the teenager had left California for a while to work on horse ranches in Pennsylvania, a job he obtained through Sue Davidge's connections. But he had eventually returned to California and was trying to put the terror of that day behind him.

Chaidez and five other men filed in for the viewing. The victim, now in his twenties, studied the lineup and said he thought either of the men in positions five and six could have been the one who shot him. Neither of those men was Chaidez.

Martinez heard about the arrests of the Chaidez brothers and the search warrants being executed at houses across the state almost immediately. After all, the Chaidez brothers were his friends.

Martinez and Mr. X couldn't believe it. How stupid could the cops be? The Chaidez brothers hadn't even been present when Martinez had killed Ayon. Martinez wasn't too worried about them though. They had good lawyers.

He had other things on his mind. He was increasingly spending time near Yuma, to be near his children, who had spent time with their grandmother in Cosalá but were now in Yuma with their mother.[3]

Martinez knew there was a lot of work for a good smuggler on the border. But he was shocked to find law enforcement everywhere.

What a difference from Earlimart, where patrols rarely came through and the cops were little more than a nuisance.

Here in Yuma and other border towns, it was not just police. The FBI was around. The DEA. The US Marshals Service. Border Patrol. US Customs. Not to mention garden-variety sheriff's deputies and police officers.

Plus, life was boring. "There is nothing good to see or to do here. Not even a fucking water park," he wrote in his memoir. Only two small Indian casinos, but they wouldn't let children in, which made family activities there difficult.

There was, however, a lot of money to be made. Crossing drugs from San Luis Río Colorado to Yuma was incredibly lucrative, and Martinez said he moved "kilos and kilos of cocaine." He also shepherded a number of people across the border—by his estimates more than a thousand in one year. These numbers are unverifiable, but this was the 1980s. Mexico's economy was in shambles, Guatemala and El Salvador were convulsed by war, and the border was fairly open, if you knew how to get across.

Martinez's family had, by this point, been bringing people for years. He knew the trick wasn't so much getting people across the line—this was before the big reinforced border fences and motion-detecting cameras and infrared heat sensors that beamed images of vast swaths of the lonely desert night onto Border Patrol monitoring screens. For the most part, it was possible to just walk across. The real trick was getting past the checkpoints on the freeways and into the cities. And to manage this, he sometimes relied on his family's old system of having someone with a walkie-talkie watching for guards to go on breaks.

One time, he said, he brought nineteen Central Americans from the border all the way to Los Angeles, netting himself $2,000 a head.

"There's hundreds of ways to make a lot of money in the border," he wrote in his memoir. "All you have to have are balls." He had soon invested in a car, a truck, and a van. He even thought about buying "a fucking bus."

And if Yuma was boring, San Luis Río Colorado, on the other side of the border, was a place where you could "do whatever you want." This, he said, included having wild sex. He also began to dabble in a new drug: cocaine.

His estranged wife still refused to take him back, but seeing his kids whenever he wanted made him happy. And periodically he would check in with Mr. X to see if anyone needed kidnapping or killing.

Cecilia Camacho had been back in the United States, working in the orange groves again, for three years when a quiet man named Antonio Alcantar joined the crew in the winter of 1985.

Cecilia could see that this new worker had no idea what he was doing. He did not pick quickly or efficiently and sometimes looked unsteady on his ladder. She decided to help him. She taught him how to balance his sack and how to pluck fruit off the branches with ease. Cecilia would have helped anyone learn the ropes of fieldwork—it was the right thing to do. But something about this man, with his calm manner and gentle smile, intrigued her.

She was still living in Lindsay, and her son, now about seven, was still back at home in Puruandiro. She sent money home to him regularly, hoping she could find a way to bring him to the United States when he got older.

Day after day that winter, she labored next to this new worker.

He wanted to learn—she could see that. He listened to her instructions and tried to follow her movements. He was from a small city in the Mexican state of Michoacán, and she saw that he was a hard worker and a caring person. They talked about their lives throughout the day, and he told her that he believed above all in the importance of family.

In no time at all, he was picking as fast as she was. He didn't need her anymore. Cecilia assumed that would be the end of it. She had become accustomed to being alone. Her sole focus was making enough money to take care of her son. And yet, this Antonio Alcantar kept finding ways to talk to her.

Finally, one day he asked her out to dinner, and within a few weeks after that they were a couple. She told him she was a widow and that her first husband had been killed. She didn't tell him much more. But she did tell him her son was back in Mexico, and she missed him desperately.

He won her heart permanently with what he said in response: "Let's go get him."

Whenever Martinez talked to him, Mr. X would ask if he was back together with his wife.

"No," Martinez would answer. "But I'm working on it."

And work on it he did, taking every opportunity "to make points, and win [his] family back." When he saw a sign for a carnival in San Luis, he asked his estranged wife if they could take the kids.

"Sure, why not," she answered.

They spent a wonderful day eating, talking, and laughing.

Then, one December day, he took his children to a big circus in San Luis Río. They had a great time watching the performance.

But when he tried to come back through the port of entry, US Customs searched his car and found a $100 bill folded around a gram of cocaine in his wallet. He was cited for cocaine possession, and because he was with the kids, his wife found out. She was furious.

"You're a drug addict," he said she told him.

Nonsense, he said.

It was a setback in his plan to win her back. And it hurt his business too. Every time he crossed the border after that, US Customs agents searched his car "real good. I mean, real good."

But it didn't put a dent in his coyote business, which he viewed as a service. "Somebody have to bring them poor people to America," he wrote in his memoir.

In that way, 1987 passed without any murders or mayhem but also without his hoped-for reconciliation with his family.

In the spring of 1988 Martinez was teaching his children how to swim at a Colorado River swimming hole when his oldest son heard his beeper go off. With great consideration, the nine-year-old climbed out of the water, dried off, and carefully brought the beeper to his father.

It was Mr. X. The coded message said to call but indicated it was not an emergency.

"What makes the beeper beep?" his son asked. "And who is beeping you and why?"

The questions made Martinez feel proud that he was an important enough person to have a beeper, and now his son would know it.

"The beeper is like my office," he said. "When it goes beep beep beep, that's my boss."

After they left the river, he took his children to the Golden

Corral Buffet on Fourth Avenue in Yuma and called Mr. X from the payphone.

"I'm sorry for the delay," he said. "I was teaching my kids how to swim. And I also couldn't take my eyes off the girls who were playing in their bikinis."

Not a problem, Mr. X said, but he had a job. There was a man in Waterloo, Iowa, who needed taking care of. The fee was $10,000.

Martinez took his kids home to their mother, gave them each a few dollars and a few kisses, and told them he would see them soon because he had to go on a business trip.

Murder was becoming almost routine, according to Martinez. The creative part was finding a way to get the target somewhere he could kill him. He was getting very good at that. With his natural ease and welcoming smile, he had an almost uncanny ability to lure his targets into his car so he could kill them.

As Martinez tells it, he drove into Waterloo, Iowa, and found the target, who was working as a car salesman. Posing as a customer, Martinez asked for a test drive.

He and the salesman headed out, with Martinez in the driver's seat. He drove them out of town, to a lonely, little-traveled road he had researched beforehand.

As they drove, the car salesman asked the usual questions.

Did he like the car? Yes, he did.

Did Martinez have a job? And good credit?

"I have the best job in the world," Martinez answered. "And no, I don't have credit. If I buy, I'm going to pay cash."

Then, out in the lonely location, Martinez announced that he had driven enough and asked the salesman if he wanted to drive back. When they got out of the car to switch spots, Martinez shot him twice in the head and took his wallet. He left the body on the ground. It was his eleventh murder.

He swung through Delano on his way back to Yuma and dropped

off some money for his mother. He was a good son. He always gave his mother money. He never told her where it came from.

While he was visiting family in the Delano area, one of his sisters asked him if he knew anyone who could help get her baby-sitter across, who was coming up from Sinaloa.

"If the woman is pretty, I can try to cross her myself," he said.

A few weeks later, his sister called him and told him the baby-sitter was waiting in San Luis.

She was beautiful, with big, dark eyes that peered from a face that was both serious and kind.

They took a taxi to the border fence. As they drove, Martinez gave her directions.

"When I run, you run," he told her. "When I jump, you jump."

Within minutes they were across, and within an hour they had arrived in Yuma.

The next morning, they drove north toward his sister's house in Richgrove, a little town a few miles east of Earlimart. His mother and stepfather had recently built a house there too. Richgrove was a little smaller than Earlimart and a little bit less violent. But otherwise it was quite similar: an unincorporated town of mostly farmworkers—a close-knit community with few municipal services where people knew each other well, looked out for each other, and also knew not to talk to authorities or ask too many questions of their neighbors. It suited the Fernandez-Martinez family well.

When Martinez and his sister's babysitter sailed through the second Border Patrol checkpoint, he smiled at her. "Welcome to America."

"It was so easy to get to America," she marveled.[4]

"It's easy when you have a good coyote." He told her that some people walked for two days across the desert near Phoenix. Other people walked three days through the mountains to reach Borrego Springs. "A lot of people get bit by rattlesnakes," he told her. "You're just lucky that you met me."

During the eight-hour drive from Yuma to Tulare County, the woman told him her life story. How her mother had died giving birth to her. How she had spent her childhood on a small rancho called Los Tigres, near Cosalá. What had brought her to California. Finally, she asked how much Martinez planned to charge for her passage.

"Don't worry about that," he told her. "My sister told you to come so you can work for her, and that means she's paying for you."[5]

Then he had another idea.

He told her he wouldn't charge his sister for her passage if she would go out with him one day.

The young woman agreed. She was young and undocumented, raised in a time and place where women had little power, and traveling alone to work for his sister. She was from the area around Cosalá. Had she heard fearsome tales about Martinez and his family? Or had she heard only good things—that they were warm and loving and also powerful and could take care of her? Or was she grateful for the way Martinez had escorted her across the border and then listened empathetically to her life story?

When they got back to Richgrove, Martinez took her on that date. And before long, she was his girlfriend, easing the pain of his separation from his wife.

But, of course, amid his romantic idyll, there was more murder. In June 1988, Martinez heard from a friend that the other man blamed for the 1979 dance hall shooting—whose brother Martinez claimed to have murdered by mistake—had been located. The man, Martinez heard, was living in a small apartment in downtown Bakersfield.

Martinez said he got the address, drove up to the complex on the morning of June 9, and shot him twice. "Victim number 12," he wrote in his memoir.

For his trouble, Mr. X gave him $5,000. And an AK-47 as a birthday present.

Then, in 1990, the law finally caught up with him. A "godfather" of his from Riverside had asked him to cross five hundred kilos of marijuana from Mexicali to Calexico in a car with hidden compartments. The pot had come up the Sea of Cortez packed into bales on a boat, and Martinez and an associate had waded out into the cerulean blue sea to unload the bales and then packed them into the car. Five hundred kilos of marijuana is not a small amount; it would take multiple trips to get it across. Back and forth across the border Martinez went, ferrying the drugs. On the third day, a customs agent wrinkled his nose at a familiar odor and waved Martinez to secondary inspection. Martinez watched the drug-sniffing dogs come toward his car. "Damn stupid dogs," he thought, as the animals stopped in front of his car and gave their handler the signal that they had caught a scent. Border officials tore the car apart, eventually discovering the hidden compartments and one hundred kilos of pot.

They sent Martinez to jail in Imperial County while he waited to be charged. While there, Martinez discussed with his fellow inmates how to proceed. Should he post bail and fight the charges? Post bail and go on the run? Or plead out?

"Don't waste your money," a fellow inmate advised him. "They won't give you that much time if it's your first time. Probably they will give you probation."

Martinez liked what his new friend and jailhouse lawyer was saying, and he decided to take his chances in federal court in San Diego. He pleaded guilty and explained to the judge— with a straight face—that the one hundred kilos stashed in the professionally constructed hidden compartments in the borrowed car were for personal use.

The judge didn't buy it. Martinez got eight months and was assigned to serve his time at the federal prison in downtown San Diego.

The jail was "very nice and clean," he noted, and he was assigned to work in the kitchen, loading the food cart. Most of the cooks were female inmates, and he got to work beside them all day long. "I was in heaven," he said. He also made some valuable drug connections. As his stepfather had discovered before him, prison was like Harvard Business School for drug dealers.

While he was in prison, his new lady gave birth to a baby girl. Martinez wrote to her and told her to move in with his mother, and he promised to buy her a house in Earlimart as soon as he got out. It was a promise he kept, he said, buying a three-bedroom house near the elementary school a few months after he was released in the late winter of 1991.

Once out of jail, Martinez went straight back to drug smuggling. He also began planning his baby girl's baptism. The event was held at the grand and historic Olvera Church in downtown Los Angeles. His family came down from the valley, and all his friends and business associates from Los Angeles also attended, he said.

From time to time, Martinez thought about Tacho Chaidez, locked up in the Santa Maria jail for a murder he hadn't committed. But he wasn't that worried about his friend. There was no way the charge would stick.

Chapter Fourteen

Back in Santa Barbara, Detectives Correll and Ortega were determined that the murder charge absolutely *would* stick. They were sure they had the right guy.

On May 6, 1991, a Santa Barbara judge ordered Tacho Chaidez to stand trial for the murder. The story made the front page of the *Santa Maria Times* the next day and included quotes from Chaidez's lawyer pointing out that the only witness to the shooting had not even picked the defendant out of a lineup.[1]

It was true. Correll and Ortega needed more evidence. And they needed it fast.

They went looking for it from an unlikely source—a convicted murderer long rumored to have been involved in the crime himself: "El Abuelo," the "highwayman" and phantom-like figure whose name kept popping up in the case and who had been spotted in Earlimart around the time of the murder. This time the detectives were able to find him fairly easily. In the intervening years, El Abuelo, whose real name was Manuel Ayon Nunez, had been convicted of homicide in Monterey County and was sitting in a maximum-security cell in California's Pelican Bay prison.

Pelican Bay, which sits in foggy and earthquake-prone isolation just south of the Oregon border in the town of Crescent City, was opened in 1989 and designed to house the California prison system's most dangerous and violent inmates, many of whom are confined to "supermax" cells twenty-two hours a day. Over the years, its occupants have included Charles Manson and record producer Suge Knight.

On May 15, 1991, Detectives Ortega and Correll took a private plane from Santa Maria to Crescent City. Their sheriff's department had a few volunteer pilots—rich men who had their own aircraft, which they made available to detectives who needed to travel a long distance in short order. Like to interview a mythical-seeming criminal locked away in a notorious, isolated prison. Though it wasn't on their flight path, the pilots swooped over the facility before they landed. They all wanted to see it. As the pilot and his friend went off to lunch, Correll and Ortega rented a car and headed out for an interview they hoped would help them clinch their case once and for all.

Pelican Bay is like a futuristic bunker on an island of concrete lapped by waves of razor wire. To the east are the forests that blanket this part of the state. To the west is the Pacific Ocean. Correll and Ortega were no strangers to cells—in the normal course of business, they went in and out of jails more regularly sometimes than they did the grocery store. But they had never seen security like this. They even had some trouble getting in. Correll had worn the wrong trousers: the zipper on his fly kept setting off the metal detectors, and he could get through without beeping only by covering it with his fingers. Obviously, Ortega found this hilarious.

Once they were through, the wardens brought the detectives to an interview room, where they sat and waited. Guards brought Nunez in a few minutes later. Finally, they were face-to-face with El Abuelo—the legend about whom they had heard so much.

His appearance did not disappoint. Correll took one look at him and thought, "Whoa, this guy is a heavy hitter."[2] They knew that he was a heinous, violent criminal—but he also appeared almost regal. He was probably in his fifties, yet still imposing, and even in his prison garb, he seemed somehow stylish. Correll looked at Nunez's brown shoes, wondering about the life he had led, the place he had come from. He let Ortega do the talking in Spanish.

Ortega, as he did with almost everyone, connected almost instantly with El Abuelo, and soon the two were chatting away. At one point, El Abuelo asked who Correll was. "He's my *jefe*," Ortega told him. "But don't worry about him. He doesn't speak Spanish."

Ortega informed El Abuelo that they were there to investigate the murder of Silvestre Ayon. Nunez replied that he had already been questioned about this murder. He offered that another detective from Santa Barbara had come to talk to him about it in the mid-1980s. This was true. When Nunez had first been arrested on his murder charges, his name had been flagged in the state system, and a Santa Barbara detective had visited him.

Either that detective hadn't had Ortega's charm, or Nunez hadn't seen any angle in talking at that point.

"I told him nothing," Nunez said.

Ortega nodded. He already knew this. But maybe now Nunez might consider talking, Ortega suggested, because Tacho Chaidez had been arrested. Left unsaid was the fact that now that Nunez had had a real taste of California's bleakest prison, he might want to consider trying to make a deal.

Nunez was noncommittal. But he told Ortega that he knew the Chaidez brothers well.

"We suspected as much," Ortega answered. That's why we're here.

Correll, who was following along as best he could, with some translation from his partner, spoke for the first time. He whispered to Ortega, "Ask him what he would do if he was investigating this case."

When it was translated, the question appeared to delight Nunez. He beamed, sunshine spreading across his face, and tossed his head back, laughing long and low. "So you have come to the famous El Abuelo for help."

Three decades later, Correll still remembered that laugh and El Abuelo's satisfaction. That was the moment, he said, when he knew they might get something.

Why yes, Nunez said, he knew all about the murder of Silvestre Ayon—Ayon was his cousin.

He knew who had done it, he continued, and he might be willing to help.

Detectives asked him how he knew who the killers were.

"I heard it from their mouths," El Abuelo answered.

But he wasn't just going to spill his information to police officers. Before he told them anything further, Nunez wanted to talk about what detectives might do for him in return. He was interested in a "prisoner exchange" program between the United States and Mexico. He could do his time in Mexico, he said.

The detectives were not fools. They knew El Abuelo wanted to be transferred to Mexico because he believed that once there, he might be able to pay a bribe or otherwise exert influence to get himself free.

Even before "El Chapo" Guzman, leader of the Sinaloa Cartel, became famous for escaping from Mexican prisons, those involved in the drug trade had remarkable success in getting out of jail. El Abuelo himself had even done it once before. In 1970, he had been arrested for alien smuggling in San Clemente, California, and was sent to a federal prison camp. He promptly escaped (which is hard to do) and stayed on the lam until 1977, when he was picked up by authorities in Oregon.

Once recaptured, he was deported in 1977 to Durango, where

officials promised he would face charges on several murders. Durango officials did accuse him of committing a number of murders, but, as El Abuelo explained to Correll and Ortega, they didn't lock him up.

"Money talks," Nunez explained.

Correll later said that the detectives didn't promise to get Nunez deported to Durango—and possible freedom—in exchange for talking to them. But they did pledge to speak to prison officials about his circumstances.

Nunez took this in. "Let me dream upon it," he told the detectives.

They had been dismissed. Ortega explained to Correll that they would have to reach out to Nunez again the next day.

They made their way out of the prison, finally exiting into the cool North Coast air. They weren't sure what to think. Nunez was an accomplished criminal—as manipulative as they came. There was absolutely no reason to trust him. He was obviously working an angle. Probably more than one. They weren't even a little swayed by his suggestion that he might help them because Silvestre Ayon had been his cousin. Silvestre Ayon had apparently been everyone's cousin—and that seemingly hadn't mattered enough to keep him safe. But Tacho Chaidez, their target, was still sitting in a jail cell in Santa Maria, with a powerful defense attorney and a ticking clock. The detectives were convinced he had committed the murder, but if they had any chance of convicting him, they needed more evidence.

The next day, back home in Santa Barbara, Detective Ortega called Nunez on the phone. I have decided to help, Nunez said, his voice magnanimous. Then he told them a story. He had been in an apartment in Cerritos, another Los Angeles suburb tucked into the city's great blue-collar southern sprawl, with two of Tacho Chaidez's relatives in 1983. And they had admitted—in no uncertain terms—that they had driven the getaway car that was used during the murder of Silvestre Ayon.

And that's not all, Nunez said. Two of Chaidez's associates had also been involved in shooting and wounding another man in Kern County whom they believed to have been the second man responsible for the 1979 dance hall shooting. The man hadn't died in that attack, but he had been murdered a few years later.

It was exactly what the detectives had been hoping to hear. But it wasn't enough. There was only one thing to do after this conversation.

It was time to go back to Earlimart.

On July 9, Detective Ortega arrived in Tulare County. He was there to meet his old friend Ralph Diaz. Diaz had left the Tulare County Sheriff's Department and was now an investigator with the district attorney's office. But he was still ready to help them. Ortega, Diaz, and Correll had one thing in common: they all lived for the thrill of the hunt. And this case, nine years in, was one great hunt.

Diaz took them to meet with the uncle of the second man believed to have been murdered in revenge for the dance hall shootings. The man Martinez said he had killed in 1988. They didn't run into the uncle at home, but they did find another relative. She told them what they already knew: word on the street was that both the second man and his brother had been murdered by the Chaidez brothers, or at their behest, to avenge the victims of the dance hall shooting.

An hour later, they found the uncle himself. They tracked him down to the middle of a field where he was working. From him, they gleaned more rumors, including that the Chaidez brothers had been spotted in Delano in a white Cadillac limousine two days before the murder of one of the brothers. He also advised them to speak with someone else in Delano who had seen the Cadillac with the Chaidezes in it with his own eyes.

This person opened his door with extreme nervousness. "There is a certain fear" involved in talking about this case because of the

Chaidez brothers, he told the police, according to their reports. After that, he would say no more, denying all knowledge of Cadillac limousines, drug trafficking, or anything else.

The Santa Barbara detectives marveled, yet again, at this world they had stumbled into. It appeared that the murder of Silvestre Ayon at the horse ranch of one of the most prominent people in Santa Barbara had been but the beginning of a breathtaking level of carnage.

In 1983, one of the other men reputed to have been involved in the dance hall shooting in Durango had been shot but not killed in the town of Shafter. Then, in 1984, his brother was shot dead in a vineyard near Bakersfield. Two years later, in 1986, the first man survived another would-be assassination in a drive-by shooting near the Kern County town of Wasco. Finally, in 1988, he had been killed in the parking lot of his apartment complex.

Almost everyone the detectives talked to blamed the Chaidez brothers for all this violence. But no one had any actual proof.

Detective Ortega picked up the phone and once again called the prison at Pelican Bay.

This time, El Abuelo wasn't very helpful. In fact, he had no new information, except for some gossip about yet another murder in Los Angeles that he claimed the Chaidez brothers may have been involved in. No one had time to follow up on that.

Ortega and another detective continued making trips to Tulare and Kern. Their days were a parade of terrified people.

"Please don't tell anyone I've talked to you," one person after another pleaded, just as they had the last time. "They'll kill me."

Some people refused to talk to the detectives at all. But others did talk, and at length, giving them more and more potential suspects.

Which is how, on July 26, 1991, Santa Barbara County sheriff's deputies pulled up to a stucco house in the little town of Richgrove.

It was the Martinez family home.

Chapter Fifteen

D etective Ortega and his partner opened the doors of their un-
marked police car. It was around one hundred degrees, and the
heat hit the officers in the face when they stepped out onto the
pavement.

Martinez wasn't there. Federal prison had been good to him.
He had made friends with "some guys from Chicago" who wanted
to pay him to run kilos of cocaine to Illinois.

The drive was hideous. The profits were amazing.

One of Martinez's sisters was home. The detectives told her
that they wanted to talk to her about a man—unrelated to either
the Martinez or Chaidez families—whose name had come up in
connection with the murders of Ayon and the two brothers.

As they explained the reason for their visit, they were "immediately struck by…her very nervous demeanor," as they put it
in their police reports. She told them she knew nothing directly
about any of those murders. However, she had heard rumors about
who had killed the two brothers.

And who would that be, the detectives asked?

El Abuelo, she answered.

The next day, the detectives came across another piece of evidence pointing toward the Martinez household: a car registered there had once been linked by police to an unsuccessful assassination attempt on one of the brothers.

This could have taken the case in an entirely new direction. It could have brought suspicion straight down on Jose Martinez. But given all the evidence the detectives already had against Tacho Chaidez, who was, after all, sitting in jail waiting for them to build a case against him, it just seemed like more noise in an already loud investigation.

On July 31, the Santa Barbara detectives took one more flight north to Pelican Bay. After their trip to the valley, they had decided they needed to talk to El Abuelo one more time.

Tacho Chaidez had hired a brilliant defense lawyer who was accusing witnesses and sheriff's detectives of fabricating the evidence against his client.

Ortega told it to El Abuelo straight: they may accuse you of lying, he said.

El Abuelo answered that he had been "entirely truthful."

Detectives tape-recorded his statement. Then, a few days later, they brought El Abuelo to Santa Barbara to testify. He moved into a cell in the Santa Maria jail and feasted on his favorite treat—"ultimate cheeseburgers" from Jack in the Box—which guards brought him as often as possible to keep him happy. And not just any guards but a tall, blonde female deputy. Correll had noticed El Abuelo checking her out and drafted her onto the case to see if she could get any additional information out of him while plying him with fast food.

Detectives and prosecutors had decided that instead of simply charging Tacho with the murder of Silvestre Ayon, they were going to try to prosecute Tacho *and* his brother Domingo *and* their cousin. They were charged not just with the murder of Silvestre but also with the conspiracy to kill the other man believed responsible for the dance hall shooting and his brother.

El Abuelo was the star witness before the grand jury. True to his theatrical nature, he gave an amazing performance. He testified that he had heard Domingo Chaidez claim responsibility, with his brother Tacho, for the murder of Silvestre Ayon. He also gave quite a few details about his own colorful life.

At the end, grand jurors were permitted to ask him questions. One man wanted to know—it's not clear why—if El Abuelo had ever killed anyone with a revolver.

El Abuelo gave an answer that became part of Santa Barbara County Sheriff's Department lore. Correll didn't have the transcript, but he said he will never forget the words: "I have killed many men," El Abuelo said, speaking in Spanish. "Some for business and some for sport, but I never brought no stinking revolver to a gun fight."

Apparently, El Abuelo was credible. The grand jury returned indictments against Tacho and Domingo and their cousin.

Then, things started to unravel.

A lawyer for Chaidez pointed out a key problem with the evidence—namely, that the prosecution's case rested, as the attorney told the local paper, on "a witness who purportedly has committed 19 murders."[1]

The lawyer added that El Abuelo's evidence boiled down to his claim that "some time in 1983 he supposedly overheard my client say he was driving a car when Silvestre Ayon was shot."[2]

Things got worse for the prosecution from there.

A second key witness, who had claimed to have overheard Tacho Chaidez say he had committed the murder, disappeared after testifying at a preliminary hearing. Detectives looked high and low for him, but he was never heard from again. Ominously, his car's license plate number was written on a piece of paper found in Domingo's possession.[3] Correll told the local newspaper he assumed the witness had been murdered. But no one could ever prove it.

And then, the case—years in the making, with thousands of miles traveled and dozens of people interviewed—completely fell apart.

The defense lawyers caught Santa Barbara authorities in a legal vise. The chief evidence against the Chaidezes rested on the testimony of El Abuelo. But there was a problem with that testimony—a problem that should have been revealed to the grand jury but hadn't been.

It was a fact that in 1991 El Abuelo had told Detectives Correll and Ortega that he had heard Domingo brag about the killings. But it was also true that the first time authorities had tried to talk to the old gangster about the murder, in 1984, he had said something quite different. He'd told detectives then that he had heard about the murder of Ayon and felt sadness about it but had no idea who had done it. The Santa Barbara detectives knew about that interview; Ortega and El Abuelo had talked about it during their conversation in Pelican Bay.

But the grand jury was never told. And they should have been.

Santa Barbara officials protested that they thought they *had* told the grand jury about this and were surprised that it wasn't in the transcript of the proceedings. They tried to argue that it didn't matter. What El Abuelo had told Ortega, what he had come down to Santa Barbara County and testified to—those were the facts that mattered.

But Domingo's lawyers argued that El Abuelo had made up stories for prosecutors in a bid to get out of Pelican Bay's solitary confinement and transferred to Mexico, where he thought he might have a better chance of going free.

In January 1992, a judge agreed that the problems with the grand jury testimony were serious enough that he dropped the murder charges against Domingo and his cousin.

Then, a few months later, in early April 1992, prosecutors announced they were giving up completely on prosecuting any of the Chaidezes. The witnesses had either disappeared or were in Mexico and too scared to testify. "We interviewed many many people who told us they were afraid of the Chaidezes," Correll told the *Santa Maria Times*. "We can't get them up here, we can't protect them.... We can't fight anymore."[4]

On April 15, Detective Ortega drove Tacho Chaidez to Tijuana and handed him over to Mexican officials, who he hoped would prosecute him there.

Martinez claims that Tacho Chaidez was shot to death in the mid-1990s in Tijuana, possibly as part of an explosion of violence between erstwhile allies in the Tijuana and Sinaloa cartels. With the incarceration of Miguel Angel Felix Gallardo, its head, the old Guadalajara Cartel, which had once controlled most of the drug trade through Mexico, broke up into different factions. The Arellano-Felix organization took control of Tijuana, with its lucrative border crossing to San Diego, and began challenging its old allies, who were organizing themselves into the Sinaloa Cartel under Joaquin Guzman Loera, famously known only by his nickname, "El Chapo."

The irony was, Tacho Chaidez may have been safer in a California cell. Still, Martinez thought it was outrageous that the Chaidezes had been in jail for almost a year before the charges were dismissed.

He was, however, impressed with the Santa Barbara detectives' dogged efforts to solve the crime. "They got so fucking close to me," he said.

Chapter Sixteen

In all his stories about all his crimes, Martinez takes extraordinary care never to name any of his accomplices or any of the people who hired him.

He makes one big exception. Martinez claims that El Chapo himself, then on his brutal rise to become perhaps the most infamous and powerful drug lord in modern history, spent an afternoon in the winter of 1991–1992 at Martinez's stucco house near the 99 freeway in Earlimart.

According to Martinez, it was a Saturday afternoon, and his second wife was at a baby shower.

Mr. X called up with a question: Was Martinez home alone?

Yes, he was.

In that case, could Mr. X drop by with a friend who needed a quiet place to make a deal and also to use the restroom?

But of course, Martinez said.

About a half an hour later, four men walked through the chain-link fence demarcating his front yard and into his house. One of them, Martinez claims, was the legendary leader of the Sinaloa Cartel.

A little older than Martinez, El Chapo had been born in a small, impoverished community in Sinaloa's Sierra Madre and had gotten his start tending opium; he parlayed this into a marijuana operation and then into handling logistics for drug lord Miguel Angel Felix Gallardo. When Felix Gallardo was arrested, El Chapo became the leader of the Sinaloa Cartel.

He was famous for his brutality. He was also brilliant at logistics.

He hired architects and built tunnels under the US-Mexico border for the purposes of transporting cocaine. He packed the drugs into cans of chili peppers. Later he put his logistical prowess to use in spiriting himself out of prison. He escaped from Mexico's most secure prison in 2015 through a mile-long tunnel that led from a shower in his cell to a construction site in the town of Almaloya, west of Mexico City. He had previously escaped from a Mexican prison in 2001 in a laundry cart and then lived on the lam, evading US and Mexican officials for more than a decade.

He was finally caught in 2016 after a gun battle in the town of Los Mochis, in Sinaloa. In 2018, he went on trial in federal court in New York and was sentenced to life in prison. US officials conservatively estimated that he had taken in nearly $13 billion over the years. They also alleged he was responsible for dozens of murders directly and for waging a drug war that left one hundred thousand people dead in Mexico.

But back in the winter of 1991–1992, he was just getting started. Guzman first became a major trafficker in the 1980s, working with Gallardo's Guadalajara Cartel. Eventually, he teamed up with another trafficker, Ismael Zambada Garcia, known as "El Mayo." The two men would lead the Sinaloa Cartel for nearly three decades.

In all the accounts of Guzman's life—which catalogue his mistresses, his wife, his private zoo, his gold-plated guns—Earlimart is rarely, if ever, mentioned. Martinez offers no proof either. But a close reading of federal court testimony from some of El Chapo's captured lieutenants indicates that such a visit is possible. At some point in the early 1990s, according to testimony given in federal court in Arizona, El Chapo took a road trip from Los Angeles to Las Vegas and then to Tucson. Such a route could have allowed for a detour through the San Joaquin Valley.

According to Martinez, a few months after El Chapo's alleged visit to Earlimart, Mr. X hit his beeper and asked him to call directly to Culiacan, the city where the Sinaloa Cartel is head-quartered.

A promotion, of sorts.

They sent him to St. Louis, which was an easy trip, because he happened to be in Chicago. While there, he invested in a silencer for his gun. "Every time I pull the trigger, is like a little kid trying to whistle. Pip Pip Pip," he wrote in his memoir.

Those killed in St. Louis were victims fifteen and sixteen.

Every day, Martinez marveled as he drove home, killing was easier and easier for him. It was so simple to be rich, he wrote in his memoir.

He also had some close calls.

On May 1, 1992, he was driving home from Chicago in a car he owned with Illinois plates. He was pulled over near Las Vegas. He offered up a fake driver's license in the name of Martin Arias, along with insurance papers and car registration.

Next the deputy asked him if he had a green card. Martinez told the truth. No, he did not. He didn't add that he didn't need one because he was an American citizen, born in California. He couldn't. Because Martin Arias had no such proof of citizenship, and explaining that he wasn't Martin Arias at all would lead to a whole bunch of additional questions, which might lead to police finding the $150,000 in cash tucked in a hidden compartment in the car. He definitely didn't want to have to talk about that.

Assuming he was in the country illegally, the deputy took him to jail in Las Vegas. The television in his cell showed Los Angeles in flames from the Rodney King riots. Watching it, Martinez was thrilled. He loved violence in all its flavors, and he especially loved watching riots against the police.

The next day, he was loaded onto a Border Patrol bus along with ten other men and deported from Andrade, California, to Los Algodones, Mexico. He took a cab straight to San Luis Río Colorado, Sonora. He stuck his fake ID in the name of Martin Arias in the bottom of his shoe and took out his real driver's license. He was an American citizen and was back in the United States in less than an hour.

He took the opportunity to visit his former wife and his children, then convinced her to come with him to Vegas to get his car—cash still hidden in the secret compartment—out of the impound lot.

His entire family thought the story was hilarious. Every time his mother looked at him, she burst out laughing.

PART THREE

El Mano Negra

1995–2013

Something sad came into my mind when I heard that lady was going crazy [over her missing son]. I said to myself, tomorrow night, I will go and unbury him, so one day they can find him. I have a mother too, and I don't want my mother to be in the same situation like that poor old woman who was going crazy.

—Excerpt from Jose Martinez's unpublished memoir

Chapter Seventeen

——

Martinez was standing in the front yard of the Earlimart house he now shared with his new wife and their children, finishing up a difficult conversation with a woman who worked for him, when his little son toddled out to find his father.

It was early 1995. Martinez, who was now thirty-three, and his second wife were settled in and building a family. Martinez had been earning good money running drugs to Chicago, making the trip as often as every few weeks.

But the drug business was full of complicated variables, and those trips to Chicago needed to pause. Martinez does not explain why in his memoir. He was breaking the bad news to the woman who worked for him. She often helped with the driving, in exchange for an excellent payout, and now her income from those trips would be drying up.

Once she understood that her job was ending, the woman, who was sitting in her car, threw her vehicle into reverse and backed out of the driveway. Neither she nor Martinez noticed until it was too late that Martinez's son was standing behind her car.

The woman ran over him.

Miraculously, the little boy appeared unharmed. But in a panic, Martinez rushed the boy to the hospital and insisted he have every kind of test. The toddler was fine. Martinez, however, was traumatized, terrified. From then on, he decreed, no one—and he meant *no one*—was to park in his driveway. The only exceptions: his wife and his mother. To make this clear even to casual visitors, Martinez put up signs warning anyone who might even think of parking on his property.

Shortly after that, Martinez and his family came home and found an unfamiliar brown Ford pickup in the driveway. Martinez found the truck's owner in the backyard, talking to one of his wife's brothers.

"Hey man," he said, polite as could be, "next time when you come to this house, can you please park your truck in the street?"

Yes, of course, the man said.

Some days later, Martinez came home and noticed the brown pickup parked in his driveway again.

It was unbelievable. It was disrespectful.

"Didn't I tell you not to park in my driveway?" Martinez asked.

The man blithely said he had forgotten.

Martinez repeated the warning: next time, he said, make sure to park in the street.

But the man didn't listen. On the morning of April 7, 1995, Martinez saw the brown truck, once again, pull into his driveway. The driver, who Martinez knew was friends with his brother-in-law, walked up to the front door and knocked.

Martinez was home alone. His family was at church, he said. Rage boiled up in him. He had asked the man—nicely—not to park in his driveway. Twice. And the man had ignored him, showing him blatant disrespect and endangering his child.

Martinez answered the door, betraying no sense of the fury seething inside him.

"My brother-in-law is not home," Martinez told the man in

the brown truck. "But since you're here, can I get a ride to the store?"

"Sure," the man said. He was thirty-two years old, with a slim build, thick black hair, and a warm smile. His easy manner, the pleasant way he agreed to drive Martinez to the store—neither of these things would help him. Martinez had made up his mind.

"Hey," Martinez asked as they walked down the driveway together, "do you mind if I drive your truck?"

"No problem," said the man. He got into the passenger seat and gave Martinez the keys.

"Your ass is mine, you stupid son of a bitch," Martinez thought, according to his memoir. He got behind the steering wheel and set off through Earlimart, whose streets were calm and peaceful because it was Saturday morning.[1]

"Hey," the man said, "you passed the store."

"No, no, not the store in Earlimart," Martinez said. "We're going to the store in the next town over, in Richgrove. But don't worry, amigo, I'll give you money for gas."

Martinez took the back roads. At 7 a.m. on a Saturday, they were all completely empty.

During the drive, Martinez asked the man questions about his life. He learned that the man was named Domingo, was from Mexico, and had a mother and sister in Earlimart. He was married but had no children. The truck, Domingo said, belonged to his sister-in-law. She was a widow. Her husband, Domingo's brother, had died in a car accident five months earlier. That's why Domingo was here: he had come from Mexico for the funeral and stayed.

"So," Martinez asked, "how come you don't listen to people when they ask you not to do things, like park in their driveway?"

"I only listen to my parents," the man replied.

It was a disrespectful answer. Martinez pulled over to the side of the road, took out his .44-caliber, and shot Domingo once in the head.

Then he spoke to the dead body slumped in the passenger seat: "I'm not your parents, but I'm El Mano Negra. When I talk, people listen to me."

Martinez started the car and drove onward, looking for the perfect spot. He found it in an orange grove, about two miles north of Richgrove.

As he dragged Domingo's body from the truck and tried to hide it, he noticed a gun sticking out of the dead man's waistband. He wasn't surprised to see it. He suspected his brother-in-law was involved in drugs, and lots of people in Earlimart carried guns. Martinez took the weapon. He thought about searching the dead man's pockets for cash, but he was more worried about time. It wouldn't do to be caught with the body.

He was back in the truck within minutes. What should he do with it? He could burn it. He'd done that before. Burn up the truck, and it would be that much harder to trace. That was a lesson learned from the Santa Barbara murder of Silvestre Ayon, when it had taken police mere hours to find the car's owner despite missing plates and a new paint job. But Domingo had just told him the truck belonged to his dead brother's wife. A widow. Martinez felt a stab of pity for her. She'd already lost her husband. Should she lose her truck too, just because her brother-in-law had failed to show the proper respect?

Martinez took back roads for forty miles to the city of Bakersfield, which sits at the southern end of the valley, and went straight to an anonymous do-it-yourself carwash. He felt fortunate that Domingo's window had been rolled down when he shot him, sending much of the gore out onto the road. Nevertheless, there was still a lot of blood. He scrubbed and scrubbed, washing most of it out. Or so he thought.

When he went to park the truck nearby, a man looked at the liquid dripping out of the vehicle. "Hey, is that blood coming out of your truck?"

Some people might have panicked. Martinez did not. It was a sign of how brazen a killer he was becoming—or how little he feared police—that he felt comfortable washing blood out of a truck in public and in broad daylight.

Smooth as could be, he answered, "No, it's strawberry soda, from my daughter." Martinez smiled, like a loving father exasperated with his children.

Then he parked the truck and walked away. At 2 a.m. he returned and drove the truck forty-five miles back to Domingo's mother's house, where he parked it in the driveway. Earlimart was a small town. He knew where she lived.

The widow would have her truck back. Even better, the whole town would hear about how it had shown up in the middle of the night, as if delivered by a dark phantom. His good deed contained a menacing message: everyone would know to keep their mouths shut, because, as he would later explain, whoever had disappeared Domingo and dropped the truck back at his home sure "had a lot of balls."

On Saturday afternoon, a few hours after Martinez had shot Domingo, Domingo's sister-in-law was beginning to get irritated that her dead husband's brother still wasn't back with the truck.

The woman called Domingo's mother and sister to figure out where he had gone. They said they hadn't seen him.

No one was that worried. It was just annoying. But the next morning, they called back in a panic. The truck was in their driveway, they said. But Domingo wasn't with it. And, they added, there was blood inside it.

The widow went over to her mother-in-law's house and looked at her truck. There were bloodstains on the passenger seat and the inside of the passenger-side door. But the truly frightening thing was a sickening pool of water and blood on the passenger-side floor.

The widow called the Tulare County Sheriff's Department.

Officer Gene Pinon got the call at about 9:55 a.m. on Sunday morning and arrived on scene about ninety minutes later, at 11:20. He examined the truck and collected a cigarette butt. He also noted a pager—which had belonged to Domingo—inside the vehicle.

When he interviewed the widow, she told him that she had no idea why her brother-in-law carried a pager.

Detective Pinon made a quick canvas of the area. As he wrote in his police report, he was "unable to locate Domingo or any leads."

Then, he wrote, he confronted the widow.

He told her that he didn't believe her story. She had to know more. It didn't make a lick of sense that someone would return an empty, blood-stained truck to its owner's home with no explanation, he said. And furthermore, someone like Domingo, who was unemployed, did not "go out and pay for pagers unless they were dealing drugs."[2]

Shortly after, he spoke to the widow's daughter, who said she didn't know anything either.

While in the house, Officer Pinon saw a poster for a band, Los Gatos de Sinaloa. He took note of the poster because a confidential informant had told sheriff's officials that the band was involved in drug trafficking. He noted that the family seemed "startled" when he asked about the poster.

Then Pinon left, no closer to discovering what might have happened to Domingo.

From a few houses away, Martinez watched them.

Martinez didn't learn Domingo's full name until a few days later, when missing posters with his photo went up around town. He spotted one at the Earlimart market.

A short time after that, he left Earlimart and went to Sinaloa for a meeting. When he got back a month later, he caught up on all the town gossip—including the news that Domingo's mother was going crazy with worry, not knowing what had happened to her son.

Martinez thought it unlikely that anyone, even the man's mother, could possibly believe Domingo was still alive. What else could have happened to him, after all? They had found bloodstains inside the truck.

Still, Martinez felt a wave of pity for the woman. He thought of his own mother. He imagined her despair if he were to disappear and then a bloody truck mysteriously showed up. "Something sad came into my mind," he wrote in his memoir.

The next day, he went to see his family in Richgrove, near where he had buried Domingo, and announced he was spending the night at his mom's house. After everyone had gone to sleep, he dressed in dark clothes, slung an AK-47 over his back, and set out in the dark. He brought a shovel and a mask—he knew the odor would be bad.

He walked two miles to where he had left the body, then moved it to a spot where he thought it would be seen. Two days later, on May 23, workers checking irrigation pipes found Domingo's corpse.

Detective Greg Hilger of the Tulare County Sheriff's Department was called to the scene. He arrived a bit after noon, and deputies showed him the body. And then, they showed him a curious piece of evidence: surgical gloves, dropped a few feet away from the body behind an orange tree.

"I was advised that no one from the Sheriff's Dept used these gloves and discarded them, nor were they the gloves that field workers would use," Hilger wrote in his report.

Hilger sent the gloves off to the crime lab to be tested.

It took another day to match the corpse's clothes to a missing person's case from April, that of one Domingo Perez.

Final identification was grisly. The body was badly decomposed, and officials ultimately removed Domingo's hands and sent them to the crime lab to get fingerprints.

That missing person's case was now a murder. But if detectives ever developed any evidence or leads in the case, they didn't note them in their case file.

On August 4—four months after Domingo was killed—the Tulare County Sheriff's Department finally got a report back from the regional crime lab on the gloves found at the murder scene. The result: no latent fingerprints could be pulled from them.

As Martinez noted, the case went cold. "There were no suspects; no questions were asked."

He wasn't far off. That was almost the end of the investigation, according to the case file. The file contains paltry if any interviews with Domingo's family members or friends about his last days or who they thought might have killed him. Police did pull phone records, which showed numerous calls to Culiacan and to Badiraguato, Sinaloa, which is, incidentally, the hometown of El Chapo Guzman. About a year after the murder, police also tried to run down a lead on one of Domingo's former associates, who was reputed to be involved in drug smuggling and had a falling out with Domingo in the months before his death. The associate's son had been murdered in Earlimart in May 1996.

Martinez insists further investigation would have been fruitless: his good deed in returning the truck, he said, also served to terrify anyone who might have known anything into silence.

Martinez had also committed this murder at a time when a good many people in Earlimart were already scared. And not because of him.

Anti-immigrant fervor had swept California, casting a pall over communities like Earlimart. The previous November, California voters had approved Proposition 187, a ballot initiative that called for denying government services, including health care and education, to undocumented immigrants. Even small children were to be turned away from school. And anyone could be reported to authorities if they tried to access services.

The state was reeling from recession, drought, and deep cut-backs in the federal defense and aerospace industries, which had provided many middle-class jobs. Immigrants became a convenient scapegoat.

"They keep coming" was the threatening voiceover on the television advertisement for Proposition 187.[3] It played over grainy footage of people running across the border.

The initiative had passed with nearly 60 percent of the vote statewide—and by an even higher margin in Tulare County. A legal challenge, filed almost immediately, blocked it from ever going into effect. In the long run, the Republican-backed proposition backfired: it galvanized a generation of Latino and progressive activists, spurred many to enter politics, and helped turn California heavily Democratic.

But that took years, and much of rural California remained Republican. In the Central Valley, always more conservative than the coastal areas of the state, mostly it served to remind Mexican Americans that they were second-class citizens. And it made many people even more fearful of talking to police or advocating for themselves in other ways.

Not that police had much bandwidth to listen, even if people had wanted to talk.

Up and down the valley, police forces were overwhelmed by a severe budget crisis, even as they struggled with rising rates of violent crime.[4] The recession and the attendant drain on public coffers hit the valley, as it always did, harder than it did the rest of the state.

Tulare County lost officers, particularly experienced ones. Detective Ralph Diaz had departed for the district attorney's office, as had so many other experienced Spanish-speaking officers that the department had far fewer Latino officers by 1994 than it did in 1990.[5]

Smaller police departments fared even worse. McFarland, the small city just south of the Tulare County line where Martinez had lived in the early 1980s, actually dissolved its police department in 1991, unable to afford it anymore. Its police chief told the Associated Press that he planned to seek work as a barber or a roofer. Mendota, another tough farming community, a bit farther to the north, also disbanded its police department. "Without police, what do you think will happen?" one woman asked the Associated Press. "Maybe we'll all have to carry our own machine guns." (In an ironic twist, the story also noted that the woman, a few days after giving this interview to reporters, was herself arrested and charged with trying to sell fourteen pounds of cocaine to undercover police officers in another city.)[6]

Because this was California, where change, disaster, and head-spinning shifts in state policy came in waves, the retrenchment in local police forces coincided with another dizzying new initiative: a new criminal justice policy that would fill the prisons for years to come.

Never mind the recession and the diminishment of public safety statewide, California voters in 1994 also approved Proposition 184, a three-strikes law mandating that people convicted of any felony be sentenced to life in prison if they have two prior felonies.

Almost overnight, many more people were headed to prison and for much longer terms. Meanwhile, state officials—drawing on bond funding not affected by the recession buffeting local departments and in some cases not even approved by voters—had been building prisons at a furious pace. One state bureaucrat called it "the largest prison building project in the history of the world."[7]

From the time California joined the Union in 1850 until 1964, the state built just twelve prisons. Between 1984 and 2013 the state added more than twenty. The prison population also swelled, growing nearly 500 percent between 1982 and 2000. Around half of these prisons were built in the Central Valley, along what became known as "prison alley."[8] Once again, the Central Valley's farmers were big winners. Many of these prisons were built on formerly irrigated agricultural land; big farmers, of course, profited, selling or leasing land they had allowed to lie fallow.

Martinez paid keen attention to the prison boom. It was hard not to. From the roof of his mother's house at night, he could actually see the lights from four of these facilities—Corcoran, Northern Kern, Delano, and Wasco—gleaming eerily in the dark.

More importantly, the trend touched his own extended family. Some served time in these new prisons. And some worked in law enforcement. This was not an uncommon story. The San Joaquin Valley—not to mention American gangster lore—is full of families in which some members have been criminals, and others, their jailers or pursuers.

As Martinez studied the prison system's explosive growth across California, he formed his own theories about what that expansion, in conjunction with the decline in personnel in local police departments, meant. His conclusion: cops wanted to fill their new prisons with people who were easy to catch. And that left them even less time to spend on someone like him.

Chapter Eighteen

One afternoon in October 1997, Martinez arrived home from a trip to find a red Astro minivan parked in his driveway.

Who *the fuck* would dare park in his driveway now?

He parked his car on the street, grabbed a bag of money out of it, and walked into his house full of ire.

He was greeted with a surprise. The driver of the minivan was a beautiful woman with black hair all the way to her knees and eyes that seemed to him to flash like rainbows. Martinez never forgot a face, and he knew he had seen this woman before. He found her captivating.

"You look like someone I knew, seventeen years ago, in Buell-ton," a small city near Santa Barbara, he told her. Then he told her he remembered her name.

The woman startled. She asked who Martinez was, and how he knew her.

"You used to be friends with my mother," Martinez explained. "When you were young."

It now emerged that the woman had moved to the Earlimart area and become friendly with his wife, a friendship that blossomed over the proceeding months. Martinez did not necessarily approve. He claims he told his wife that he could "see the devil" in the woman. He didn't tell her he found the woman irresistible.

Then, as quickly as she had appeared, the woman was gone. She had headed north to Dutch Harbor, Alaska, for a seasonal job in a fish-processing plant. Many farmworkers went up in the off-season for work there. It was backbreaking, monotonous, and repetitive— in short, much like fieldwork. Except you were on an island in the Bering Sea in the dead dark of winter, sleeping in a crowded dorm room and spending twelve to eighteen hours a day standing at a conveyer belt chopping and packing frozen blocks of fish.

Martinez said he thought little of the woman's absence, continuing his "normal happy life" of contract killing and drug smuggling, spending time with his wife and children, and seducing other women when possible. But after committing a series of murders, including one in Oklahoma, he began to feel, for perhaps the first time, that "the heat was hot," and things were "out of control." He was worried that police were after him. He decided he needed to get out of town. And then he took a truly radical step: "I decided to go to work for the first time in my life."

Using a fake ID, he applied to a fishing company in Dutch Harbor under an assumed name. He passed the drug test and was hired.

Maybe it was the woman who gave him the idea. Or maybe it was his wife's cousin, who had also headed north. Or maybe it was that Alaska was unimaginably far away.

Martinez doesn't provide much explanation for why, two decades after he began killing with impunity, he suddenly got nervous. He wasn't aware that police were after him for anything specific. But there was no doubt that law enforcement had suddenly taken a keen interest in him. This had happened before, obviously. The wrinkle this time was that he didn't know why. And because he didn't know what crime they suspected him of, he couldn't, as he had after previous murders, gauge where detectives were in their investigation or how close they were to him.

As so many outlaws had before him, he fled to the frontier. Alaska. They called it "the last frontier."

His wife was delighted. "It's about time you got a job," he said she told him. He kept to himself the fact that he wasn't interested in gainful employment but rather wanted to flee the law.

On January 2, 1999, he flew out of Los Angeles International Airport, bound for Dutch Harbor. With him on the plane were numerous farmworkers from Earlimart seeking seasonal work in the fish plants, including his wife's friend, the woman with the long dark hair, returning for a second season.

The work at Dutch Harbor was hard. A conveyer belt full of frozen fish, waiting to be chopped. And when you weren't chopping up frozen fish, there was nothing to do except drink beer in the freezing darkness.

Martinez called home and learned from his wife that police had come by the house looking for him. They didn't say why.

"Don't tell anyone where I am," he told her.

He went back to his conveyer belt.

A month into his job, there was a surprising turn of events: Martinez was promoted. He was now the lead safety officer. He was overjoyed. It was, he decided, the best job in the world after selling drugs or collecting money from or murdering deadbeat drug dealers. He liked managing people. His duties included making sure the workers had proper safety gear, including safety glasses and earplugs. He also had to check forklifts to make sure they were in working order and ensure that workers hadn't disabled the smoke detectors in their bedrooms. When people got injured on the job, Martinez shepherded them to the hospital. He took pride in the responsibility.[1]

When he called home to report the good news, he learned from his wife that police had come by the house two more times looking to talk to him. Each time, his wife told them she had no idea where he was.

Martinez insists he still has no idea what the cops wanted with him. Whatever it was, he was convinced they would eventually give up and move on. Still, he decided it would be prudent to stay up in Alaska a little bit longer, safely hidden under his assumed name.

As an added bonus, the friend of the captivating woman with the long dark hair had departed Alaska.

Now this woman is "alone on my island," Martinez wrote.

All the dockworkers began to hit on her. Any single woman on this island was like gold, let alone a beautiful one. Of course, Martinez began to hit on her too.

When they returned home to their families in June 1999, Martinez had a cab drop the woman at her home in a small town about five miles north of Earlimart. He noted that the woman's husband did not look happy to see him.

When he got home to his own family, his younger daughter, then about eight, ran up to him. "Daddy, Daddy," she cried. "The police came looking for you five times!"

"Don't worry," he consoled her. "Probably they are looking for another man who looks like me or has the same name."

"No, Daddy," his daughter said. "They had a picture of you."

"Oh shit," Martinez thought. This must be serious.

The next day, he decamped to his mother's house for a week and then, as soon as he could, returned to Alaska.

It was king crab season. Out in the ocean, fishermen caught the crabs, which live more than fifty fathoms below the surface. It is among the most dangerous of fishing jobs, memorialized in the show *Deadliest Catch*. Work inside the plant was safer but no less frenzied. Workers wearing rubber gloves stood at conveyor belts, pulling the innards out of steaming hot crabs and then yanking their legs off. Martinez was again in charge of his fellow workers' safety.

Two weeks after he arrived, his wife reported that police had come looking for him again.

"What is going on?" she asked him.

Martinez wasn't about to tell her. "I don't know what the fuck they want," he said. Which was true, up to a point. He neglected to mention that they might be interested in his role in so many different murders he could barely keep track.

Like his first wife, Martinez's second wife—who also did not provide her story for this account—had come from Sinaloa to California at a young age, arriving alone and undocumented.[2] Martinez said he went to great pains to hide his violence from her. "I don't tell my wife or my family about the crimes I done in my life," he said. "My family thought I was the nicest person in the world."

Martinez said he never found out why detectives were so hot to get their hands on him in 1998 and 1999. There are no active case files from that period linked to him. When asked about it years later, several detectives who worked for the Tulare County Sheriff's Department during that time said they didn't have a clue.

In any event, Martinez was right: eventually police did move on. His family reported that interest in him had faded away, and in October 1999 he returned home to his family in Earlimart.

Chapter Nineteen

⟵

The poison came drifting off the fields and across the houses and apartments of Earlimart just as the sun was setting. It was Saturday evening, November 13, 1999, and many folks in town were getting ready to sink into the pleasure of a weekend evening. Children were playing in the street. Families were gathering for dinner.

And then, without warning or explanation, residents began to wheeze and cough and vomit.

The sickness started on the east end of town and spread west with the pesticide that caused it—the soil fumigant metam sodium. Eventually, the sheriff's department came and announced that people had to leave. Just take what you can and go, officials said.

Teresa De Anda had driven to Delano from her home in Earlimart to run an errand. She got back just as the sun had set and found a sheriff's deputy standing at her gate. "We need to get out because there's something happening," her husband said.[1]

De Anda could smell something, but it wasn't terribly strong. She did, however, feel deep dread. "It's a horrible feeling, getting told you've got to get out, that there's something you shouldn't be smelling."[2] She and her husband collected their children and her uncle, who was blind, along with their eighty-seven-year-old compadre, or close family friend. And then they fled.

De Anda didn't find out what had happened to the people who had stayed behind until later. The sheriff's department had gathered up the people who were sickest and told them to go to the center of town. Then they told them all to strip down.

People were still coughing and vomiting, their eyes burning, and now they were standing naked in the center of the town. Hazmat officials from the county trained water hoses on them and sprayed.

The idea was for people to get sprayed down and then be loaded into ambulances. But enough ambulances hadn't yet arrived, and so they stood there in the dark, naked and sick and frightened.

When transport finally did come, there was no system for making sure families stayed together. In some cases, small children had their parents' phone numbers written on their stomachs in Sharpie pen before they were sent off. In the end twenty-one people were hospitalized.[3]

What's more, they learned later that the humiliation of having to strip and the discomfort of having a fire hose trained on them had been completely unnecessary and in fact harmful: water didn't counteract the pesticides at all.

People in Earlimart had been living for years with so-called pesticide drift, the phenomenon of chemicals sprayed on crops wafting off the fields and making people sick. Cesar Chavez and the United Farm Workers (UFW) had raised concerns about pesticides as far back as 1970. In the late 1980s, having lost many of its contracts and members, the union focused more on the issue. In 1988, Chavez underwent his third and final lengthy public fast in an attempt to draw public attention to the issue. "The growers are using pesticides to kill our people," Chavez said.[4] When he died at age sixty-six in 1993, many believed the weeks-long fasts had shortened his life.[5]

The Earlimart event six years later—so traumatic and so widespread—galvanized the community.

Leading the charge was Teresa De Anda. The daughter of a Filipino farmworker father, who later became a contractor, and a Mexican farmworker mother, she had been raised in Earlimart. She had, she said, "no idea what an activist was," but she was furious about the poisoning of her town and how the fire and hazmat officials had treated the people in the aftermath.[6]

People had been forced to strip naked in front of their neighbors. One woman tried to refuse, referring to her rights, and a fire official had told her, "Listen, you have no rights tonight; you've lost your rights."[7]

After the incident, De Anda started making phone calls, trying to find out what exactly had happened to the people in her town.

"She went up and down the yellow book pages," her daughter, Valerie Gorospe, recalled. "She was calling every single agency."

Call after call, she got the runaround. No one was responsible. Everyone sent her somewhere else.

Finally, someone told her that the correct treatment for metam sodium inhalation was not rinsing the skin.

How could officials not know this? How could they have done it anyway? "That really pissed her off," her daughter recalled. "And she was like, No, we can't do this anymore. This has to change."

The answer, De Anda decided, was stronger laws and greater education about the dangers of pesticides, how to respond to them, and what protocols and punishments should be put in place if accidents happened.

Following De Anda's lead, women who had never dared speak out before were suddenly showing up at community meetings to demand answers from officials about how this could have happened and what they were going to do about it. They were willing to state, in public, their full names and addresses, as required by law at many public meetings. This was no small thing in the years after Proposition 187, especially for people who may have been undocumented and feared any interaction with authorities. Even for those with legal residency or US citizenship, speaking out as a farmworker still carried risks. If employers found out, they could fire you.

Meeting after meeting, people followed De Anda's lead and stood up.

At first, they didn't get very far. They asked repeatedly for a meeting with county supervisors to no avail. On December 8, a contingent of Earlimart residents drove forty miles to the Tulare County seat, Visalia. No county supervisor would meet with them. But the story of the residents' anger—and their fear and confusion following the pesticide gassing and the county response—made the front page of the next day's *Visalia Times-Delta*. That spurred the women to organize more. As De Anda put it, "We started having our own meetings, monthly meetings. The ladies…were just very outspoken." One woman, she noted, had always been quiet, and "now she was speaking her voice."

Despite the pall cast by Proposition 187, despite their fear of making waves, despite the many times they had asked for change before and been denied it, for the first time in a long time, the women of Earlimart were speaking out.[8]

Martinez didn't take much notice of either the environmental catastrophe or the activism it sparked among the women of his town.

He was too focused on the woman with the long dark hair. He had decided to kill her husband.

In February 2000, the woman went to Palm Springs to visit her mother. On the eve of Valentine's Day, Martinez went to her house. He crept into her husband's bedroom but found him sleeping with their youngest daughter.

He left without doing anything. He would never kill a man in front of his little girl. That would traumatize her! And he certainly didn't want to do anything that would harm an innocent child.[9]

The next night, at 3 a.m., he went back and found the husband, Santiago Perez, sleeping alone.

Martinez shot him three times in the back of his head. He said he used the gun he had pulled off the body of Domingo Perez, after he shot him for the crime of parking in his driveway. The killing gave him an extra jolt of satisfaction because of where Santiago Perez and his family lived: just across the street and down the block from the Tulare County Sheriff's Department's Pixley substation. If detectives had looked out the window, they could have seen him sneaking into the house and sneaking back out a few minutes later.

He went straight home and pretended to be asleep. He was still pretending at 4:15 a.m. when his sister-in-law asked for a ride to work in the fields.

He knew an alibi when he came across one. He happily agreed.

Later that morning, he said, he called the woman with the long dark hair in Palm Springs. "Happy Valentine's Day, my widow," he told her.

Her answer, according to Martinez: "Stop the games, what do you mean widow?"[10]

Chapter Twenty

B ecause it was only one block from their station, sheriff's deputies were at the scene of the murder by 3:48 a.m., just a few
minutes after it happened.

The Perez children, aged six to sixteen, all told a version of the
same story.[1]

The oldest, sixteen, said he awoke to the sound of gunshots and
then heard footsteps pounding down the hallway. When he ran
out of his room, he saw a man in dark clothes bolt from the house,
jump into a car, and speed away. Then he found his father, shot
to death in his bed. His younger brother, fourteen, added that he
heard his oldest brother yelling, "There were people here.... They
shot dad."

Initially, police suspected drugs were a motive. They found
drug paraphernalia in the house, along with guns. What's more,
Santiago—as police noted in their reports—dressed "like a
Sinaloan cowboy" and was wearing a pendant of Jesus Malverde,
a legendary Robin Hood figure from Sinaloa whom drug dealers
had adopted as a patron saint.

But details that didn't fit that picture quickly emerged.

The house, for one, had been locked, meaning whoever had killed him had a key—hardly typical of a drug hit. They also heard from relative after relative that Santiago, far from being a hardened criminal, was like "Mr. Mom."[2]

Among the first people to seriously question Martinez about the murder of Santiago Perez was his second wife.

A few weeks after the killing, she confronted him. Was he having an affair with the widow?

"No," he said.

She didn't accept this for an instant.

"You *are* having an affair," she insisted. Did you hire someone to kill Santiago?

Martinez found the question stunning. He almost snapped back, "Why should I hire someone, when I do that job?" But obviously, he couldn't say that.[3]

"No," he answered, "I did not hire someone to kill Santiago."

But his wife was not satisfied. Every single day, he said, she said the same thing: if he had had Santiago killed, she did not want to live with him.

As Martinez tells it, one day he could take it no more. "I can see you want to be alone," he said he told his wife. "When you ask me a question and I don't give you an answer, you get mad so easy. I'm moving out to my mother's house."

Martinez did not record what she said in response, but she did do something that shed light on her thinking: she asked Martinez to stay away from their children.

Martinez moved in with his mother. But he also took to spending more and more time at the home of the woman with the long dark hair—although never in the bed where he had shot her husband.

*　　*　　*

Eventually, police hit upon the same suspicions as Martinez's wife. Ironically, she and Martinez's own sister had inadvertently tipped them off.

Soon after the murder, according to their reports, police heard rumors that an unknown woman had confronted Santiago's wife and accused her of having an affair with her husband. By March 7—three weeks after the killing—they had heard that the woman in question was married to a "Manuel Martinez, who lived in Earlimart."[4]

By March 27, police had two names: those of Martinez's wife and one of Martinez's sisters, who had driven his wife to the woman's house for the confrontation.

On April 10—nearly two months after the murder—police showed up at Martinez's house to talk to his wife.

The police report on this encounter is terse. Martinez's wife confirmed that she had confronted the woman she believed to be her husband's lover. She also said that she had separated from her husband. And she gave them his full name: Jose Manuel Martinez. Police asked if her husband had any guns. She said she didn't know of any.

Two days later, on April 12, police showed up outside Martinez's mother's house. Martinez watched Detective Mario Martin get out of his car and told himself he wasn't worried at all.

"This is a stupid cop," he later wrote that he thought. "I can tell one when I see one."

Detective Martin wanted to know about his relationship with Santiago Perez's wife, the woman with the long dark hair.

Smoothly, Martinez told him he'd known her a long time, through his mother and his wife. He also provided his alibi about driving family members to work in the early-morning hours of the murder, which family members backed up. And he added—truthfully—that yes, he had talked to the widow after the murder. He said he had spoken to her children, at her request, to counsel them to stay out of trouble.

Martinez agreed to take a polygraph, a lie-detector test. It was inconclusive. Police suspected he was guilty, but they didn't have enough evidence. So they set out to get more.

Detective Mario Martin stayed on the case for months. In September 2000, eight months after the murder, he filed search warrants for phone records on five numbers, including several at homes where Martinez stayed, as well as flight records from Alaska Airlines for Martinez and the woman with the long dark hair.

The records came flooding in, hundreds of pages of phone calls and plane ticket after plane ticket, from Los Angeles to Puerto Vallarta to Anchorage to Seattle and back. But they did not yield the conclusive evidence that Martin needed.

In such a circumstance, there are things police can do to try to get more information out of people they suspect are not telling them the truth or giving them the whole story.

Interrogating people is one of them. Police are allowed a fair amount of leeway in this endeavor. They are allowed to lie to suspects, to make them think authorities have evidence they do not, in order to elicit confessions.

There are also some things they are not allowed to do. One of these is familiar to anyone who has ever watched a police procedural. The so-called Miranda warning, which stems from the 1966 US Supreme Court ruling in *Miranda v. Arizona*, requires that police must advise people being taken into custody or interrogated of their right to remain silent and to have an attorney present and that police must stop questioning them once these rights have been invoked.

In practice, this means that anything a suspect tells police before being read his or her rights is not admissible in court. It also means that once a suspect asks for a lawyer, police have to cease questioning.

Good detectives, therefore, walk a fine line: try to get as much information as possible before people know they are suspects, but don't go so far as to get them to confess before they have been read their rights, lest the confession be unusable in court.

In the summer and fall of 2000, it is possible that no officers in California were more conscious of that fine line than Detective Mario Martin, the investigator on the Santiago Perez murder, and his supervisors.

While investigating a 1999 homicide, Detective Martin had found himself on the wrong side of the line. And the California Supreme Court called his department out for it, with one judge issuing an opinion that described the approach to questioning the suspect in the case as "unconscionable" and a "fiasco."[5]

The case in question had involved an eighteen-year-old former foster child, Kenneth Ray Neal, who was invited to live with a former child-care worker at a group home where he had lived, a sixty-nine-year-old man named Donald Collins. Collins plied the young man with vodka and then tried to touch his penis. On the night of April 3, 1999, Collins was strangled with an electrical cord.

Neal quickly became the prime suspect. He had apparently watched police procedurals. Neal told Martin he didn't want to talk. And he asked for a lawyer. In fact, he asked for a lawyer at least nine times. Just one ask is supposed to do the trick.

But Detective Martin hadn't gotten Neal a lawyer. Instead, he locked Neal up overnight, without access to food, water, or a toilet. He also badgered and threatened him, according to transcripts of the interrogation that later made their way to the California Supreme Court. Eventually Neal confessed. Those confessions were used against Neal at trial, and he was subsequently convicted of the murder.

Martin testified that he was aware that the suspect had asked for a lawyer and that he had continued the interrogation anyway. He also said that he viewed such continued interrogations as a "useful tool" and, he added, one he had been taught by his supervisor.

The California Supreme Court was outraged and issued a rare decision to vacate a murder conviction. "The consequence of the officer's misconduct…is severe, but is intended to deter other officers from engaging in misconduct of this sort in the future," the chief justice wrote.[6] The opinion made headlines across California.

This particular ruling had not yet been handed down when Martinez killed Santiago Perez and Martin picked up the case, but there were signs that a storm might be brewing. When Neal's case reached a Tulare County courtroom in the spring of 1999—about nine months before Perez was killed—Detective Martin was grilled in court. The judge stated that he was "very concerned about the questioning activity in this case and I think it comes very close to coercion." A second judge echoed those concerns in December 1999.[7] Not close enough, however, for Tulare County judges to throw out the confession. It would take the Supreme Court to do that.[8]

Once again, Martinez had gotten lucky. He'd committed a murder at a moment when the Tulare County Sheriff's Department was perhaps particularly squeamish about squeezing people during interrogations. So they came and asked him questions, and he told them lies. In the end, that was the end of that.

The case went cold.

For once, though, someone in Earlimart scored a partial victory.

The day of Santiago Perez's murder was also the day that Teresa De Anda and the group of Earlimart residents furious about the pesticide drift decided they had finally had enough. It had been two and a half months since the fumigant had wafted over their town, and they still hadn't been able to get a meeting with the county supervisors.

What's more, nearly two dozen residents were experiencing ongoing health problems from the poison. And although the company,

Wilbur-Ellis, had promised to cover their medical expenses, the residents claimed the bills hadn't been paid, leaving them on the hook for hospital tabs and harassed by collection agencies.

The residents filed into an open supervisors' meeting and made their complaints during the "public comment" section. Four of the five supervisors refused to even reply to them. The fifth, board chairman Bill Sanders, told them the issue was not on the agenda, and so the supervisors could not respond to their complaints.[9]

"When you just show up, it makes it difficult for us," he said.

"We have waited too long," shot back one of the Earlimart women.

The women fighting for relief from the pesticide poisoning never did get much official recognition from the board of supervisors. But they did get organized. With assistance from the United Farm Workers, the women formed a group, El Comite para el Bienestar de Earlimart, or, in English, the Committee for the Wellbeing of Earlimart.

In May, they held a community meeting in Earlimart and convinced someone from the state Department of Pesticide Regulation to come.[10] Confronted with the committee's insistent and well-organized members, the county created a hotline for people to call if they suspect their communities have been sprayed with pesticides. It was a simple idea. It hadn't existed until De Anda's group argued for it.

Meanwhile, the farmer who owned the vineyard where the pesticide had been sprayed agreed to pull his vines one hundred feet back from the community, creating a buffer zone to protect residents.

But De Anda and her group weren't done. They kept pushing. And in September 2000, around the same time that Tulare detectives were searching through phone and travel records in the Santiago Perez case, the state of California stepped in. The state and the pesticide company, Wilbur-Ellis, entered into a $150,000 settlement, at the time the largest such settlement over pesticides in California history.[11]

The money, the state announced, would be used to pay for the ongoing medical expenses of the people of Earlimart. This was necessary, officials said, because ten months later, twenty-eight people were still suffering because of what had happened to them.

It was a victory for the women of the town.

It just pushed them to work harder.

De Anda had started organizing in Earlimart. But now she was going to Weed Patch, and Arvin, and Lamont, and other little farmworker towns scattered around the southern part of the valley, talking to people there too. Have you ever been sprayed? Have you ever gotten sick? There are things you can do about it. I'll show you how.

It was inspiring to many people in Earlimart. Among them was Melissa Morales, the little girl whose father had helped build Earlimart's swimming pool in response to the explosion of murders—some committed by Martinez—in 1982.

As a young woman, Morales had worked at the local grocery store—an establishment where Jose Martinez was a regular, and unfailingly courteous, customer. She had been appalled to watch how the people in her town had been treated after the pesticide accident—"like animals," she said. She was exhilarated by the way De Anda was organizing residents to force government officials to make change.

Now in her twenties, Morales was well aware of the deprivations and problems of her town. But remembering the lesson of the swimming pool, she chose to focus on the positive. As De Anda moved from house to house, organizing her neighbors, Morales found her own way to make her community better. She went to college and became a teacher. And when it came time to get a job, she chose the Earlimart schools. She planned to dedicate her days to showing the town's children how much they were loved.[12]

At the end of October 2000, about nine months after Martinez murdered her husband, the woman with the long dark hair asked him to drive her and her family to Santa Ynez to visit a cemetery and pay respects to a dead relative.

Of course Martinez said yes.

The family set off in the morning in Martinez's white Suburban and made the three-hour drive out of the San Joaquin Valley and over the coastal range into the softer, lusher green of the Santa Ynez Valley. There was already a crowd at the cemetery when they arrived.

Martinez got out of the car, smiling and friendly, greeting the assembled relatives, shaking hands, and giving hugs. Then, not wanting to intrude on their sorrow or their rituals, he hung back as the family took flowers to the grave. The women stood over it, weeping and lighting candles. Martinez noticed that his girlfriend was among those who were emotionally overcome. Her tears touched him, and he walked over to give her a supportive hug.

Then, he glanced at the gravestone. He read the words, and then read them again, lest he was seeing things. "Silvestre Ayon," it said. And it listed the date he had died: October 1, 1982.

"Oh shit," Martinez thought, his heart starting to pound. "I killed that man."

A more terrifying thought popped into his brain. What if the guy he had wounded was here too, paying his respects? What if he recognized Martinez?

Martinez's head began to spin. He walked slowly away from the grave, the weeping of his girlfriend's mother echoing in his ears like a rebuke.

He reached into his pocket, taking out his cigarettes. He lit one and walked to his Suburban, trying to figure out what to do.

When he reached his car, he did the only thing he could think of that would calm him down. He opened the hidden compartment he had installed and took out his gun. Holding the cold steel in his hands steadied him slightly.[13] But his mind was still racing. How was it possible? What was the universe trying to do to him?

Finally, after what seemed like hours, his girlfriend and her family finished their ritual and returned to the car. Martinez took them for a meal and then drove them back home. They appeared not to notice how subdued he was, because they were emotionally wrung out themselves.

A day later, Martinez got his girlfriend alone, with no other family around. Tell me about your relative who died, he said.

He was shot, the woman answered. He was working, driving a tractor, and three men came up and shot him.

"How did you know it was three men?" Martinez asked.

Because there had been a witness, the woman said.

"Did they catch anyone for the crime?" Martinez asked.

They tried and failed, she answered. But it didn't matter: she knew who was responsible.

As soon as Martinez left the woman's house, he called Mr. X, who was now living down in Los Angeles.

"I'm on my way to your house," Martinez told him. "I have something very important to tell you. You're not going to believe it, because I don't even believe it myself."

When he got to Mr. X's house, he told him to sit down "because this is a long fucking story."

"Compadre," Martinez began, "this is a story about a woman."

After explaining the story of his affair with the woman with the long dark hair, Martinez finally got to the point. "Three days ago, she came to me. She wanted a ride to Santa Ynez with all her family." He continued, "I took her to a cemetery. To put flowers on a grave. And the man she went to see was Silvestre Ayon. The man we killed in 1982."

"What?" Mr. X exclaimed.

"That's what I said," Martinez answered.

The course of action was clear, Mr. X advised: Martinez needed to stay away from this woman. Especially because she had any number of brothers and cousins who might take revenge into their own hands.

Martinez knew Mr. X was right. And he tried. He began to see other women. But he was still captivated by the woman with the long dark hair, and he kept seeing her too. He also acted as a coyote to bring some of her family members across the border. He didn't quite trust her. This didn't lessen her appeal in the least.

As his fortieth birthday rolled around, he felt happy with his life. He felt he had a good relationship with his children, the three raised in Arizona with his first wife and the three in Earlimart with his second. After the murder of Santiago Perez, his second wife had restricted his access to his children in Earlimart, but he had found a way to see them anyway. He would wait on the street as they were walking to school and accompany them, giving them gifts and making sure they were OK.[14]

He had also found a new source of income: methamphetamine, also known as crank, speed, ice, or crystal. By some estimates, more than 50 percent of the nation's meth labs were in the valley, with many local entrepreneurs linked to drug cartels in Mexico. Just as, in an earlier generation of the drug business, the valley had been a perfect place to land small planes loaded with marijuana, it was also the perfect place to make meth: wide, open spaces, sparsely patrolled by police, meant you could cook several million dollars' worth of the drug in a clandestine lab set up in a trailer or two and disappear before anyone was the wiser. Some farmers, hard hit by a drought that stretched from 1986 to 1992, were even willing to rent land to park that trailer on without asking too many questions, provided the money was good. Police stumbled across one lab where the farmer provided everything but the chemicals.[15]

Hard statistics were, of course, impossible to come by, given that the trade was illegal, but so much meth was being cooked in the valley that officials estimated that the drug had surpassed peaches as a cash crop.[16]

Cooking meth was a process that used gallons of toxic chemicals and posed an ever-present danger of deadly explosions. And while this was going on, someone had to guard the labs to make sure another band of criminals didn't swoop in and try to steal the final product. At some labs, the meth cookers themselves needed to be guarded as well: some of them were farmworkers who had signed on for what they thought was a lucrative gig, only to discover they were virtual slaves, working a low-paying job in which they could die in an explosion or get burned by toxic chemicals at any moment. In addition to his drug-debt collection and his smuggling trips to Chicago, Martinez signed on for work in meth labs too. His brush with legitimate employment in the fish factories of Alaska hadn't stuck. He had children to support, and his skills were much more valuable in the black market.

Family members noticed that Martinez lost his teeth—a common side effect of the drug, stemming in part from the way it dries out people's salivary glands. Martinez insists he never had a problem with the drug.[17]

What Martinez chooses to emphasize from this period of his life is not his family's concerns about him or the difficulties of a troubled love life but his growing fame—at least around Earlimart.

There had been whispers of his dark dealings for some time among certain circles in Earlimart. But after the murder of Santiago Perez, those whispers grew louder. "The whole town of Earlimart called me 'El Mano Negra,'" he wrote in his memoir with pride. *Narcocorridos*—danceable ballads that celebrate figures and episodes from the drug world—were being written about him.

Sometimes, he said, he heard them driving through town and felt his heart swell.

*   *   *

In July 2002, Teresa De Anda, the Earlimart woman who had led the charge against pesticides, saw a TV news report that there had been another incidence of pesticide drift in the Kern County farm town of Arvin involving the same chemical: metam sodium.[18]

The news said that only one person had been hospitalized and downplayed the incident. De Anda didn't believe it for a minute. Arvin, a desperately poor and blighted town hunched at the southeastern end of the San Joaquin Valley, had a population of about twenty thousand. If residents had been exposed to the same kind of pesticide in the same way, there had to be many more people who were sick, people who were confused and frightened and didn't know how to advocate for themselves.

She began calling Kern County's agricultural commissioner, demanding to know whether his office planned to investigate the incident. He put her off, pointing out that only one person had been sickened. Then he put her off again, saying that what was important was how the accident had happened, not how many people had been affected.

Fed up, De Anda got into her car the next day, drove sixty miles south to Arvin, and began going door-to-door. After hitting just a few houses on Judith Street, nearest to the field where the pesticide had been applied, she and the people she was with counted forty-two people who had been sickened. It was like a flashback to Earlimart: they heard about burning eyes and coughing, parents feeling powerless as their children suddenly began to vomit, how all of a sudden a strange odor descended and no one could breathe. But it was worse: county officials hadn't even done an evacuation. And they still couldn't be made to care.

De Anda and the others went back to the neighborhood for a second visit to take a more thorough count. But this time they brought a reporter and a cameraman. After the journalist's interview with a young woman whose little baby had developed asthma after the incident, the case finally got the regulator's attention.

The California Department of Pesticide Regulation stepped in. Eventually, 250 victims were identified, 84 of whom ultimately sued and won $775,000 from the pesticide company, one of the largest awards of its kind.[19]

Soon after that, De Anda got a job offer. Californians for Pesticide Reform, an advocacy group working to regulate pesticide spraying, hired her as its Central Valley coordinator. Amid its troubles, Earlimart had created one of the valley's most effective environmental justice advocates.

Chapter Twenty-One

Martinez was in Chicago during the first week of November 2006, when Mr. X called from Culiacan. Martinez's "special services" were being requested in Florida.

Martinez landed in Orlando the next afternoon, the steamy Florida air a welcome change from the biting cold of Chicago. His local contact picked him up at the airport and got him up to speed.

It seemed that a guy named Javier Huerta, a masonry contractor with an apparent side business in cocaine, had been accused of stealing ten kilos from another drug distributor. The alleged thief was just twenty years old.

"Damn," Martinez wrote that he thought when he laid eyes on the kid. "This punk stole ten kilos?"

The local contact took Martinez to a motel room, where he met the drug wholesaler whose "little problem" they were there to solve. The drug wholesaler explained what had happened. He had received a call from Huerta, asking if he had ten kilos of cocaine that he could buy at a wholesale price.

The wholesaler replied that of course he could. He had ten kilos right here, he said.

An hour later, there was a knock at the wholesaler's door. But it wasn't Huerta, as expected. It was two men, one of them wearing a ski mask.

The wholesaler was at home with his nine-year-old sister. One of the men put a gun to the little girl's head. "Give me the ten kilos or I'll blow her fucking head off," he said. The wholesaler handed over the cocaine. Ten kilos at $17,000 a kilo meant the thieves had made off with $170,000 worth of product.

Martinez had one question for the wholesaler. Since this robbery, had he heard from Huerta? The wholesaler said he had not, which was unusual, since they were friendly.

That was proof enough for Martinez. There was no doubt in his mind that this punk kid had ordered the robbery that had threatened the life of an innocent nine-year-old girl. Intolerable!

Martinez and his accomplices watched Huerta for a few days and came up with the perfect trap for him. They rented a house in the town of Deland, a rural community known for its downtown historic district, about thirty miles from Orlando at the edge of a swamp.

Martinez called up Huerta and said he was in need of a new brick wall to prevent his children from running into the street. Could Huerta come bid on the job?

When Huerta showed up, Martinez told him and the worker he brought that inside he had blueprints showing a gas line running through the property, which might be helpful to see. He welcomed them into the house, incredulous that the "two idiots" were stupid enough to follow him in. They sat on the sofa.

Martinez locked the front door. Then he whipped out not one but two guns concealed inside his waistband.

"Get on the floor, motherfuckers," he said. He swiftly bound their hands with zip ties.[1]

Martinez told the men they had stolen cocaine and needed to

pay it back. He also informed Huerta that he had been watching his family for days.

"This morning," he told Huerta, "I was at your house. Your wife was in the shower. Your little baby was lying on the bed. It came into my mind to get the baby, but I change my mind. It's not her fault that you do stupid things."

While Martinez dealt with Huerta, one of his associates searched Huerta's truck and found $20,000 in cash. Martinez then asked Huerta if he had any money in his truck. Huerta replied that he did not.

So Huerta was lying, even now. Martinez hated lying. He hated disrespect even more.

Martinez walked over to Huerta's partner, Gustavo Olivares, and pulled his zip ties so tight that his arms pinched back in pain. This is the way I work, Martinez said. If you lie, your partner pays.

Gustavo began to yell. "Give him what you took from him," he said.

"I'm going to get my money the easy way or the hard way. You pick," Martinez shrugged.

Huerta asked to use the phone. He called his wife and told her to go into their backyard and dig up the safe of money he had buried out there.

His wife called him back and said she had extracted $160,000 in cash from the ground.

In short order, Martinez had arranged to pick up the cash. Once Martinez retrieved the money, he asked Huerta's partner how many home-invasion robberies of drug stash houses Huerta had carried out. The partner counted four. The partner also told him that in addition to the safe containing $160,000 in the backyard, there was at least one more box stuffed with cash.

Martinez demanded to know from Huerta how much money he had buried in the backyard. Huerta told him $300,000. And he told Martinez where to get it.

Martinez claims he was in the process of driving Huerta back to his home to let him go. At one point, he said, he lit a cigarette, and Huerta asked for one as well.

"No," Martinez answered. "It's bad for your health."

Huerta asked not to be left in front of his house with zip ties around his wrists. "I will be embarrassed in front of my wife and kids," he said.

"You weren't embarrassed when you sent those men to steal ten kilos and put a gun to a little girl's head," Martinez said, his anger growing.

"That was the easy way to get the kilos," Huerta answered.

It was the wrong answer. Martinez hated the notion of anyone hurting children. It filled him with the same kind of fury he felt when he learned his sister had been killed. His rage consumed him, and right there, while driving, he shot Huerta.

In the backseat, Huerta's partner began screaming and begging for his life. Martinez believed the partner was innocent of stealing the cocaine from his associates. Possibly he wasn't even involved with drugs but was just what he appeared to be: a masonry worker who had accompanied his boss to bid on a job and had some knowledge of his side business involving cocaine. But Martinez didn't believe in witnesses. So he shot the partner too.

Then he drove out of town and parked his victim's Nissan truck on a swampy stretch of road at the edge of the Ocala National Forest.

Martinez's associate was following behind and picked him up.

"Did you let them live?" Martinez's partner asked.

"No," Martinez answered. He offered a justification. "Once a thief, always a thief," he said.

Then he and his partner drove through the night to Atlanta.

Huerta's family reported him missing to the Volusia County Sheriff's Office the next morning, but authorities didn't take it too seriously, since the family neglected to mention that they had dug up tens of thousands of dollars buried in their backyard in a state of panic right before he vanished.[2]

A day later, on November 8, the family again called to report Huerta missing. The sheriff's department didn't take a written report because Huerta hadn't been missing long enough and what the family told police about his disappearance didn't suggest to them that he was in danger.

Then, at about 4:15 p.m. that afternoon, a passerby found Huerta's black truck, parked at the edge of the Ocala National Forest. The location was just over the county line, in Marion County. Concerned about the abandoned truck, the passerby called authorities.

Sheriff's deputies pulled up on the scene about 5:15 p.m., and when they opened the door of the truck, they "immediately smelled a foul odor." Inside were two bodies. They had been shot to death. Their hands had been bound with zip ties.

Police traced the car's registration and soon arrived at Huerta's house. They found his wife, who was hysterical and refused to speak to them. No one else would speak with them either, except for Huerta's father, who insisted that his son was not involved in any illegal activities and that he could not imagine why he had been killed.

But by the next day, police were starting to hear differently. From sources in the Drug Enforcement Administration, police learned that Huerta was known to be running large quantities of drugs. Then one member of the family broke the silence and told the police about the box full of cash that Huerta had come to pick up, just before he disappeared for good.

The killing suddenly had all the signs of a drug hit. It was only a matter of time before informants told them about the stolen cocaine.

When detectives tried to follow that trail of stolen cocaine, however, they were warned off, told that it might interfere with a bigger drug investigation. For some reason—in a decision another detective in that department later criticized—authorities decided that this other drug investigation trumped a cold-blooded murder.

Even so, police had picked up another piece of evidence. In Huerta's truck, they found a cigarette butt inside a Mountain Dew can in the center console. They bagged it and tagged it as evidence.

It could have cracked the case. Martinez's fingerprints should have been on file in the national computer system, along with his DNA, because of his arrests over the years on various charges.[3] But there was no DNA analysis on the cigarette butt. And overwhelmed with mountains of physical evidence from the investigation, no one noticed or asked for it to be tested.

The case went cold.

Martinez and his partner drove into Atlanta at about 6 a.m. on the day after the murder. Martinez's take from the Huerta collection and hit was $70,000 in crisp bills.

As he prepared to head home, he got an idea. "How far is Alabama?" he asked his Atlanta associates, naming a town he had never visited.

His oldest daughter from his first marriage lived there with his granddaughters. He hadn't seen her in a while and thought it would be a wonderful time to visit.

Then it was time to go home, for his other daughter's *quinceañera* back in Earlimart.

When Martinez got home, he went straight to visit his mother and gave her some of the cash from the Huerta job—without, obviously, telling her exactly how he had come by it. He passed more around to other family members. This is what he did with his blood money: he gave a lot of it away. He loved to be generous.

Showering his family with gifts and money made him happy, and it made him feel powerful and protective of them too. Much of the rest of the money, he said, he stashed in various secret places or invested in real estate in Mexico. On paper, Martinez was poor.

When it was time for the party, his younger daughter wore a beautiful dress, and the entire family gathered for photographs. Martinez took his place in the bottom row on the right and smiled with his lips closed, hiding his teeth. He looked proud and shy, like a man who couldn't quite believe his luck in being there.

Chapter Twenty-Two

By the time he had settled back in after his Florida murders and his daughter's *quinceañera*, Martinez had been playing cat and mouse with law enforcement for decades. Detectives had pulled him over and questioned him. They'd been to his houses and his family's houses; they'd interviewed his friends and family members. He'd been locked up in jail for short stints on drug charges. Martinez had also had some daring escapes. There was the time he'd used an assumed name to get work in Alaska to dodge being questioned. Or the time he'd avoided arrest by pretending to be an undocumented immigrant, got himself deported to Mexico, turned right around and reentered the country legally, and reclaimed his car from an impound lot, still stuffed with undetected ill-gotten cash.

But in the spring of 2007, Martinez's games of cat and mouse with law enforcement ratcheted up to a whole new level.

By the late 2000s, any number of detectives within the Tulare County Sheriff's Department suspected Martinez was a killer—they even knew his nickname around Earlimart was El Mano Negra, for heaven's sake. But the evidence needed to make a murder charge stick was as elusive as ever, especially because law enforcement in the valley had so much else to contend with.

There was a growing, increasingly violent gang problem, one that Tulare County's biggest newspaper, the *Visalia Times-Delta*, decided to pay close attention to in the spring of 2007. "Gang Wars," blared the banner headline across the front page on March 3, 2007—a headline no local elected politician wants to see, especially as part of an ongoing series, like this one. The sheriff's department was overwhelmed with gang violence, the story reported—half of the fifty-eight murders in Tulare County in 2005 had been gang related.[1] Innocent bystanders, including children, had been caught in the crossfire. In response, the sheriff's department stepped up antigang efforts.

Another big priority for both the Tulare and Kern County Sheriff's Departments was agricultural crime: the theft of everything from fruit and nuts to farm equipment and metal. (As meth swept through the valley, so-called tweakers were stealing every piece of metal they could get their hands on, occasionally getting electrocuted in the process; metal prices were high, and it was easy to sell at scrap yards to get cash for drugs.) Powerful farmers screamed for more attention from law enforcement. And, as they often did, the farmers got what they wanted.

All this left authorities with little time to build a major case against a criminal like Martinez, who was not a gang member, did not associate with street gangs, killed people whose family members and associates were terrified of talking to police, and left little evidence in the process.

But Martinez was on police radar, and sheriff's officials could and did pull him over with some regularity, searching his cars thoroughly. In the late spring or early summer of 2007, Martinez was pulled over and caught with some kind of stolen property. Then—finally—he was packed off to prison. The court record on what landed him behind bars is dizzyingly complicated, but it appears that he was sent away because he had violated his probation on an earlier charge. He was sent to the Sierra Conservation Center, a small prison in the foothills of the Sierra Nevada mountains near Yosemite National Park. He was sentenced to fourteen months.

While there, Martinez began attending church—because, he admits, the pastor was an attractive female minister he was trying to seduce. The seduction failed. But amid his churchgoing, Martinez did something extraordinary for a serial murderer who had managed—over more than twenty-five years of killing—to avoid serious trouble with the police: he wrote homicide detectives a letter, offering to help solve the murder of a young man from Kern County who had been missing since early 2007.

Martinez sent his letter to the Delano Police Department, which eventually passed it on to the Kern County Sheriff's Department, which was responsible for the case. It wound up on the desk of Kern County homicide detective Kavin Brewer.

The Kern County Sheriff's Department is, by many accounts, a troubled agency. Some of its officers have proven vulnerable to the corrupting influence of drug smugglers. The county's officers are also, by some measures, America's most trigger-happy. A series by the *Guardian* newspaper found that the county's officers, in both the sheriff's department and the Bakersfield Police Department, had killed more people per capita than those in any other American county.[2] Year in, year out, the county also posted some of the highest murder rates and lowest solve rates in the United States.[3] Many residents, particularly those who were black or Hispanic, had no trust in the department—a problem that went back decades.

But Brewer, the investigator who eventually picked up Martinez's letter, was a dedicated homicide detective, beloved by some victims' families for the concern he showed in solving their cases and supporting them as he did so. He gave out his personal cell phone number. He came in on his days off to sit with victims.

Brewer, who was then forty-seven, with brown eyes, thinning brown hair, and a slight limp that seems exaggerated because he is so tall, knew Earlimart and its surrounding towns well. His grandparents and his mother had run a cafe there, before such businesses stopped being viable in the town. And his mother and grandmother had grown up in the Sierra Vista Labor Camp, when it was still run by the DiGiorgio grape corporation as housing for white farmworkers. As a child Brewer, like Martinez, had roamed the banks of Deer Creek, fishing and shooting at rabbits. As an adult, he mourned the violence that had overtaken the once peaceful farm towns of his youth—or at least they had seemed peaceful to him.

He'd become a police officer in 1980, working for departments in Shafter and McFarland, then joining the Kern County Sheriff's Department. Being a homicide detective was all he'd ever wanted, an urge that grew stronger the longer he was a cop. "I got tired of arresting the same people sixty times," he said. "And I thought, 'Those homicide guys, when they get them, they don't ever come back out. No cop will ever have to write your name on a report again, because you're done.'"[4]

Brewer read Martinez's letter and decided to drive up and see him. Martinez was in his favorite prison. A trout fisherman, Brewer loved the nearby lakes and streams of the foothills and the gorgeous views visible from the sun-dappled forested roads leading up to them. Plus, in his years as a detective, he had developed an old-school belief in the power of sitting across from people and taking their measure.

Brewer arrived at the prison on February 21, 2008, and met Martinez in an interview room. In keeping with his style, Brewer did not get right down to business. He made small talk. He and Martinez chatted about Earlimart, about life in farmworker communities. Martinez made Brewer laugh with his keen descriptions of life in a labor camp. The ways in which people were hilariously in each other's business. Brewer, like many police officers before and after, was struck by Martinez's calm and polite demeanor. He did not seem like a killer. He seemed like a humble farmworker, who would do a few months in prison on a minor charge and then go back to his family and his life.

"I sent you a letter," Martinez finally said. "Did you find the kid?" Brewer had not.

Martinez told Brewer that the young man was dead. And he told him he knew who did it.

Brewer perked up. This was just the kind of break he had been looking for in the case.

Martinez gave him the name of the person he said was responsible.

Brewer knew the name well. The person Martinez had told him about was a suspected contract killer and a prime suspect not only in the disappearance of the young man but in another murder as well.

Brewer was investigating both cases—and many more besides. Murders were piling up in Kern County, just as they were in Tulare. Detectives could barely keep up with them—actually, they often couldn't keep up. Bodies were found in lonely fields. People were gunned down as they lay in their own beds. And, of course, a scourge of violence plagued the streets. In these years, Brewer said, he was routinely up for twenty-four, sometimes forty-eight, hours at a time, running from crime scene to crime scene. He developed diabetes, a condition his wife blames on the stress and the punishment his body took.

Amid the body count, the man Martinez was telling him about had captured authorities' attention, both in the Kern County Sheriff's Department and in the Delano Police Department. The man was rumored to be a methamphetamine dealer and a vicious killer for hire. His recent exploits included leading police on a high-speed chase through Delano that ended in a car crash; the man had jumped from his smashed vehicle and, although clearly injured, hurled himself over a fence and disappeared, the black steel of a handgun visible in his waistband as he hoisted himself up and away. Behind in his car, police found ammunition for a Russian gun—unusual on the streets of the United States but quite common in Mexico among members of drug cartels.

In other words, no matter how violent it got out there, catching this man was a priority.

Here was Martinez, helpful, humble Martinez, just offering up information on him and, unusual for someone in prison, not asking for any special treatment in return.

Martinez told Brewer that he had known the man since he was a teenager, when both were living in the old Sierra Vista camp— the very same camp where Brewer's family had lived long ago.

He told Brewer that he had seen the man drive away with the victim and described the location where he had last seen him.

Then Martinez said something even more surprising. "I saw him kill a person in front of me in McFarland," Martinez said, adding that the killing took place around February 2007.

What was happening? Brewer had thought Martinez wanted to talk about the death of a young kid. But now he was talking about an entirely different murder and claiming to have witnessed it.

Martinez said he didn't know the dead guy's name. But Brewer did. From Martinez's description, the victim had to be Jose Alvarado, a twenty-five-year-old farmworker who had been found dead in February 2007.

Brewer had been working the Alvarado case for months. The man Martinez was speaking to him about was a prime suspect because several people had said that he was furious with the man for dating his wife, and because no one had seen Alvarado since the man drove up to his house and asked him to get in his car. Alvarado was found two days later, shot full of bullets from two different guns.

Why was Martinez telling him he had seen it happen?

Before Brewer could figure it out, Martinez kept talking. He told Brewer that he had been driving from Earlimart to Delano when his own car broke down. He got out and began walking down the freeway to seek help when the man happened to drive by and motioned for him to get in.

Martinez said the man agreed to give him a ride to his brother-in-law's house in McFarland, but as they were driving there, he suddenly pulled over and motioned to someone to get in his car. It was Alvarado.

Once Alvarado was in the car, Martinez said, the man made a U-turn and began to drive out of town. As he drove, the man accused Alvarado of having an affair with his wife. He took them off the major road and onto land empty of everything but orange groves and irrigation, then got out and shot Alvarado, first with one gun and then with another.

Most of what Martinez told Brewer that day about that man was true. He left out one tiny, crucial detail: the other man hadn't fired the second gun. Martinez had. He claims the motive was some form of twisted self-defense: if he hadn't helped shoot Alvarado, either the man would have shot him, or, had he survived, Alvarado might have come after Martinez.

Brewer didn't have the history with Martinez that Tulare County did. He had never heard of him. But he wasn't a fool. He knew the story of this second murder didn't add up. Homicide detectives learn quickly that people with information to give about heinous crimes are often far from angels themselves. Martinez seemed truly disturbed about the murder of the young man he had written police about, whom he thought was a teenager. Martinez explained to Brewer that he was helping him in part because his own sister had been murdered when she was young, and he hated for bad things to happen to young, vulnerable people.

Brewer appreciated the information about his prime suspect;

he was anxious to stop him before he killed more people. It never occurred to Brewer that, sitting across from him, Martinez had killed far more people than his prime suspect was accused of hurting. Or that Martinez had just managed to learn a lot about whether police suspected him of involvement in Jose Alvarado's murder, while also keeping police attention firmly focused on the other man.

In a way, Martinez's gambit succeeded for everyone. Brewer got information on his murder. The suspect fled Kern County and, according to Kern County authorities, wound up working for a drug cartel in Mexico.

And Martinez? He had taken a big gamble in summoning Brewer. One part of his motivation was genuinely altruistic—he hated to see teenagers caught up in drug violence. But it was also true that sitting in jail, cut off from the world, he worried about what police might know about the other recent Kern County murder, the one he had helped commit. Thanks to his conversation with Brewer, Martinez left prison in July 2008 with the knowledge that he had probably dodged real trouble for the murder of Jose Alvarado.

It was good to be free, Martinez thought. He had enjoyed a delicious meal cooked by his mother and a wonderful time with his kids.

Then he met his parole officer. His first thought was that she was beautiful. His second was that she was a bitch, and she was lucky she was a woman or he would kill her.

No drugs, she said.[5] No alcohol. No guns. No leaving town without telling her. Even worse. His parole officer summoned him again and told him she was sending him to a ninety-day drug treatment program.

He protested—as he always did—that he didn't do drugs. And he hadn't been convicted of doing drugs.

His parole officer didn't believe him, perhaps in part because he was showing signs, including missing teeth, of a serious methamphetamine problem. She sent him off for three months.

In his own narrative, Martinez glosses over his drug use, insisting he never had a problem. Some in his family have said they believed he did at times abuse drugs and lied about it because he didn't want to admit that he had a problem and because, despite the family smuggling business, actually doing drugs was frowned upon.[6]

On the last day of rehab, Martinez claimed, he went to his required daily Narcotics Anonymous meeting and unloaded about the uselessness of drug treatment programs.

"I would love to say a few words," he said. "When people want to change their lives, or stop using drugs, they don't need a program. All you have to do is tie your balls and say I don't want to do drugs today." And he added, "I've been smoking weed since I was fifteen-years-old. I'm not going to stop just because [the head of the program] says so."

He collected his certificate showing that he had completed the program and took it to his parole officer. Unimpressed, he said, she continued to give him drug tests once a month. That meant he could smoke marijuana only one week out of every four before abstaining from the drug to clean it out of his system.

Being on parole crimped his style in other ways too. He couldn't drive to Los Angeles to visit Mr. X or travel elsewhere. It did not, however, prevent him from committing murder.

In March 2009, a consortium of small farmers hired him to recover money from a man who had allegedly promised to sell their fruit on the black market and then stiffed them for about $132,000.

Black-market fruit deals were not unheard of in the San Joaquin Valley. Fruit and particularly nuts were valuable commodities and, unlike many lucrative products, virtually untraceable. The absence of barcodes or manufacturing stamps had facilitated an epidemic of nut theft in a region known for its walnuts, pistachios, and almonds. Farmers themselves sometimes played the black market. They typically sold their first harvest to a big buyer, such as a grocery chain or a food processor. The second or third pick, which was typically smaller, was sometimes offered on the black market to evade taxes. Sometimes the farmer could declare a loss on the product and collect a subsidy, while also taking cash under the table.

Because it was the black market, there was little legal recourse if a deal went bad. What's more, some farmers in the valley, according to law enforcement, were not really farmers at all. Or rather fruits, nuts, and vegetables were not their primary product. They had bought farms in order to launder drug proceeds.

Both arrangements yielded a potential job opportunity for someone like Martinez.

Martinez said he was told to find a man named Juan Bautista Moreno to collect money for wandering fruit profits. To get his hands on Moreno, Martinez used one of his most innovative ruses yet.

Martinez drove a Crown Victoria, the same car used by many police departments. He followed the man in it and flashed a red light at him. Moreno thought he was being pulled over.

When he saw Martinez and realized he was no police officer, Moreno locked his door. Martinez shot out his tires so he couldn't drive, then told him to open up, or he would burn the car. Then he kidnapped the man and took him to a house he had on a ranch.

"The reason you are here is you owe money to a lot of people," Martinez explained. "They are tired of your lies. You keep promising that you are going to pay them. And you never do. That's not good."

He added that he had been to Moreno's house. He knew it was nice. "Listen," he said. "And listen very good. I'm going to get the money the easy way or the hard way."

Moreno made some calls. Martinez left him under the watchful eye of an accomplice to get some food. While he was out, he burned Moreno's truck. No sense leaving evidence around. Then he brought Moreno a meal. And he asked him, "Why did you steal that money from those people in Delano and Earlimart?"

Moreno answered that those stupid people didn't have the balls to do anything to him. He added that Martinez was stupid for listening to them and that he didn't think Martinez had the balls to actually kill him either.

As prosecutors later noted, Moreno had just made a "big mistake."

"I'll show you my balls, you motherfucker," Martinez said. "Fuck the money and fuck you too."

He took Moreno out to the countryside and shot him.

A few hours later, Martinez went back to the body and removed the black zip ties he had used to bind his hands. He had used black zip ties in local murders before—no sense making things too easy for police. Then he drove to lunch at El Tapatia, in his opinion the best restaurant in Porterville, and dined on chile rellenos, washing them down with a cold Pacifico. After lunch, he spent a lovely afternoon at Lake Isabella, and then he went to visit his children.

Later on, he contacted the people who had hired him to collect the fruit money from Moreno and confessed that he hadn't gotten their money. Instead, he said, he had murdered Moreno because the victim had accused him of not having the balls to do so.

There was little his employers could do about it.

Jose Martinez was almost forty-seven years old. This was, by his count, his thirty-fourth victim.

Farmworkers found Moreno's body the next day.

The case was clearly a weird one. Investigators took note that Moreno's hands and wrists showed signs of having been bound, but the ties had been removed. They also noted that he was not the typical drug-hit victim. He was a fifty-two-year-old family man with a fancy house in Bakersfield.

Moreno's body was found as law enforcement officials struggled with yet another pressure: economic freefall.

The Great Recession had slammed into the San Joaquin Valley harder in most parts of the country. People were losing their homes to foreclosure in record numbers—several valley cities frequently topped national lists for the most foreclosures.[7] Unemployment was skyrocketing. A severe drought compounded the problem, hurting agriculture and parching the landscape. Police and sheriff's departments were being decimated by budget cuts. If they had struggled in good times to keep up, now the number of unsolved crimes seemed overwhelming.

By chance, the detective assigned to lead the Moreno case was Kavin Brewer, the Kern County homicide detective who had earlier interviewed Martinez in prison. Brewer and his partner had, for several years running, posted the department's highest solve rates, closing upward of 70 percent of their cases some years. That would have been a great rate in any department, but it was phenomenal in an area beset by so much violence and a history of unsolved crimes, untrusting communities, and uncaring public officials.

By the time Brewer got called out to the scene of Moreno's murder, he had been up for forty-eight hours straight. He was so tired he actually fell asleep standing up at the watch commander's desk in the station. Moreno's murder was the third he had picked up in two days.

Despite his fatigue, he took a deep breath, poured himself a cup of coffee, and got to work.

A few days after he killed Moreno, Martinez took off for Las Vegas—Martinez loved the Mirage—bringing with him a girlfriend, an accomplice, and the accomplice's girlfriend. They stayed for three days. But before long, Martinez's mother called on his cell phone: "Your parole officer is at my house, and she wants to talk to you."

"Put that bitch on the phone," Martinez spouted.

The parole agent came on the line. "Martinez, you have thirty minutes to get to your house," she said.[8]

No can do, he answered. "I'll be back in two days. I'm in Las Vegas, and I'm having a lot of fun, winning money and fucking my girlfriend."

"You've just violated your parole," she told him.

"Fuck you," he answered. "You and the parole board, you're like my fucking babysitter."

Then he asked her how much money it would take for her to leave him alone. She ignored the question.

"When you get back, come to my office," she said.

He said he'd see her next year.

Despite his bravado, he realized his vacation was over. He was a parolee at large now. And he did not want to go back to jail.

Some criminals might have hit the road at this point. Martinez, after all, potentially had access to numerous family properties in Mexico, apartments in Chicago, houses in Yuma, friends who could offer shelter in Los Angeles and Atlanta— and more.

But he came home. He got a camping trailer and parked it first in Delano and then on some land next to a small stream in Tulare County owned by some of his family. He would bring his children out to swim in the river, and he would also bring women there— albeit separately.

He stayed on the lam for months. But one night, while he was sleeping at his mother's house, she woke her son up and told him his parole officer was in the living room, asking for him.

"Mr. Martinez, I'm taking you in," the parole officer said.

"The only way I'm going in is dead. You're not taking me alive," he said.

His parole officer ran to her car to call for backup.

Martinez took the opportunity to go out the bedroom window and over the fence into the next-door neighbor's yard. Luckily for him, his mother's next-door neighbor was also one of his sisters. She gave him a ride back to his trailer. As they were driving, they passed police cars speeding toward his mother's house in the opposite direction.

The law didn't get him that day. And, as often happened, law enforcement's interest in him appeared to fade away.

Chapter Twenty-Three

In September 2009, Martinez got a call from a friend in Delano.

"Mano Negra, we have a little problem in Earlimart," the friend said. "There's a snitch in that town. And we want him dead." Martinez claims his prospective employer also told him the snitch, Joaquin Barragan, was also a child molester. (Police said they had no such record.)

Because the crime was local, Martinez agreed to do it for $8,000. However, he added, because Earlimart was his hometown, he would have to tread carefully.[1]

On visits through the community to see his children, he began keeping an eye out for Barragan. But Barragan was apparently hiding from Martinez. Martinez would have to get creative. He heard that a young woman, who he suspected was a drug addict and a prostitute, hung out with his target.

He found her walking on the street, told her to get into his car, and asked where she was going. She replied that she was going to a friend's house to smoke some dope.

He told her he needed her to take Barragan out on a date for him, because he needed to talk to him. She refused, saying that Joaquin was her friend, and she knew enough about El Mano Negra to know Joaquin might want to stay away.

Martinez tried to argue with her. Barragan had done bad things to a woman in Mexico, he explained. But she was unmoved.

Finally, Martinez lost his patience. "Get the fuck out of my car," he snarled. "And if you tell anybody that I talked to you about Joaquin, you'll be in big trouble."

He watched her walk away. He needed a new plan.

It didn't take him long to come up with one. He brought another lady friend to the Swap Meet in Earlimart, a place he knew Barragan liked to frequent. Indeed, Barragan was there. Martinez pointed him out.

"That man has done a lot of bad things in Mexico," Martinez told her. "I'm going to give you one thousand dollars so you can help me catch him."

He laid out his plan. She was to buy $20 worth of dope from him. Then she would invite Barragan to come with her to smoke it. "Only a blind man won't get in a car with you," he added gallantly.

"Once he gets in your car," he said, "call me, and say, 'Wrong number,' when I answer."

On the afternoon of September 27, 2009, when the call came in, Martinez recalled that he was indisposed—holed up with a woman in a motel in McFarland. But still he raced to the point on Deer Creek where the rendezvous would take place. "I came running with my gun in my hands."

Three evenings later, two brothers training horses along Deer Creek came across a pair of boots sticking out from under a blanket. They whistled and yelled, and when they got no response, they began to fear the boots were on the feet of a dead man. They ran to seek help.

When police showed up, they discovered Barragan's body. And they noticed that his wrists were bound with zip ties. Few things said professional hit like zip ties. Police began the usual routine, trying to retrace Barragan's last movements and identify his friends, hoping to figure out why someone might have wanted him dead.[2]

On the morning of October 5, they got a visit from Barragan's brother, who wanted to pass on information gleaned from one of Barragan's friends. The friend thought he knew exactly who had killed Barragan: a menacing figure with the moniker "El Mano Negra."

And that wasn't all. The friend had talked to a woman, another of Barragan's friends, who claimed El Mano Negra had offered her money to lure Barragan to him.

Detectives went straight to the friend and begged for his help. They appealed to him to please tell them what he knew, to think of his dead friend and the man's grieving family. The friend appeared terrified and denied knowing anything.

Detective Cesar Fernandez, a longtime Tulare County investigator who was well respected by his homicide colleagues, tried again, with a more specific question.[3] "I heard that someone had a bounty on your friend."

Well, yes, the friend admitted. He had heard that.

Had anyone offered him a bounty?

Oh no, the friend said, and he never would have taken it if they had, because Barragan was his friend.

But now, the friend started talking. He told Fernandez that Barragan had told him personally, before he died, that someone known as "Mano Negra" was trying to kill him.

Why, Fernandez asked.

No idea, the friend answered. But he could tell detectives this: El Mano Negra lived in the town of Richgrove but was often spotted in Earlimart. And he drove a white Suburban.

Detective Fernandez began to ask his colleagues if they had ever heard of a guy who went by the moniker "Mano Negra." It didn't take long to get a real name, a name well-known by that point to some in the department: Jose Manuel Martinez.

They tracked down his parole officer. Why yes, she knew him too. He was a parolee at large, she told them. And should be considered armed. She confirmed that he drove a white Suburban but added that he also had a yellow Jetta and a gray PT Cruiser.

It had taken years of suspicions and missed opportunities. But finally the detectives were getting somewhere. The pieces were slotting into place. By 5 p.m. that same day, they were back at the friend's house with a "six-pack" photo lineup. Martinez's face was in the number two position. The friend immediately picked him out.

Two days later, detectives caught another break. The female friend whom Martinez had offered money to lure Barragan to an isolated place had been arrested by police for her own legal issue: suspicion of being under the influence of a controlled substance.

Detectives went to question her. At first, she would tell them only that "someone" had offered her money to lure Barragan, but she wouldn't say who. She said she was too scared of the person. A detective told her she owed it to Barragan, to herself, and to the other members of the Earlimart community to tell them who it was "so we could arrest him and get him off the streets" before he hurt anyone else.

This persuaded her. "I know him only as Mano Negra," she told him. "But I do know he drives a white Suburban."

She also offered police a motive: it was obvious to anyone who was paying attention, she said, that Barragan was giving the police information about drug dealers and their crimes. "Everyone" had noticed that Barragan was frequently picked up by the police, but within a day or two, he'd be back in town. People put two and two together and assumed he was a police informant.

Less than two hours later, a detective was cruising the streets of Earlimart when he saw a white Suburban parked on Front

Street. He ran the plate, and it came back registered to a man in Fresno.

The detective was not deterred. He called headquarters and asked for backup to conduct a business-to-business search down Earlimart's Front Street for one Jose Martinez. But just a few minutes later, before the search could commence, a man walked down Front Street, got into the Suburban, and drove away. Was it Martinez? The detective followed the car; meanwhile, from around the county, deputies streamed toward Earlimart to help.

Martinez was driving home from visiting his kids in Earlimart when he saw two sheriff's cars headed his way. He stayed calm but surreptitiously took the memory chip out of one of his cell phones, steeled himself against the terrible sensation, and swallowed it. Then he pulled over and waited to see what the sheriff's deputies would do.[4]

They would wait for backup, that's what.

From a loudspeaker mounted on his car, an officer ordered Martinez to keep his hands hanging out the window, where police could see them. Ten minutes later, about fifteen sheriff's cars arrived and officers announced they were taking him into custody. Because he had violated his parole, they had the legal right to take him back to jail.

"They had their guns out, pointed at me, as if I was a criminal," Martinez said indignantly.

Detective Fernandez let Martinez sit in the county jail in Visalia for nearly a week as officers worked to gather more evidence.

Finally, after lunch on Tuesday, October 13, detectives went over to the jail and picked up their prime suspect in the murder of Joaquin Barragan. Detective Fernandez started off by reading Martinez his Miranda rights, telling him he had the right to remain silent and that anything he said could be used against him. This was a signal that the police were serious.

Martinez magnanimously declined to have a lawyer present, saying he'd be happy to talk because he had "nothing to hide."

Did he know Joaquin Barragan?

Martinez said he did. He added that he had heard Barragan was "a rat and a dope dealer."

How did he know that?

"Earlimart is a small town," Martinez answered. "Everyone likes to talk."

Fernandez asked if he knew Barragan well and if he knew of anyone who might have wanted to hurt him.

"Many people would have wanted to hurt Joaquin," Martinez answered, cool as could be. "He burned people for money and for dope."

Did Martinez know anyone personally who might have wanted to hurt Joaquin?

Martinez said he really couldn't answer that question. Why not? Because he feared for his own well-being.

Fernandez got to the heart of the matter: Would Martinez be interested to know that lots of folks in Earlimart said it was Martinez himself who had wanted Barragan dead? In fact, Fernandez said, he had heard from one person that Martinez had actually offered a $1,000 bounty to deliver Barragan.

If Fernandez thought that would rattle Martinez into a confession, he was wrong. Calmly, Martinez told Fernandez that he had been misinformed.

"Well, if you didn't kill Joaquin, then who did?"

Martinez said he heard it was someone named Pedro, who had ties to a Mexican drug cartel.

Fernandez countered that the only person who had offered this story was Martinez. Everyone else in Earlimart said it was him. Could he explain that?

Martinez said he really couldn't, except, obviously, "everyone in Earlimart is lying."

That was the end of the interrogation. Detectives had Martinez transported back to the Tulare County jail. But he wasn't going home. He was going back to prison for violating his parole.

And while he served out his term, detectives would keep trying to gather evidence against him. At long last, they finally had a chance to bring him to account for his crimes, or so it seemed.

On October 28, while Martinez was in jail, a detective asked technicians to extract the data from the two cell phones found in Martinez's car. Cell phones can often provide valuable evidence for police, including, of course, text messages and contacts, as well as information about a suspect's location history.

Martinez's phones, however—not so much. One of the phones was missing a SIM card. The other had only two phone numbers saved in its address book, neither of which proved interesting enough for police to draw conclusions about whom they belonged to.

Where was the other SIM card? Detectives went back to Martinez's Suburban to see if maybe they could find it. They didn't.

But a second search—more than two weeks after Martinez had been arrested and his car impounded—revealed that their first hadn't been as thorough as they thought. While poking around for the SIM card, an officer put his hand on the cup holder in the center console and inadvertently revealed a hidden compartment containing a Smith and Wesson 9mm semiautomatic pistol.

The gun was registered to a rancher in the farm town of Hanford, who had been unaware that it was gone but told police his house had been burgled a few months earlier.

They searched the car more carefully, but still, no SIM card.

Officers later tried putting a police department SIM card into the cell phone, but—as almost anyone with a modicum of technological skill could have told them—it didn't get them anywhere.

In February 2010, Martinez was released from jail, having served out his original sentence. On March 29, he voluntarily headed straight back to the Tulare County Sheriff's Department.

He wanted his Suburban back.

He agreed to speak with Detective Fernandez again about the murder. According to Fernandez's notes, this time Martinez was a little more forthcoming both about his own background and about the murder of Barragan.

He told police that he worked for "a group of Mexicans from Guadalajara" and was "the collector" for the group. He refused to come out and say what business his group was in but "in a round-about way stated he worked for a drug cartel."

He also said Barragan was murdered not because he owed money but because he was "a rat." Still, he denied any personal involvement in the homicide.

When Fernandez asked if Martinez would be willing to take a lie-detector test, he readily agreed. Lie-detector tests are generally not admissible in court in California, but police often use them while conducting investigations as a technique to gauge suspects' credibility and pressure them to tell the truth. Martinez was asked several questions about the murder, including whether he knew who did it. The examiner found that "deception was indicated" when Martinez said he did not know who murdered Barragan.

The examiner asked to do a second test, which would focus more on whether Martinez had carried out the killing.

"Did you murder Joaquin?"

Martinez said no.

The result: "Deception was indicated."

A second investigator did his own analysis of the results. He came to the same conclusion: Martinez was lying when he said he hadn't killed Barragan.

Following the test, Fernandez tried again.

He showed Martinez a photo of a Smith and Wesson 9mm handgun.

Martinez smiled and said the gun looked familiar.

Fernandez told him that made sense, because the gun had been found in the hidden compartment in his car.

Martinez then denied that the gun looked familiar and said he had just bought the car "from some guy" and hadn't known about the weapon.

Martinez was allowed to leave the station.

Police kept trying. They went back to the woman who said she had been offered $1,000 to lure Barragan to an isolated place but had not done it. They put pressure on her to admit that she was lying, that she was responsible for the murder. "You're the only one Barragan trusted," they told her. "We heard *you* took the bounty. Did you take him to be killed?"

She would not break. She was telling the truth. And she readily agreed to a lie-detector test, which indicated she was not being deceptive.

Police also talked to another young woman who had been rumored to have lured Barragan to an isolated place. She too denied it.

Alas, the cops still did not have enough proof. Martinez was not charged with the murder.

"They let him go," said Barragan's brother, who gave police credit for working the case hard but noted that after Martinez was released, he continued to kill.

Tulare County sheriff's officials maintain they did the best they could.

Fernandez worked the case particularly hard—and refused to give up. In April 2010, he began looking for other potential victims.

He called his old friend, Kavin Brewer from the Kern County Sheriff's Department, with a question: Had he heard of any zip tie murders?

As a matter of fact, Brewer said, he had an open case from March 2009. Juan Moreno, found in an orange grove near the county line. No zip ties found on him but marks suggesting they had been cut off. Weird case. The victim was a family man, with a nice house in Bakersfield and a legitimate business. Case had gone completely cold. The police still had no clues and no ideas.

Detective Fernandez found that very interesting. He said the MO was the same in his department's case and described the murder of Barragan. But, Fernandez added, they had a suspect. A guy named Jose Manuel Martinez. Went by the moniker El Mano Negra. Or the Black Hand.

Brewer started in surprise. That humble farmworker he had visited in prison? The one who'd had information on the 2007 homicide? The one who was so funny on the topic of life in Earlimart?

Brewer thought back to what Martinez had told him about his association with the suspected hit man from Kern County. His mind raced. He and Fernandez kept talking. It seemed possible they had, in Martinez, another contract killer on their hands.

But what could they do? No district attorney would bring charges based on such slim evidence and risk an acquittal. The "double jeopardy" clause of the US Constitution meant that, once acquitted, Martinez could never be prosecuted for the crime again— even if police eventually came up with stronger evidence.

"He was known. He was interviewed many times," said former Tulare County assistant sheriff Scott Logue, who is now retired. Still, barring a confession, there was little they could do. "He's a sociopath. He's a good liar. There's no corroborating witnesses. There's no physical evidence....He got away with it."

Chapter Twenty-Four

As the first decade of the twenty-first century came to a close, the San Joaquin Valley was struggling in ways that it perhaps had not since the Great Depression and the dust bowl had made the region a symbol of deprivation and broken dreams.

Even as the Great Recession lessened its grip elsewhere, it showed no signs of letting up in the valley. The Brookings Institute found that the valley had been hit harder than almost any region of the country and that many of its cities—including Fresno, Stockton, Modesto, and Bakersfield—were more economically depressed, according to many indicators, than almost anywhere else.[1]

People were losing their homes, their jobs, and, in higher-than-average numbers, their sons and daughters to war, as young people flocked into the military seeking a steady paycheck and then died on the battlefields of Iraq and Afghanistan. In July 2010 one town near Fresno posted a grim measure of the toll: the community turned out in force to mark the seventh death of an alumnus at one high school.[2]

And another menace was looming: drought. It felt as though

the rains had simply stopped. Year after year, the skies stayed dry, and the land was parched.

Martinez, meanwhile, kept winding up behind bars—but never for very long or for very serious crimes. If they couldn't get Martinez on murder charges, the Tulare County Sheriff's Department now seemed hell-bent on finding other ways to get him off the street.

Martinez was out of jail only for a few months when he was arrested again. After being packed back to prison, following the failure to get him on the Barragan murder, he had cleared his debt to society on the parole violation. But law enforcement still had a hold on him for various other convictions. In the summer of 2010, police picked him up again and sent him back to county jail for 180 days.

Within three weeks of his release in January 2011, he had committed another murder.

Gonzalo Urquieta, a longtime Earlimart resident, was supposedly "a snitch and a child molester," according to Martinez, although officials could find no evidence for the second allegation. When police notified Gonzalo Urquieta's mother of his death, she fainted and had to be rushed away in an ambulance. The rest of the family watched in horror. But no one was much help when asked who might have killed him.[3]

His family didn't know who his friends were or even whether he had any friends, except for a girlfriend. They also said he was a drug user, spent his time with thieves, and had "a criminal past." Some family members also said he was dealing drugs out of the family's garage, leading to a stream of people at the home and upsetting his mother.

When police found the girlfriend, they learned she had a number of boyfriends, most of whom supplied her with drugs or money. She told them Gonzalo did not have any enemies and speculated that he could have been killed because of his habit of stealing prizewinning fighting roosters. Maybe he had pissed off someone in the world of cockfighting? This wasn't as crazy as it sounded. Cockfighting had long been a big, if illicit, enterprise in the valley.

The girlfriend also told police that "due to her continuous drug use of Ice [crystal methamphetamine]," she did not sleep; nor was she able to stay in one place for long. "Also, due to her chronic narcotic use, she was unable to recall specific events."[4]

But while her memory was flawed, detectives immediately remembered one thing: her name had also come up in the Barragan investigation. Police also heard that Martinez was seen at Urquieta's house the day before he disappeared.

Armed with that information, police picked up Martinez on February 11, 2011.

On February 18, Detective Bari Molyneux fetched Martinez from lockup and brought him to an interview room.[5] Molyneux asked Martinez how he got the nickname "Mano Negra." He said it derived from a wholesome experience: he took his children camping (as all good parents do, he later told detectives), and while making a fire, one of his hands was blackened.

Detective Molyneux didn't buy it. He noted that his Spanish-speaking colleagues had told him that the phrase actually refers to the hand of death or the hand of evil.

The conversation turned to Martinez's family and friends. They talked for a while about how much Martinez loved his children, and Martinez told detectives that Gonzalo was his friend. They'd known each other for several years and had even been in jail together at one point. Martinez said he last saw Gonzalo on February 5, when he went to his house to pick up a part for his car. At that time, he said, he encountered a woman he knew and gave her and her husband a ride.

He denied any involvement in the murder. Then, with characteristic pluck, Martinez suggested that Detective Molyneux should hire him as an informant, because he knew a lot of people and could find things out.

Molyneux replied that Martinez hadn't told him anything about the murder, and it didn't seem like a good idea to hire him.

The next day, police showed up at Martinez's home. They called on him in jail for permission to search. He gave it to them. They found nothing incriminating, as Martinez knew they would not.

As Tulare County sheriff's deputies hit the streets of Earlimart and Delano searching for evidence, they saw firsthand the devastating impact of the recession and years of gang violence. At one home in Earlimart, Detective Molyneux was forced to clarify that he was asking about the death of Urquieta on February 6, not the double homicide that had taken place at the home a few days before that.

Finally, after days of door-knocking, he found the couple that Martinez had given a ride to. Initially, he was met with lies. The man first claimed to be the brother of the person Detective Molyneux was looking for. Molyneux left. When he came back a day later, the man admitted he had lied and apologized.

Molyneux arrested him and his wife, who had an outstanding warrant on drug charges. Back at the station, they told more lies. The pair said they had been at Urquieta's house on the night in question but had gotten a ride back to Delano with fieldworkers. The husband said they drove a white truck. The wife admitted it was a blue Honda.

Finally, they both broke down and admitted they'd been lying about everything. They were scared, they said, of a person they knew as El Mano Negra.

They said they had been at Urquieta's house when someone came to talk to him about stealing two hundred pounds of marijuana. They weren't sure of the person's name but said he drove a purple van. Eventually, they went to sleep at Gonzalo's. But in the middle of the night, they heard knocking on the garage door. It was El Mano Negra.

Gonzalo left with him, the two men claiming they were going out to steal cockfighting roosters.

As in the Barragan case, detectives had a great deal of circumstantial evidence against Martinez. But it was not the kind that would necessarily hold up in a courtroom under cross examination. Once again, authorities decided it was not enough to charge Martinez. He was released from jail on March 19.

"Fuck Tulare County Cops," Martinez wrote. "They are the most stupid punk cops I've ever seen. A bunch of idiots. Out of 10 crimes that happened in that county, they only solved one, and that's because people told them it was me."

Still, he was sick of being hauled off to jail. And now that he no longer had to check in with his parole officer, he decided it was time to get out of town. He went to his mother's ranch in Sinaloa.

Police continued to work the Urquieta case. Unable to get any evidence against Martinez, they turned their attention to a man who had also been seen at Urquieta's house in the days before his death.

On May 19 they served a search warrant at the man's house and found evidence of drug dealing: a .45-caliber handgun and a dealer's pay/owe sheet. At the wholesale level, many dealers hand over the drugs first and then get paid back with the profits from their sales. Pay/owe sheets are just what they sound like: a way for drug dealers to keep track of what they are owed.

When police talked to the man, they inadvertently created a terrible misunderstanding. He thought they were there to investigate a different homicide. It seemed Delano police officers had shot and killed his brother a few years back, and he was desperate to discover the circumstances of his brother's death.

"I advised that I was not there to investigate his brother's death," a detective wrote, but rather an entirely different murder. But on this, the man could not help them. The case remained unsolved.

A few months later, police heard from an Earlimart guy who was facing a "third-strike" conviction that could, under California's punitive law at the time, put him behind bars for the rest of his life. He said he was willing to do anything, "even testify," to get out of it. He had information on two murders, he said: the killings of Joaquin Barragan and, two years later, of Gonzalo Urquieta.

Both men, he told police, had been killed by the same person: El Mano Negra.

Detectives believed him. But, they said, their hands were tied.

Then Martinez, home from Sinaloa, got arrested again, this time by the McFarland Police Department.

Officers had pulled him over in his BMW on May 27 as he drove through the small, blighted city. Martinez had lived in McFarland in the 1980s, around the time it was grappling with an unexplained cluster of cancers in young children, but this time he was just passing through.

Police claimed Martinez had drugs in his car. Martinez swore that he didn't and claimed the cops had planted them. Martinez managed to win that one. In October 2012, the Kern County district attorney dropped the charges against Martinez, saying it was "in the interests of justice" to do so.[6]

One of the officers involved in pulling him over had developed legal troubles of his own. In July 2012, several weeks after Martinez's arrest, the officer, along with several others, was involved in what local newspapers called "a wild chase" through McFarland and the nearby town of Delano, in which they had pursued a suspect at speeds upward of seventy miles per hour. At one point, the chase blasted through a construction site, forcing workers to dive for safety. When the chase finally ended, the officer fired at the suspect.[7] Following an outcry, the officer was placed on paid administrative leave. He eventually left the police department and, in an unrelated case, pled no contest to identity theft as part of what appeared to be a bizarre scheme to avoid paying his utility bill.[8]

It was only the latest bit of insanity for the troubled McFarland Police Department, which the previous year had suffered revelations that four of its officers had left their previous police departments under clouds of suspicion but were hired in McFarland anyway. In fact, an investigation by the University of California, Berkeley's Graduate School of Journalism later found that one in five officers working for the department from 2009 to 2019 had previously been fired by another police department, sued for misconduct, or convicted of a crime. That tally included two of its most recent police chiefs.[9]

Once again, Martinez had gotten lucky.

The corruption had even ensnared McFarland's hometown hero, Damacio Diaz, a high school cross-country star whose life story was so inspiring that Disney had made a movie about it, *McFarland USA*, which premiered in February 2015. It told the story of the McFarland High School running team, farmworker kids who put in hours in the fields and then ran through the dusk, winning state championship after championship and besting rich kids from fancy towns. Weeks after the premiere, the real-life Diaz, who had grown up to become a narcotics detective in nearby Bakersfield, was put on leave and eventually charged with accepting bribes from drug dealers and selling meth that police had confiscated. He pled guilty and, in the course of his adjudication, told the court he was far from the only corrupt officer.[10] He detailed a series of practices he said were widespread—including leaking information about investigations to drug dealers who were also police informants, drinking on duty, and seizing narcotics from smugglers during traffic stops and then stealing the evidence.

Following Diaz's conviction, other Bakersfield officers and Kern County sheriff's deputies were also charged.[11]

Perhaps Martinez would have gotten away with his murders anyway, but that he committed so many of his crimes in communities plagued by mismanagement and corruption certainly worked in his favor.

While the chaos in law enforcement agencies close to home helped Martinez evade capture, problems were brewing for him on the other side of the country—although it would be months before he learned of it.

At 5 p.m. on October 9, 2012, Detective Tony Watts of the Marion County Sheriff's Office in Ocala, Florida, who was earning overtime by reexamining cold cases, grabbed a thick case file labeled "Huerta," sat down, and began to read. The case involved two construction workers from Deland, Florida, who had been executed, their bodies found, hands bound with zip ties, at the swampy edge of the Ocala National Forest in the fall of 2006.[12]

Watts, a former college football player, believed he had a "God-given" ability to solve cases. Supremely confident of his intelligence and investigative skills and so loquacious he could probably make conversation with a rock, he did everything at lightning speed. A friend laughed at the fact that he would cut conversations in the middle, wandering away to jump on a phone call or simply because his brain, always two steps ahead, had moved on to something else.[13]

But that night in 2012, Watts went through page after page of the report, methodically if not exactly slowly. As Watts read, he deduced that the original detectives on the case had figured out fairly quickly that they were dealing with a drug hit. Through a network of informants and from the victims' families, they heard about the stolen cocaine and the money dug up from the backyard.

But the original detectives got nowhere when it came to figuring out who had ordered the hit or who had carried it out. They were further stymied, Watts said, when their attempt to investigate the murder collided with a long-running narcotics investigation, and they were asked to tread carefully so as not to jeopardize it.

Then Watts came across something startling. Some of the evidence, including a cigarette butt found in a Mountain Dew can, had not been fully analyzed. Watts filled out paperwork asking the Florida Department of Law Enforcement to rerun the evidence.

Chapter Twenty-Five

The engines roared as the plane tore down the runway at Los Angeles International Airport, lifted off over the Pacific Ocean, and made a big swooping turn toward the east.

Martinez sat back. He was done with Earlimart. Done with the Tulare County Sheriff's Department, and the Kern County Sheriff's Department too. And the McFarland Police Department. Done with all of them.

Those idiots. They were too stupid to get him on a murder charge. But they seemed determined to keep El Mano Negra in jail. Fine. He would leave. He was going to visit his oldest daughter in Alabama.

His oldest daughter waited for her father to arrive, her heart full of hope. Her father was actually coming. And for an extended visit, he had said.

This latest reunion had come about almost by chance. She had called her grandmother to say hello, and her father happened to be there and jumped on the phone, full of cheer and love.

As she often did, she invited him to come out for a visit. Usually her father put off such entreaties. But this time, he'd readily agreed, and then he'd bought a plane ticket.

Her father had always been a distant and yearned-for figure for her. Her parents had split when she was five or six, and her father had been in and out of her life. He would come into Yuma, all funny and playful and full of excursions and gifts. And then he would be gone again, leaving her mother to handle the day-to-day raising of her and her brothers, putting food on the table, keeping children in school. It hadn't been easy for her mother; she'd toiled in the fields for years. Martinez's oldest daughter had known that her dad had a new lady and more kids back in Earlimart, whom he saw all the time. She used to imagine what life would be like if he lived near her.

As a child, she had known he didn't work much, at least at any kind of traditional job, except as a mechanic. He was a genius with cars. As a young adult, she sometimes heard dark talk about him on visits to California, but it was never specific, and she brushed it aside.[1]

She knew he had been to prison for a stint. She'd heard he occasionally smuggled drugs and people across the border. But anything worse than that was impossible to believe. He was so loving and so sweet, not just with her but with the rest of the family. She saw how much he took care of her grandmother, always giving her money. And she saw how generous he was with everyone around him. She remembered one time seeing him with a backpack full of cash. Within an hour, the backpack was empty. He had given all the money away.

Mostly, she didn't want to know too much about any of it.

In her own life, she had determined to walk a very different path. She had always followed the rules, even when it seemed like those rules were set up to keep people like her extended family of farmworkers down. After high school, she got as far away from home as possible. She enlisted in the army and was delighted when she was stationed in Germany. It was so different from Yuma or the San Joaquin. The tall trees. The pretzels and the beer. The snow that blanketed everything in winter.

When she took the Armed Services Vocational Aptitude Battery, a test the US Army uses to help guide recruits into jobs within the army, they told her the results indicated she was well suited to certain kinds of office work, which didn't excite her, and also to be a "light vehicle mechanic."

This seemed like a sign. "I'm going to make my dad proud," she thought.

She had fallen in love with a fellow service member. When she got out of the army, they came to Alabama and started building a family.

But she and her husband had split up, and now she had four children to support (although their father contributed as well). As if that weren't enough, she was trying to launch her own roofing business.

Her dad was coming at the perfect time. Her father was a whirl of energy, labor, and fun. He spent hours and hours and hours with her children. He took them to school and soccer practice. He made them healthy snacks. He allowed himself to be dressed up as a Disney princess by the little girls and submitted to a game of "spa day" with the older ones, letting the girls put cucumber slices on his eyelids and then gobbling up the avocado facial while the girls howled with laughter.

He attached a cart to the lawnmower and turned mowing the lawn into a fun train ride. He took the girls walking by a creek and then jumped in, explaining that it was a "Mexican water park." He taught them to make grilled cheese sandwiches and how to fold pizza in half the better to eat it. He made them laugh and laugh and laugh. One afternoon, she even found him mowing the neighbor's yard, so anxious was he to be helpful to her.

She began to entertain dreams of a future in which her dad

gave up his criminal activities—not that she wanted to know too much about those—and lived with her for at least part of every year. He would be a steady, loving presence in her children's lives in the way he had not always been in her own.

His oldest daughter believed in hope and redemption. And for the first weeks of that visit, those hopes and prayers were realized.

Her father was desperate to help with her business too. She would find him trying to sneak onto roofs to help attach roof tiles.

"Get down," she would say. "You're not on the insurance."

"*Mija*, I want to help," he would say. "I want to learn."

"No," she would say. "You're doing so much with the girls already."

And it was true. They adored him, and they blossomed under his care. They played soccer with him. They played practical jokes on him. They sat around the kitchen table doing homework. But still he wanted to contribute more, a desire that only grew when his oldest granddaughter, who was then eleven and suffered from an autoimmune condition, had to go to the hospital for an infusion.

Martinez sat by her bedside all night, seemingly never once shutting his eyes.

"I want to get extra money to help you," Martinez said.

His daughter explained that they didn't need money. The girls' father had excellent insurance. All the medical care was paid for. But her father couldn't seem to believe it.

Around this time—early February 2013—he came to her with an idea: a friend of her boyfriend's needed help collecting a debt. And, her father said, he was good at debt collection. He could help.

His daughter was against it. "You didn't come out here to do that," she said. "Let it go."

Her father told her boyfriend, "That's why you don't tell women everything." This pissed her off. But she had too much on her plate to think hard about it.

On February 27, 2013, Detective Tony Watts finally—six years late—got the crime lab report on the forgotten cigarette butt.

It revealed that Evidence Item 28, a cigarette butt from a Mountain Dew can, had hit a match against a man once held in prison in California: Jose Manuel Martinez, of Richgrove, in Tulare County, California.

Watts did not assume the information meant anything. Huerta had been a masonry contractor, after all, and had driven untold numbers of people in his car. There was no immediate reason to suspect that a nonviolent offender from California was the murderer just because he'd been smoking in the same vehicle.

He made a note to call out to California to find out a little more about this Jose Martinez. But it wasn't a top priority. It was a cold case, after all. There was no reason to think that faster action might save someone's life.

Although his daughter told him not to, Jose Martinez decided he would help her boyfriend's friend, a man by the name of Jose Ruiz, collect on his debt. One of his motivations was that he had begun to have concerns about her boyfriend.

If he helped Ruiz collect on the debt, he could also do a little investigating, to make sure his daughter's boyfriend was good enough for her.

"I didn't like him since the first minute I saw him," he later said. "But he was my daughter's 'friend.' I can't kill my daughter's friends."

When Martinez got into the car with Jose Ruiz, he asked him about his daughter's boyfriend. Ruiz's answer made clear that he had no idea who Martinez was—or, more crucially, who his daughter was. Ruiz said something to the effect that the boyfriend was OK but that his girlfriend was a real bitch.

Saying this was a mistake, to say the least.

Martinez stewed on the comment, growing more and more enraged. On March 4—five days after Tony Watts had received the lab report on Evidence Item 28 and begun wondering about this criminal defendant from California—Martinez arranged to go on an outing with Ruiz and his daughter's boyfriend.

They drove into the country through ever smaller towns that petered out into fields of hay. Ruiz and his daughter's boyfriend were talking about something, but Martinez could barely follow the conversation. He wasn't paying attention. He was consumed with fury. How could that man have insulted his daughter?

When they reached the edge of the Bankhead National Forest, a dense stand of old-growth trees cloaking mossy green canyons and sparkling waterfalls, Ruiz said he needed to stretch his legs. When Ruiz got out, Martinez followed him, clutching his gun.

That woman you said bad things about "is my daughter, you stupid son of a bitch," Martinez spat. He shot Ruiz twice in the head. He watched him crumple to the ground. He thought about shooting his daughter's boyfriend too (he'd decided he was bad news) but stopped himself. Instead he got back in the car and glared at him. "Drive," Martinez commanded. "And keep your mouth shut."[2]

Chapter Twenty-Six

Martinez figured it could be a while before anyone found Ruiz's body. But he still needed an alibi for the day the man disappeared.

When he got back to his daughter's home, he bustled into the house and told everyone to get ready to go out for a special treat. "I'm going to take you to the movies," he announced with a big smile. Movies were fun—not to mention the perfect alibi.

Then he looked down at his clothes and realized he needed to change. There was a spot of blood on his pants.

After they came out of the theater, he thought he saw his daughter looking at him oddly.

Martinez had taken care to shoot Ruiz in a remote spot. In California, it had often taken days or weeks for someone to find his victims' bodies. But this time, Martinez was unlucky. As it turned out, some off-duty police officers were hunting nearby. They heard the shots and responded almost immediately.[1]

Shortly thereafter, the chief investigator for the Lawrence

County Sheriff's Office, Tim McWhorter, was standing in the dirt at the edge of a hayfield, staring down at Ruiz's body.

Tall, with a boyish face, soft brown eyes, and fluffy brown hair, McWhorter favored polo-collared shirts, dad jeans, and sneakers. He looked a little bit like a human golden retriever. And his job as chief investigator often left him feeling a little bit like one too. He spent all day running from thing to thing, like a dog after a ball. He was in charge of investigations, but he was also responsible for personnel, and evidence, and ordering office supplies. One day he might find himself investigating a rape or a murder, and the next, a stolen lawnmower. He spoke with a thick drawl, peppered with local sayings. His slightly distracted air and stream of idiomatic expressions belied a shrewd intelligence about people and a creative approach to getting things done.

As he looked at Ruiz's body, he exclaimed in surprise, "I know that guy."

One of his colleagues shook his head. McWhorter had to be mistaken, his colleague demurred, because all Mexicans looked the same.

But McWhorter was right. He did know Ruiz. He had hired him to put a new roof on his home. McWhorter knew a lot of folks in the area. He had spent his whole life there, first in Moulton, the county seat, then in nearby Hartselle, and then, after high school, again in Moulton, where he followed his father into the sheriff's department. He started at age nineteen, as a jailer, then worked as a school resource officer and patrol officer, and finally as an investigator. Along the way, he had four boys.

He didn't make much money—even after nearly two decades on the force, his salary was only around $50,000 a year. To generate extra income, he had a side business building cabinets. Sometimes his day job, with its constant exposure to the worst of human behavior, made him so cynical that he would sit in church, look at his fellow parishioners, and wonder what evil things they had done. Still, whenever other departments tried to lure him away to better-paying jobs in bigger places, he turned them down. He was proud of his department: during his eight years as chief investigator of the Lawrence County Sheriff's Office, he said, he and his team had not failed to solve a single killing.

What's more, "this is home," he said. "You know the people here."

McWhorter recalled Ruiz as a nice guy. Who would want to kill him?

Clues fell into place very quickly. But they did not point to Martinez. Next to Ruiz's body, officers found a Walmart receipt. One of the store's many surveillance cameras led them to images of Ruiz's friend, the one who was dating Martinez's daughter, a man named Jaime Romero.

They tracked down Ruiz's truck in a parking lot in Decatur and found more surveillance camera footage showing a truck pulling up next to Ruiz's vehicle not long before the murder. They ran the license plate. It came back registered to Romero.

"Jaime's the guy that done this," McWhorter said he thought.

On the afternoon of March 11, 2013, McWhorter and his team trailed Romero to Martinez's daughter's house and banged on the door.

In a voluntary statement he signed that day, Romero wrote that he had been with Jose Martinez all day. They had gone to Decatur and eaten tacos, he said, and then come home and gone to a movie. He said he had no recollection of what movie he had seen.

"I don't know why anyone would have wanted to hurt Jose [Ruiz]," he wrote.

When he heard that his daughter's boyfriend had been called down to the station, Martinez tried to help. Full of genial humility, he presented himself at the police station as a loving father visiting his daughter from California. He swore that Romero had been with him at the time of the murder.

McWhorter recalled being taken in, as so many cops had

been before, by Martinez's "aw-shucks" persona. He didn't suspect Martinez of involvement in the murder but was hoping to get from the exchange something that would catch Romero in a lie and thus make the case against him that much stronger.

But as they were wrapping up their conversation, McWhorter, perhaps fishing for a compliment about Alabama, asked Martinez whether he found people to be more courteous than folks in California. Martinez answered that for the most part he did, but he had recently had "a bad encounter." Dropping one of his grand-daughters at school, he had been so focused on waving good-bye that he had bumped into another parent, who refused his apology and told him to "watch where the hell you're going."

McWhorter vividly remembered what Martinez said next: "I looked at her and said, 'Bitch, get out of my way.'"

"You could see the anger," McWhorter marveled. "It was like you flipped a switch. It caught us off guard."

Then Martinez reverted right back to his usual twinkly-eyed self.

After Martinez left the station, McWhorter and his fellow investigator, Bill Burke, talked about the strangeness of that moment—how Martinez's anger had flashed up out of nowhere and then just as quickly receded.

It turned into a joke. Maybe Martinez was the killer, they would say after he'd left. But they didn't really suspect him. McWhorter told Martinez he was free to go.

Easter came early that year, on March 31, and the next day Martinez headed back to California. He left behind his beloved eldest daughter with her life in shambles. Her boyfriend was in jail. And she was stupefied with shock and horror. She, who had always tried to do right, was now somehow tied up in a violent murder.

* * *

Martinez, trying to keep a low profile, took a Greyhound bus to Yuma and stopped to visit his first wife and two sons. He also picked up a car, driving himself the rest of the way back to the valley.

He checked in often with his daughter to see how the investigation into Jose Ruiz's murder was going. His attempt to provide the boyfriend with an alibi hadn't worked. He learned that Alabama prosecutors had charged her boyfriend with the murder. He predicted that the boyfriend would soon "snitch" on him. And, indeed, on April 11, Romero did, reaching out to McWhorter and asking to speak to him in person.

Because no one in the tiny Lawrence County Sheriff's Office, located in an area with few Spanish-speaking residents, spoke that language, investigators relied on the local high school Spanish teacher and football coach to translate.

Romero told them that Martinez had committed the murder. The reason, he said, was that Ruiz had made "a sexual comment" about his daughter.

Alabama detectives thought this was ridiculous. All the evidence pointed at Romero, not at Martinez. And while police understood that making a sexual comment about a young woman to the young woman's father might provoke anger, a cold-blooded, execution-style murder seemed like an over-the-top response, to say the least.

When Martinez heard about this turn of events from family members, he later wrote that he had thought, "Fuck, I should have killed the boyfriend when I had the chance." But he also saw no indication that he was in imminent danger of arrest. Police didn't seem to believe the stupid boyfriend. He decided he didn't need to flee immediately. He was on edge, though, watching his back, alert for signs of trouble.

A few days later, while visiting his sons at his second wife's house in Earlimart, he heard a loud series of knocks on the door.

Martinez had sent his sons out for cappuccinos and was waiting for them alone in the kitchen. Who the hell could it be?

He went to the front of the house and saw police officers massed. Adrenaline rose up in him. They were there for him! He had to get away.

He ran to the back door and tried to take off through the backyard. But there were police there too.

When they saw him running, they did what police do: they gave chase. He was caught.

Chapter Twenty-Seven

‎‎‎

Soon Martinez realized he had run for nothing. They weren't even looking for him. They were investigating a series of violent drug "stash house" robberies sweeping across Earlimart. Gangs would break into houses to steal dope or cash being held there in transit to points north or south. Officers wanted to talk to Martinez's son—not because they suspected him of involvement but because they believed he might have some information. Once Martinez had run and they had gone to the trouble of chasing him, however, they realized they could bring him in because they had found a gun in the house, making him—by proxy—a felon in possession of a gun.

Martinez once again found himself loaded into the back of a police car. "I'm fucked," he later wrote that he had thought, as the car sped toward the sheriff's substation in Porterville. What if they somehow found out about Alabama? What if they had finally developed some evidence against him on one of his local murders? Even if they hadn't, if he was locked up, he couldn't monitor the investigation in Alabama and wouldn't be able to flee if he decided it was time to go.

The officer who had arrested him was a woman. He was pretty sure she didn't have a good sense of who he was. An idea came to him. "I'm sorry I tried to run from you," he told her. "It's just that I'm scared of police officers."[1]

Martinez was right. When Detective Christal Derington had chased Martinez, she hadn't known about his reputation. As officers were cuffing him, a colleague whispered that he was El Mano Negra, the reputed phantom who had terrorized Earlimart for years. Derington looked at Martinez in surprise.[2] This man? With his pleasant air and wry humor? It didn't seem possible.

As she drove him to the sheriff's station, Derington told Martinez about the string of stash house robberies she was investigating. She now knew the man sitting behind her was a criminal, possibly a violent, manipulative one. She knew he was working some kind of angle, although she didn't know what it was. But he was also a fascinating conversationalist. As she told him about a young woman threatened with gang rape in one of the robberies, Martinez appeared almost on the verge of tears. He told her he couldn't bear the idea of men hurting women.

Then Martinez said he had a proposition for her. "If you let me go, I'll give you a couple of rifles and guns that I took from the gangsters in Earlimart," he said. "I'm cleaning up the town for you."

Martinez said Derington told him she was on the lookout for a "Glock 45 that did a crime in Pixley a couple of months ago." He promised he would get it for her—if she let him go.

At this point, the Tulare County Sheriff's Department made a decision that officers in some other departments found flabbergasting. They agreed to let Martinez walk in exchange for guns and the promise of information about crimes. He had become a police informant.

Martinez said he couldn't believe his luck. He was out. "I brainwashed her," he said to himself.

Two days later, as a good-faith gesture, he said, he took two .22 rifles to the Pixley substation of the Tulare County Sheriff's Department, the one across the street from where he had murdered Santiago Perez thirteen years earlier. He also continued chatting with Derington.

On Thursday, April 25, 2013, Detective Tony Watts, on the cold case beat in Florida, reached the Kern County Sheriff's Department. The agency had popped up in his computer as one of the last to have dealings with Martinez.

Watts had a few background questions. Martinez was not a prime suspect in the murders he was investigating, of the two men found in an abandoned vehicle parked at the edge of a Florida swamp, but Watts was just curious about how and why a cigarette butt with the DNA of a California man had been found in Florida.

That phone call changed things.

Watts got Detective Kavin Brewer on the phone. And Brewer had a lot to say. Brewer told Watts about Martinez's history, including that he had been suspected in not one but two recent murders involving zip ties, one in Kern County and one in Tulare. Such ties had been used on the victims in Watts's Florida murders too.

Brewer also told him Martinez had been a suspect in as many as five murders in the area in recent years. Watts hung up the phone, his pulse quickening with the thrill of a case breaking open.[3]

"That gave me clue number one, that I may have my man," Watts said. "It was far-fetched, but I was starting to think, this guy could be one of those cartel guys."

But Watts still had a number of unanswered questions. Who had summoned Martinez to Florida? Why was there no record of his travel there?

In a subsequent phone call with Tulare officials, Watts learned that Martinez was back in California and working as an informant for that department in order to stay out of jail.

That left Watts in a rare state: speechless. "I was more than shocked by it," Watts remembered. "I said, 'Man, this guy ain't no informant, he's a killer.'"

Watts wanted to fly to California immediately to pick up Martinez, but his bosses told him to hold off. Martinez wasn't going anywhere, they pointed out, especially since Tulare officials had a close eye on him. They were talking to him almost every day.

Watts flagged Martinez as a person of interest in a national law enforcement database and went back to trying to find other leads.

In mid-May, Martinez talked to his daughter again. She was in despair. She told him that her boyfriend was "going crazy" in jail. And she also told him that Captain McWhorter wanted to talk to him again.

Hearing that, Martinez figured his luck had run out. He drove to meet his sons in Earlimart. "I have a big problem," he told them. "I want you to know that if anything happens to me, you're always going to be in my heart."

He also told them that they weren't boys anymore. They were the men of the house now.

Then, as the sun dipped behind the hills to the west and darkness swept over the mountains in the east, Martinez headed south down California's famed Highway 99. He cut through the bottom of the vast San Joaquin Valley, past the fields where his parents and siblings had spent years hunched in the heat picking grapes. He sped by dusty migrant labor camps, where his stepdad had taught him to smuggle heroin and shoot guns. He left behind the towns where he had raised his own children. As he drove, he passed spot after spot where he had killed men and left their bodies in the ground.

In Bakersfield, he dumped his car and picked up a different vehicle that couldn't be traced to him. Within hours, he covered the three hundred miles to Yuma, Arizona, to spend time with his sons there.

Despite officials' assurances to Detective Watts that they had a close eye on Martinez, no one tried to stop his flight. Eventually he crossed into Mexico, out of reach of US law enforcement. He said he settled into a beach house that his family owned, taking a moment to appreciate the marble countertops and then enjoying himself, he said, with a beautiful woman half his age and a steady supply of cold Corona. The turquoise waves of the Sea of Cortez lapped lazily under the sun.

Then his phone rang.

It was his daughter in Alabama. She was furious. Alabama police had just told her they intended to question her twelve-year-old daughter about Ruiz's murder. It was horrible enough— unfathomable enough—that her father had committed a murder. But now her children were getting dragged in.

"Do *not* bring her to him," Martinez told his daughter about the prospect of his granddaughter being hauled in for questioning.

He tried to think what to do. He didn't deliberate long. "Fuck Sinaloa," he said to himself. "Fuck everything around here. I'm going to go back," he resolved. "I can make her happy."

Sometimes when he talks about this, Martinez says he was coming back to talk his way out of trouble, as he had so many times before. And sometimes he says he was coming back to fix the problem a different way, by executing McWhorter.

He got in the car and drove north, to his preferred border crossing, at San Luis Río Colorado/Yuma. From there, it would be a long day's drive to Alabama.

Alabama detectives didn't really think Martinez's grandchildren knew anything. In fact, investigator Bill Burke, a detective with the Alabama Bureau of Investigations who was working with McWhorter on the case, said he felt awful that the girls had been dragged into the mess and had to watch detectives execute a search warrant at their home. Seeing them cry had been upsetting.

But they needed some leverage over Martinez, and they hoped that bringing the grandchildren into it might convince him to present himself for questioning.

They had another trick up their sleeve too. A bigger one. They had convinced their district attorney to issue a murder warrant for Martinez.

They knew they didn't have much evidence against him. Martinez had no obvious motive. No tie to the crime scene. In fact, the only allegation against him came from the very man they had accused of the murder.

"We knew, as far as a conviction, we were lacking a whole lot," McWhorter said.

But Alabama was not California, where district attorneys had been reluctant to file charges against Martinez for fear that he would beat them at trial.

"If you let it go like some people might," added McWhorter's boss, "you let a murderer walk off totally free, just because you didn't want to get embarrassed a little bit in court by having a weak case."

McWhorter thought he could get Martinez back for questioning and maybe lock him up for a few days on the murder warrant, with the hope that he would slip up and say something incriminating on the jail phone.

They entered the warrant into the national system on Friday, May 17, 2013.

Martinez left his car on the Mexican side of the border and got to the pedestrian bridge in San Luis Río just a few hours later.

If he had gotten there a bit earlier, he would have crossed without a problem. Maybe he would have been arrested anyway if he had showed up in Alabama to try to talk his way out of trouble. Or maybe he would have tried to kill McWhorter, and maybe he would have succeeded.

Whatever his intentions, fate had a different plan for him. His long, improbable string of luck had finally run out.

Border guards ran his ID and stopped him. They told him he was under arrest. He was wanted for murder.

Martinez was calm. "Murder warrant?" he asked. "Warrant from where?"

It was an honest question. There were so many possibilities. The answer: Lawrence County, Alabama.

They took Martinez to jail in Yuma to await transfer to Alabama. "My life is gone and over," he wrote that he thought. His first wife came to visit him, he said, and so did his eldest son.

"Contact Mr. X," he told his eldest son. "Tell him I'm done. And pray for me."

McWhorter and Burke began making arrangements to bring Martinez to Alabama. Detective Watts from Florida, meanwhile, had been closely following the developments.

He'd been outraged when he heard Martinez had fled the country. But on learning that his suspect had returned to the United States and was in custody in Arizona awaiting transfer to Alabama, Watts sprang into action with characteristic speed. He jumped in his car and drove nine hours straight from Marion County, in the flat, swampy middle of Florida, to Lawrence County, Alabama.

He was determined to get his man. He had DNA evidence and a lot of circumstantial evidence that Martinez was a bad guy. But it wasn't enough. This was a man who had somehow managed to escape plenty of other murder charges in the past. Watts needed something that would put Martinez in Florida at the time of his crime. Not to mention a motive.

Maybe, he thought, family or friends in Alabama could help him get it. First, he spoke with Jaime Romero, Martinez's daughter's boyfriend, who was conveniently available because he was locked up in the Lawrence County jail.

Romero had decided to tell what he knew about Martinez. And what he knew was very interesting to Detective Watts. He learned that Martinez always carried a gun. And he learned that during the time Romero had seen Martinez in Alabama, he had constantly been on the telephone with an associate in California. Most interestingly, Romero told Watts that Martinez had freely admitted to Romero that he had committed a murder in Florida.

Romero also told Watts that he did not believe Martinez's daughter knew anything about any of this. Most of the time, Romero said, Martinez was "a very normal person"—but, he added, "if he doesn't like something…his behavior just changes instantly."

Next, Watts sat down with Martinez's daughter, without Romero, to talk about what she knew about Florida. It was a tough interview. She could not stop sobbing.

"You don't know why you're here?" he asked her.

"No," she said. But she had some dark clues. She knew her dad was in jail in Arizona. She knew her boyfriend had told Watts some things about her father. And she had a shiny memory, now clouded with suspicion, of her father swooping into Alabama from Florida years before to visit her.

"I want to talk to you about a case that involves your dad."

"OK," she allowed.

"Your dad is Jose Martinez?"

"That's him."

In his methodical way, Watts ran Martinez's daughter through her childhood. She had been born in Tulare County, spent a few years living in Mexico with a grandmother, and then gone to school in Yuma. These were simple biographical facts, but Martinez's daughter delivered them through such a torrent of tears that Watts became concerned.

"You need to relax," he pleaded. "You're getting nervous for no reason. Are you sure you don't want water?"

She took a breath and tried to control her tears. After high school, she said, she had left Yuma, joined the army, then settled here in Alabama. She sounded helpful and respectful and also brokenhearted and very nervous.

"You don't need to be stressing," Watts said. "Just relax. There's no reason for you to be nervous. We're just trying to figure some things out." He remained calm and collected, as if he were trying to figure out something other than whether her father was a contract killer.

"Be relaxed. Smile," he exhorted, as if smiling would lift her mood—or be at all appropriate in this situation.

Watts delivered the boom. "I'm not going to lie to you," he said. He told her he was conducting a murder investigation.

Martinez's daughter broke into fresh tears. She'd had such high hopes when her dad had been living with her earlier in the year. He had been so loving and wonderful with her children. They had been so happy.

"I just want you to be relaxed," Watts said again. "I think you know a little bit more about why we're here, and even if you talked to someone else, or they told you about Florida, we want to know about that, OK?"

At that point, Martinez's daughter broke down again. "Me and my dad don't have that type of relationship," she said.

As if sensing that the conversation was taking a turn and they might finally get Martinez's daughter to open up, another officer in the room jumped in. "Has your dad ever told you any of the stories about some of the things he's done?" he asked.

"No," Martinez's daughter said firmly. They didn't have that type of relationship, she said again. It was true. She knew her dad had been in trouble with the law. But her father never said anything about murder. Martinez's daughter began sobbing so hard that Watts became concerned. "What's wrong? You alright?"

She kept sobbing. "I...this is my dad. I mean, my God."

PART FOUR

Catching a Killer

2013–2018

Marion County Florida Detective TJ Watts: "Your confession has been made freely and voluntarily." Pause. "Why is that, if I can ask you?"
Jose Martinez: "It's time for me to pay for all the things I've done in my life." Pause. "If I didn't do the job, somebody was going to do it."

—Partial excerpt from a police interrogation,
June 3, 2013

Chapter Twenty-Eight

On June 2, 2013, Detectives Tim McWhorter and Bill Burke took a small plane out to Arizona to bring Martinez back.

Guards from the jail in Yuma brought Martinez to the tarmac early on the morning of June 3. As Martinez was shackled into the plane, McWhorter found himself surprised by how unconcerned their captive seemed about being arrested on murder charges. Martinez didn't yet know about Tony Watts and his DNA evidence, but even so, a murder charge was a serious thing.

The detectives did not attempt to talk to him in the plane, which would have been impossible in any event. It was so loud in that thing.

Burke was wearing sunglasses, and the entire way to Lubbock, where they stopped to refuel, he felt Martinez staring at him. He thought, "Great, this is how it's going to be."[1]

But when they landed in Lubbock, McWhorter ordered a pizza delivered to the tarmac. McWhorter and Burke offered to share it with Martinez. This kindness impressed him, and he told them so.

They returned to the plane and flew to Muscle Shoals, Alabama, and then drove to Lawrence County. Arriving in McWhorter's office, they sat down—McWhorter behind his desk, Martinez and Burke in the two chairs opposite him.

Watts was waiting elsewhere in the station. Because he had flagged Martinez in the national system, he had received an alert about the transfer from Arizona to Alabama. He had jumped in his car, once again sped across four states, and been waiting at the sheriff's station when they arrived. But McWhorter had put him off. "No hard feelings, buddy," he told him, "but you got DNA. We need a confession."

McWhorter started the interrogation. He figured it would go nowhere, that Martinez would tell him to "pound sand" and then sit in jail. He was still pinning his hopes on Martinez's saying something stupid on a recorded jail phone. Best-case scenario, McWhorter mused, was that Martinez might admit to being at the murder scene but try to pin it all on Romero.

At first, McWhorter got nowhere.

"Look, Jose," McWhorter finally said. "The fact is, you're being charged with murder." Did Martinez want to tell his side of the story?

Martinez, who had slipped out of so many charges by playing the part of the simple farmworker or by trading information, offering tantalizing facts about guns or drugs, or spinning outrageous stories to turn the spotlight somewhere else, seemed to make a decision.

"You guys have been real respectful to me, and I appreciate that. Do you want me to tell you the truth?"

McWhorter nodded.

"Yeah, I killed that son of a bitch." Martinez's eyes, so friendly moments before, suddenly turned black and cold. "He said some bad stuff about my daughter. I stand up for my family. I don't let anyone talk about my family."

McWhorter was still trying to make sense of that when Martinez delivered a much bigger bombshell: he had killed three dozen people in twelve states. For more than three decades, he told them, he had been a debt collector for drug cartels, recovering hundreds of thousands of dollars and resorting to violence when necessary. Along the way, he'd also committed a number of kidnappings and smuggled untold amounts of drugs, weapons, and people across the border in one direction or another.

If Martinez was remorseful, he gave no sign of it. In fact, he repeatedly suggested those he had killed had deserved it. He wore his nickname proudly: El Mano Negra. The Black Hand.

Beside McWhorter, Burke listened, stunned. He was surprised, he said, not so much by the man's words as by his affect. He had seen men confess to murder before, and they usually all reacted the same way.

"Guys will get quiet," Burke noted. "You can physically see the weight being lifted off their shoulders when they confess. With him, it wasn't like that at all." All the lives he had taken didn't seem to weigh on him at all.

Watts had tried to follow the interrogation from an office near McWhorter's, pacing and trembling with agitation. Now, finally, it was his turn.

Watts agreed to meet with Martinez outside, so that Martinez could smoke while they talked. Watts and his partner, along with McWhorter and Burke, took Martinez to a little wooden gazebo just next to the station. It was about 8 p.m. on nearly the longest day of the year, but dusk was finally beginning to gather, and Martinez's cigarette flared orange against a blue-black sky as he drew deep on it.

Betraying no trace of the agitation he felt, Watts calmly told Martinez he had come to Alabama to ask him about a 2006 case from Marion County, Florida.

"What happened?" Watts asked.

Martinez's answer was shockingly direct. "He stole ten kilos of cocaine from another guy. And they hired the best."

"They hired who?" Watts asked, just to be sure.

"They hired me," Martinez said. "And I went and got them."

Watts tried to get Martinez to tell him who had hired him. "Do you know who they stole ten kilos from?"

Martinez wasn't playing. "Yeah," he said, "but I ain't going to tell you about it, because I tell you, they're going to hurt my family."

Watts ran Martinez through the details of the murder, and Martinez got every single detail right. Then Watts turned to the matter of the cigarette butt.

"Do you remember smoking in the truck?"

Yes, he did.

"Did you drink Mountain Dew?"

No, he did not.

"How did you get rid of the cigarette butts?"

"I took them with me," Martinez said with absolute certainty.

Watts revealed that, in fact, he probably hadn't and showed him a photo of the interior of the truck, with a Mountain Dew can stuck in the center console.

"There was a cigarette butt found inside that Mountain Dew can that had your DNA on it."

If he was expecting a big reaction from Martinez, he didn't get it.

"Could be," was all Martinez said. He wasn't interested in the evidence Watts had against him, and anyways, Watts didn't need it. Martinez was confessing.

At the end of the interview, as the last of the long summer's day faded out of the sky, the men were finally in the dark, the only light coming from the flicker and flare of Martinez's cigarette.

Martinez had been up since before dawn. He was exhausted physically. And he was exhausted emotionally too, because after years of successfully jousting with police officers, he had finally given up the game.

Watts gave him another cigarette, and then he asked the question many police officers would be wondering about in the days to come.

"Your confession has been made freely and voluntarily," Watts noted for the recording. And then he added, "Why is that, if I can ask you?"

Martinez answered quickly and without emotion.

"It's time for me to pay for all the things I've done in my life," he said.

And then, as if explaining himself, Martinez suggested that as far as contract killers go, he was one of the nobler ones. "If I didn't do the job, somebody was going to do it," he said. "And I'm going to be honest with you, we do not all think the same thing, OK, there's some friends that I know, they can go into that house, knock the door down, and kill everybody." He wasn't like that, he said. "I respect family."

Detective Burke's phone rang early the next morning. It was McWhorter. He told Burke that he had spent a bit more time talking with Martinez late the night before, after Burke had finally gone home.

McWhorter was agitated, so keyed up he could barely get the words out.[2]

"You're not going to believe it," McWhorter practically yelled. "We have a serial killer on our hands."

"What?" Burke replied in disbelief. Martinez had told both men, during his confession the day before, that he had killed "over thirty-five men in [his] life." But people said all kinds of crazy stuff to police that usually wasn't true—and claiming responsibility for three dozen murders was simply ridiculous. "That only happens in the movies," Burke said. Then, he added, as if to underscore how improbable it was. "This is *Lawrence County.*"

Still, Burke got in his car and drove over to the sheriff's headquarters. When he got there, he began to understand why McWhorter was so excited.

It seemed that Martinez had begun to offer specifics about some of his wild claims. In his careful handwriting, Martinez had made a list of states, twelve in all, from Oregon to Idaho to Arkansas to Florida, and by some states he had written a number to indicate how many people he had murdered there. California had the most.

Burke listened but remained skeptical. A practicing Catholic, he said, "I didn't want to believe him, because I didn't want to believe he was that evil."

Martinez told them about his black-market fruit murder of Juan Bautista Moreno and the time he killed Domingo Perez for parking in his driveway. Burke almost broke into prayer: "He's got to be lying, or making this stuff up."

Then Martinez asked McWhorter to call Christal Derington, the female officer who had arrested him in the spring and acted as his contact after the Tulare County Sheriff's Department decided to make him an informant. McWhorter dutifully made the call. He didn't get Derington right away. Instead he got another department official on the phone. And when he mentioned Martinez's name and why he was calling, he got an earful.

McWhorter had been right. He and Burke had caught themselves one of the deadliest contract killers in American history.

Chapter Twenty-Nine

The next day, the detectives let Martinez see his daughter. They were letting him have almost anything he asked for that they could get for him in jail—to keep his confessions coming.

Martinez watched his little girl walk toward him. Tears streamed down her face. She couldn't talk. She couldn't get words out. She just cried and cried and cried. For a second, he wondered if someone could die from crying.

"I love you, father," she finally told him. "I promise not to give up on you, as long as you don't give up on yourself."

When she left the jail, her boyfriend left too. Police released him without charges now that they finally had Martinez.

When Martinez's daughter told one of her girls that her beloved grandfather had been charged with murder and actually confessed to the crime, the little girl burst out laughing.

It had to be a joke. A prank. Grandpa loved to pull pranks! Like the time he ate Cheerios with lime juice. Once it became clear that her mother wasn't joking, the little girl began to cry.

This was so far from the girls' reality. They went to church every week. They got As in school. They only ever acted aggressively on the soccer field. And their grandfather was so lovely. He played Barbies with them. He cooked grilled cheese sandwiches. He sat by their bedsides and stayed awake all night when they were sick. When he was around, it was as if his whole purpose in life was to make them happy.

Martinez's daughter emphasized the loving side of her father for her children. He had done a terrible thing, she told them. In fact, many terrible things. But he was a wonderful person, and he loved them, and they loved him, and they would focus on and remember that.

It was Detective Christal Derington's day off. Her boss called her at home.

They needed her to get to Alabama, her boss said. Jose Martinez had confessed to a murder there, and now he wanted to talk to Derington. The bosses thought he was finally going to come clean.

Derington wasn't a homicide detective, and she wasn't particularly familiar with the open murder cases in which Martinez had been the prime suspect. But he had asked for her by name, and her bosses were telling her to go.

She got herself to the Fresno airport, and from there she took a series of planes that carried her east through the night. At around noon the next day, June 5, she walked into the Lawrence County Sheriff's Office and soon found herself sitting across from her former informant.

"How have you been?" Derington asked Martinez.[1]

He didn't answer her. Instead, he said, "Have you seen my kids?"

She replied that she had, and they talked for a minute about his youngest son, who had recently been arrested but later released.

"I think it was a good lesson for him," Martinez said, sounding like nothing more than a concerned father hoping a tough-love moment of discipline would stick.

"Good," Derington said. She paused. "You doing all right?"

"Yes," Martinez said immediately.

"I've heard you've had a lot of stuff going on here." This was a typical Derington understatement. She had short blonde hair and a serious demeanor that managed to seem friendly without her ever cracking much of a smile. She was also easy to talk to, absorbing other people's stories without giving up much of her own.

Martinez dove right in. "I started a race, and now I almost got to the end of it," he said. "I have a chip in my head," he continued. "It's full of information, things that I have done over there in your county, and probably you want to know about, yeah?"

"I mean, that's why I'm here," Derington admitted.

"I'm going to be honest with you," Martinez said. "I killed a lot of several people in your county, OK? There was a reason for them and somebody had to take them out."

He admitted to killing Joaquin Barragan and Santiago Perez and Gonzalo Urquieta, who he claimed—without evidence or specifics—was a child molester. He admitted to killing Domingo Perez for the crime of parking in his driveway. He also said of some murders he had committed in Tulare County, "I ain't gonna tell you about those guys."

The Tulare County victims spilled, one after another, from his lips so fast that Derington could hardly keep track. Sitting across from Martinez, she frantically texted her bosses back in Visalia with names, dates, and descriptions of roads, orchards, and ditches where Martinez said he had left bodies.

Throughout their interview, her phone vibrated constantly with return texts, and sometimes she had to step outside to take calls from her bosses back in Visalia.

"Do you feel relieved?" Derington finally asked him.

"I don't know," Martinez answered, sounding confused. "I don't feel sad. Like, this is like a—it was a job for me, OK? Like…I wasn't the kind of person that I just go and kill somebody, OK? My real job was to collect money from people that owe money."

"From the cartels?" Derington questioned.

"Yes, something like that," Martinez said, avoiding, as he always did, any specifics about drug cartels. He told her he'd been out of town on one such venture when she had called him up and offered him money in exchange for the information he was giving the department. He also told her he had feared that offer was a trap.

"I had $100 in my hand," she said.

Martinez laughed at the absurd notion that he would traffic in such small amounts. "A hundred dollars," he repeated, almost with pity.

"Well, we're broke," Derington said, referring to the sheriff's department.

Martinez laughed again. "If an ice-cream truck parks in front of my house I go out and buy $100 worth of ice cream for the kids. But thank you anyway."

At one point, Derington asked Martinez the question that was on every detective's mind.

"How come you are talking to me? I mean, what's made you come clean?"

This time he did not speak of the moral weight of his violent acts. He seemed to say, in fact, that he wanted to help Tulare officials clean their own ledgers of unsolved murders. "Well, so you can clear all the records off."

"Really?" Derington asked him.

"I know they going to send me to the electric chair," Martinez answered, as if it didn't matter. "I already done what I done in my life."

Martinez also stressed, again and again, that he believed some of his violent acts were in service of bringing justice to a place that had little of it. Some of the people he killed, he insisted, were child molesters and rapists. "I hate people like that," he told Derington. "I hate people who rape girls. I hate people who take advantage of little girls."

Once again, he brought up the murder of his older half sister when he was about sixteen. "That's why I do things like that, for my sister, okay?"

The police officers who chased Martinez and his family members who love him all have their own ideas as to why he confessed.

His daughter in Alabama thinks the confession was part of a conversion experience, an attempt to come clean, to release some of the weight of so much violence and killing. One of his brothers takes the same view. His daughter had no doubt of something else either: his love for her family had given her father the grace to confess. The simple comfort of their lives, the joy of sitting down for dinner every night, laughing, and taking care of each other, had touched something in his heart.

He had been in Mexico, driving toward Sinaloa, and those feelings of love had overwhelmed him; that's why he had returned. He had sacrificed himself for her and for her children. Overwhelmed with gratitude to him, she was determined to focus on that love and to push away thoughts about crimes he had committed—so much so that she deliberately avoided learning too many details about them.

Some police officers subscribe to a more hard-boiled version of this theory. Watts, for example, said he thought Martinez, once caught, decided to clear his conscience. Some officers, too, are somewhat convinced by Martinez's assertion that he killed mostly people he believed were bad or somehow had it coming—although they also note that he never seemed to ask for much evidence of his targets' immoral acts.

Others take a more cynical view. Some detectives think Martinez felt no remorse at all, that he was trying to work the system, to get himself out of Alabama and its notoriously brutal prison system and back to California, where he could serve out his time close to his family.

A few officers wondered whether maybe Martinez was confessing to more murders than he actually committed. Since he was going down anyway, maybe he had decided to "clear all the records off," as he'd put it to Derington. And in the process, clear the records for other people by taking the rap.

One thing was clear to almost everyone: Martinez was at least partially after fame and adulation.

Chapter Thirty

On June 12, 2013, the sheriff's department in Marion County, Florida, went public with a story about how Detective Watts had caught a vicious contract killer.[1] The story was picked up by national media outlets.

Police elsewhere were dismayed. They had hoped to keep the story quiet for a bit while they continued to investigate Martinez's claims. And some didn't appreciate how Florida seemed to be getting all the credit for the arrest.

From jail in Alabama, Martinez called his mother, who told him she was looking at him on the television.

"And I said, 'turn it off,'" he recalled, laughing sadly at the memory. "Mom, I'm sorry for that. I know I've been a bad boy."

Then he reminded her that he had given her money from his Florida job, money she had used to go on vacation.

"Had I known that," she said, "I would never have accepted it."[2]

That same day, veteran detective Rodney Klassen and a Spanish-speaking colleague showed up on the doorstep of Martinez's second wife's Earlimart home.

Klassen, whose family had farming roots in Tulare, had a stocky build, white hair, and a jolly manner. It was easy to imagine him playing Santa in his spare time. "Ask her if she is the wife of Jose Martinez," Klassen told his colleague.

The question was dutifully translated.

"Yes," she answered.

Tulare County sheriffs believed Martinez was telling the truth about all the people he had killed. After all, they had known Martinez was a killer for years—they just hadn't thought they could prove it. But they still had to investigate and verify all his claims—no mean feat given that the string of killings stretched back nearly thirty-five years and Martinez sometimes didn't even know the names of the people he had murdered.

Heading up that effort fell to Klassen. Raised in the Mennonite Church, he was soft-spoken and affable, with an interviewing style so smooth and respectful that when he interrogated suspects, it was possible to believe that he either didn't actually believe they had committed a crime or was prepared to believe they had a very good reason for having done so—right up until the moment he handcuffed them.

"You catch more bees with honey," he liked to say. "And I want to catch more bees."

Finding out what Martinez's wife knew was an important step in the investigation. But Klassen didn't speak Spanish, and so he was paired with a brand-new homicide detective who did. It fell to the other detective to translate all the bad news.

Martinez's second wife does not have an expressive face. She tends to fold in on herself, as if trying to hold herself together, and to say as little as possible. The officers stepped into her small stucco house, its yard ringed with a chain-link fence. But they were never asked to sit down, and the conversation wasn't very long or very detailed.

The woman confirmed that she was married to Martinez but quickly added that they had been separated for "many years."[3]

How many?

"Maybe ten, maybe twelve," she said. "Many, many years."

"Does she know his current status?" Klassen asked. It was a nice, euphemistic way of asking if she knew that a week earlier the father of her children had confessed to dozens of killings.

"Yes, his mother came to see the kids and told me."

"What did she tell you?"

"That he is in jail in Alabama."

The two detectives were silent for a minute. What did that mean exactly? Did she know only that he was in jail? Or did she know he had admitted to being a contract killer?

Finally, Klassen dove in. "Explain that he has admitted to committing several murders," he told his Spanish-speaking counterpart. "She's not in any trouble. But we're hoping she can help us."

The other detective found himself unable to be that blunt. "We sent a detective there," he said. "And when the detective talked to him, he said he had done," he paused, "everything he did. You know what he did, right? You know?"

Martinez's second wife said that she did not.

"He said he was responsible for many assassinations."

The woman gasped. "No! I didn't know. Ay, *dios mio!*" Although probably unnecessarily, given the gasp and cries of denial and *dios mio*, the other detective faithfully translated for Detective Klassen. "She said she didn't know anything about this."

"Is it true that you knew nothing?" Klassen prodded. The question was translated.

"No, I knew nothing," she insisted. "I had almost no communication with him. He would come see the kids."

Then the conversation got even more awkward. Did she remember her husband having an affair with a woman in the town of

Pixley? The woman with the long dark hair who was married to a man named Santiago Perez?

Yes, she said, she did remember that.

Did she know anything about the details of that affair?

No, she did not.

Klassen tried again. "Her husband admitted that he was a murder-for-hire assassinator…" he trailed off. "Well," he told the other detective, "explain that first."

The other detective took a deep breath. "Your husband was very frank. He told us. He said he was an assassin."

Martinez's second wife gasped again. "Ay!" And she began to cry.

Detective Klassen interjected, "None of this is your fault."

But she kept weeping. "I know it's not my fault," she finally said, almost impatiently, while the other detective translated. "But it's so ugly. My kids."

Detective Klassen tried to turn the conversation back to the murder of Santiago Perez. "Explain to her that when we questioned her husband, he admitted that he shot and killed [the woman's] husband."

Yet again, she seemed shocked. "For her?" She gasped.

"We don't know why."

Martinez's second wife said she couldn't help. She didn't know who his friends were. She didn't know what he did for money. She didn't know where he spent his time. She knew, it seemed, almost nothing about the man she had lived with for years and with whom she had had three children.

This went on for a few minutes, with Klassen and the other detective asking questions and Martinez's second wife insisting she had no idea what the answers might be, until finally the detectives asked her to call if she heard or thought of anything else.

In the car on the way home from the interview, Klassen and his partner talked about whether the sobbing woman had been telling the truth. Was it possible that the whole town knew her husband as El Mano Negra but she had no insight into his crimes?

They decided it was. "If I was him, in his shoes, I would never tell a wife or girlfriend," Klassen said. He sat down to write up his report on the encounter. "No further information," he concluded.

Closing at least nine murder cases—and maybe many more—that took place over a span of thirty-five years was no easy task. Each and every case had to be reinvestigated. Witnesses had to be found and reinterviewed. Physical evidence had to be dug out of musty boxes and reexamined.

On the one hand, Martinez was making it easy. He had confessed, after all. And not only was he cheerfully telling police anything they wanted to know, but he seemed to have an almost photographic memory of his crimes. He knew the number and caliber of the bullets used in every killing, the angle at which the bodies had dropped, and the likelihood of police having recovered shell casings at the crime scenes.

But Detective Klassen, who was responsible for closing the six killings that had taken place in Tulare County, had another secret weapon: "The wise men" of Tulare County Violent Crimes Division, Ralph Diaz and his old partner and friend, Jay Salazar, back from retirement and helping with cold cases.

The detectives were in their sixties now and in fading health. But they were still legendary. They knew it all. They knew the county and its history, they knew murder, and they had the patience and gumption to keep working cases until they closed them.

Like most detectives, Klassen revered the two men. He felt relief that they were helping. And then that relief turned to wonder.

They all gathered in the violent crimes conference room one day to go over the case files on some of Martinez's early murders. Klassen was astounded to hear that the detectives knew the old cases backward and forward off the top of their heads without ever having to consult the files. How could this be?

It emerged that Diaz, when first a detective, had worked the 1980 murder of David Bedolla. Then Diaz and Salazar together had worked the 1982 murder of Raul Gonzalez. They hadn't pursued Martinez at the time, Klassen said, but as time went on and Martinez's reputation grew, they began to wonder if he was good for those murders.

Yet Martinez had eluded the wise men too.

Diaz, Klassen recalled, was happy that Martinez had finally brought himself to justice by confessing in Alabama. But a sense of frustration lingered in the room too.

"Every detective that came into the homicide unit was told about Jose Martinez, and knew something about him," Klassen marveled. And yet, "we just didn't have the evidence."

By mid-June, Detective Derington was on another plane to Alabama. With her this time was Scott Logue, then the department's head of violent crimes. They were heading back to gather more information on certain killings.

Martinez started off the interview unhappy that Tulare County officers had been trying to talk to his family.[4]

Why did they need to mess with his family? His family didn't know anything. They thought he was a nice person, he told detectives. They had had no inkling he was a killer. They couldn't possibly be helpful. Plus, why did they even need anyone else? He was talking, telling police everything they could possibly want to know. His own lawyer, a public defender appointed by the state of Alabama, had advised against it, he said, but still he was talking. So why was it necessary to involve his family?

"I made two phone calls," he told Derington right off the bat. "They told me you've been looking at my family. That you went to my house, talked to my wife. I don't know why you want to interrupt my family."

Sergeant Derington tried to explain that officers had followed up with a few questions.

"My mom is sick," Martinez interrupted her. "Every time she hears my voice, she starts crying. Please don't go to her house, for her safety."

Derington and Logue answered that officials had to perform some due diligence to check out Martinez's stories. They believed him—but people falsely claimed to have committed crimes more often than one might think.

Derington moved on. "There's a lot of stuff we got to talk about. But you remember your constitutional rights?" she asked.

Martinez laughingly recited the Miranda warning. Apparently, that was good enough; the detectives plunged into talk of murder.

Martinez answered Derington's questions cheerfully, carefully, and with chilling matter-of-factness. For example, his description of how he had restrained Joaquin Barragan while pulling him out of the car to kill him was so emotionless that it took a minute for the horror of it to settle in.

"What did you do with Joaquin?" Derington asked him.

"I always have my zip ties with me," Martinez answered, as if zip ties were everyday necessities, like umbrellas or sweaters. He bought them in bulk from Home Depot. "And I tied him down…and then I shot him two times in the head." He added, "There was a red blanket right there, and I went and grabbed it."

"Do you remember what the blanket looked like?"

Martinez was annoyed at the question. "Come on. When you do a crime, you want to get out of there."

"Do you remember what color the zip ties were? Did you always use the same kind?"

"I'm not sure," Martinez answered, "because I have white and

I have black ones. But they were the long ones." He added, as if trying to be helpful, "In Home Depot, they have all sizes."

"Fair enough," Derington responded. Beside her, her boss, Logue, felt a wave of revulsion.

Martinez paused. He seemed troubled. "I don't understand why they investigate too much," he finally said. "Don't you believe a person when they tell you, 'I killed this guy?'…I done it, OK, I done it," he said, shaking his head at the way police insisted on making things more complicated than they had to be.

"I believe you," Derington soothed him. "I know you're telling the truth."

Martinez didn't answer her directly. Instead, unprompted, he jumped into a long digression about his daughter. The whole time he talked, he stared into the middle distance, behind the two police officers' heads, as though talking to a third person only he could see.

"My daughter came here yesterday, and she said, 'Why are you saying all this stuff?' I said, 'Sit down. I will tell you the truth. I was enjoying my life, OK? I lived like a king outside. And I was in Mexico, OK? And one night you called me up crying, telling me that I had come here and destroyed your life. That your company is going down because of me. That your boyfriend is in jail because of me.'"

He reminded police of how he had been in California and then fled to Mexico. But something kept nagging at him. "I was still thinking of my daughter," he said.

"I made a U-turn," he said. "I said to myself, 'Fuck Sinaloa; fuck everything around here. I'm going to go back, and I can come here; I can make her happy this time.'"

And then, after he got to Alabama and made his confessions, police finally let him see his daughter. "I said, 'Daughter, I see the happiness in your face. You got your happiness back.'" He paused, and that pause hinted at his anguish that his daughter still wasn't happy. That this gesture, as much as it moved her, hadn't fixed everything.

Derington spoke to Martinez softly. "She's having a hard time?"

Martinez nodded. "Yes, she's having a hard time."

After a sip of water, he collected himself and resumed telling police about murder after murder. It was a brutal litany. Often he either didn't know or didn't remember the name of the person he had killed, but he recalled precisely the type of gun used to dispatch each victim and the lonely fields where he had dumped the bodies.

When it came to the murder of Santiago Perez, Logue grilled him, trying to get him to say that the victim's wife—the woman with the long dark hair—had put him up to it. Again and again, he denied it.

At another point, he told police about the Kern County killing he had committed with another contract killer, the murderer Detective Kavin Brewer had been so interested in.

That man was "a stupid killer," Martinez scoffed. "If he has a gun, he will shoot you fifteen shots. This is the guy that is almost like me; they send him around [to kill people], but this mother-fucker, he will go and shoot your family."

This gave Logue an opening. "Can we talk about you?" Without waiting for an answer, he continued, "Do you have remorse for what you did?"

Martinez leaned forward. "What does that mean?"

"Are you sorry?" Logue asked.

Martinez nodded like a student who knew the right answer. "Yes. Yesterday the priest came and talked to me."

"How about before the priest came—were you sorry?"

"No," he shot back, staring straight at Logue's face. "I hated those guys. For example, when they molested a little girl, the little girl is going to have that on her mind, the rest of her life, every time she sees a man."

Logue didn't find that answer acceptable. "Did you hate Santiago?"

"Santiago, yes. Because he wanted to know who I was, probably would have sent someone to shoot my ass. Because I'm not the only one out there." He added, pointedly, "There's worse people than me."

Logue wasn't having it. "Did you hate Raul?" He was referring to the drug dealer Martinez said he had murdered in 1982.

"Raul, yeah, I hated that fool."

"He just owed you money, though. Two thousand dollars," Logue said, implying that wasn't really a good motive for murder.

"How about if it would have been more?" Martinez answered. "How about if it would have been a hundred thousand dollars?"

"I don't know. Is it enough? I don't have a limit," Logue answered. "You do."

Martinez sighed and paused for a long time. Finally, he said, "Can we finish the conversation?"

"Yeah, if you want to," Logue conceded. "I'm just trying to see about you. Why you did what you did. The psychology of it. Does it anger you that I asked you these questions?"

"Yes," Martinez answered.

"You don't want to talk about yourself?"

"No," Martinez said. "You're not interested in what happened in Kern County?"

"No, Kern County is coming to talk to you about that. I want to know what happened in our county. You're responsible for it, so I want to ask you about why you did what you did. How you feel about it?"

"I did that for a reason," he repeated. "Because they were bad people. Raul was selling dope to fifteen-year-old kids. That's not good. How about if he would be selling drugs to my kids?"

Logue refrained from pointing out that Martinez had been involved in the drug business for almost his entire life. He ignored

Martinez's point altogether. "Those are decisions that you made. I didn't make them. I'm not trying to judge you. I'm just trying to find out why."

Martinez lost his patience. "You want to know who killed them all? I killed them all, and that's it."

That, finally, shut down Logue's line of inquiry. "I can see you're getting agitated," he said. "You don't have to answer."

Martinez spoke quickly. "I don't want to talk anymore."

They were no closer to understanding Martinez's psychology. But the conversation with Logue was closed—and with it any possibility of further confessions that day.

Chapter Thirty-One

In the early-morning hours of June 25, 2013, Cecilia Camacho woke up in her bedroom. The night seemed unusually dark, and the room felt icy cold even though it was summer.

The remnants of her dream remained vivid: She had been in a tunnel. But when she got to the end of it, an angel stopped her. She realized the angel was her murdered husband, David Bedolla. The man who had been shot by Martinez in the fall of 1980—his first murder for hire. In Cecilia's dream, her dead husband was beautifully dressed, and he had little angel wings.

His death had devastated her, and she thought of him almost every day. But she had also built a new life for herself. With her new husband, she'd had three more children. One had grown up to become a teacher. And after working in the fields for three decades, she was retired now, enjoying caring for her grandchildren.

In the dream, David was young again. Her first husband, her first love, was unchanged. As beautiful as ever. She walked toward him, and when she reached him, he turned to her. "It's been so long," he said. "And all this time, I've needed you."[1]

She put her arms around him, and he spoke to her. "Do you want to come with me?"

She had to tell him no. "Because I'm married," she explained. Married to someone else.

When she said that, he disappeared, and she woke up in the dark, and the bed was cold. "I'm freezing," she thought. "Like I'm dead."

The next day, the remnants of the dream still in her head, she was sitting on her front porch when a small, dark car pulled up. A man she hadn't seen in thirty years got out: former Tulare County sheriff's detective Ralph Diaz, back on the cold case beat and helping close the Martinez cases.

Diaz smiled at her. He told her he had finally found her. And then he asked if she knew who he was.

She knew exactly. She would never forget how he had accused her of complicity in her husband's death. They were both older now. Diaz himself only had a couple more years left. He would die in 2015.

To show Diaz that she did remember, she said, "What do you think I did now?"

He looked abashed. He told her that he hadn't come to punish her. And then, maybe because he thought it would please her or maybe because it just popped into his head, he added that she hadn't lost her beauty. He told her that she was beautiful back then, and she still was.

Cecilia ignored the compliment. "Why are you here?"

Instead of answering, he replied that he hadn't forgotten what he had done to her, how he had treated her. He apologized.

Then he gave her the news. He was here, after three decades, to tell her that they had finally arrested the man who had murdered her husband.

The killer was a man named Jose Martinez. A man who killed for money. He had killed many people. And her husband had been his first murder for hire.

If Diaz knew what the motive was, he didn't tell her. Instead, she recalled, he asked her how she felt.

"How do you think I feel?" she said. In fact she felt like she had "fallen back in time." Like it was 1980 and she had to relive it all again.

The Martinez family, meanwhile, was reeling. Antonio, two years Martinez's junior, had been closer to his brother than anyone else—or so he had thought. They had lived on the wrong side of the law together. He had thought they were "two black sheep." He knew his brother was a drug trafficker. He knew he was capable of violence. But he saw his brother in the warm embrace of family, taking care of his children and his nieces and nephews, driving people to the hospital, giving them money, doing everything he could to make everyone laugh. He knew his brother had a dark reputation, but he had pushed the rumors aside as so much talk. Now his brother was claiming to be a contract killer responsible for murder after murder in their hometown. How was it possible?

"You can't imagine it. It's like, damn..." he said, trailing off, unable to find words. His friends asked him about his brother, he said, and he could only think to explain it by saying, "It's like Dr. Jekyll and Mr. Hyde."

Antonio and some other family members had another question: Could Jose really have done all the murders he was now claiming credit for? Did police really have the evidence? Police had never seemed to care much about these victims when they were killed. Were they really after justice now, or just the chance to close a bunch of cases and boost their statistics?

"He's saying things that aren't true," Martinez's mother told the *Los Angeles Times* when a reporter appeared at her house shortly after the story became public.[2] Even years later, tears came to her eyes when the topic came up.

His family also worried that the confessions put them at risk.

Martinez was claiming to have killed a lot of dangerous people. And many of those people had fathers, brothers, nephews, sons. What if one of them decided to take revenge and went after his mother or someone else in the family?

Some detectives had questions too. Bruce Correll, the Santa Barbara detective who had spent a decade trying to solve the murder of Silvestre Ayon, was long retired and living in Idaho. Correll had climbed steadily up the ranks of the Santa Barbara County Sheriff's Department, eventually reaching the rank of chief deputy. But police work lost some of the joy for him when his former partner Leo Ortega died in 1999.

Santa Barbara sent other detectives out to Alabama to take Martinez's confession on the Ayon killing. When they got back, a detective called up Correll to tell him they had closed the case. The murder had been committed not by the Chaidezes, they told him, but by Martinez.

When he read the transcript of the Santa Barbara detectives' interview with Martinez, Correll was apoplectic. Where was the proof? They hadn't asked Martinez any hard questions. They hadn't pressed him or tried to catch him out on inconsistencies in his story. They'd appeared almost awestruck during their interview, like they were blown away to be in the presence of someone who had killed so many. True, Martinez had given them details of the crime that only a perpetrator might know, Correll acknowledged, but they didn't understand that in this crowd of drug smugglers, "these guys all get together and shoot the shit and throw out details—we did this, and we did that." That would make it possible for someone who wasn't even there to glean enough information to claim responsibility for the crime.

"You're dealing unfortunately in too many cases with a bunch of inexperienced detectives who are all excited because they are going to solve a homicide," he complained. Correll said it was possible Martinez was there and committed the murder. And it was also possible that, knowing he was going down, he was trying to take credit for a few more murders along the way. The problem was, nobody seemed to be trying to get to the bottom of what had really happened. Maybe, Correll theorized, Martinez had a brain tumor. Or maybe he "wants to go down as the most prolific hit man in history."

"Quite frankly, I don't know if I believe what this guy has to say," he sighed.

Few who were not directly involved in the case seemed to care much either way. After the Florida detectives had gone public with the case, Tulare officials had expected it would be only a matter of time before the story exploded.

But news of Martinez's prolific killing did not blow up into a media sensation. A few national outlets picked the story up, but then it faded from the headlines. Tulare County's hometown paper, the *Visalia Times-Delta*, didn't even run a follow-up when the news broke in Florida.[3]

In some ways, this was shocking. After all, if Martinez's claims were true—and police believe they were—he was one of the deadliest contract killers in US history. Yet even his hometown paper could not be bothered to take note. But in another respect, the lack of attention to Martinez's crimes was entirely predictable. Few in power had cared about his victims, either when they were alive or when he killed them. Of all the people he murdered in Kern and Tulare Counties, only a very few even received mention in newspaper briefs. Mostly they died as they lived: powerless and obscure.

Martinez's younger brother Antonio put it bluntly. He was not shocked that detectives never caught his brother or didn't care too much about the victims once he had confessed. And he wasn't surprised that most folks in Tulare didn't seem to care much about a contract killer living in their midst. The attitude of the police around Tulare had always been clear, he said. "They're Mexicans. Fuck 'em. Let 'em kill each other or die."

Chapter Thirty-Two

In the fall of 2013, as Martinez sat in jail in Alabama, waiting to plead guilty to murdering Jose Ruiz there so he could be transferred back to California to face nine more murder charges in the Golden State, a scandal rocked the Tulare County Sheriff's Department.

A patrol deputy, William Nulick, was accused of pulling a Spanish-speaking woman over and, upon learning that she did not have a driver's license, responded to her legal vulnerability by demanding a blow job. He forced her to drive to an isolated area of orange groves, where he sexually assaulted her.

The woman had complained, and the sheriff's department had taken the allegation seriously, launching an investigation. They had found video surveillance footage from a convenience store that supported the woman's allegation. Within the week, the district attorney had filed criminal charges against Nulick.[1] The department had, by most accounts, handled a terrible breach of duty by one of its officers with professionalism and care.

But then, in the spring of 2014, the case appeared to be

headed back into the news. On March 4, the woman served the department with notice that she intended to file a lawsuit. Her lawyer, a fancy Los Angeles plaintiff's attorney, knew how to work the media to generate outrage that would help his clients. What's more, the story was getting worse. The district attorney's office was investigating numerous additional felony charges against the officer involving more women. And the same fancy Los Angeles lawyer eventually represented them, too, in a lawsuit against the department claiming that the problem was not just one rogue officer but "a pattern and practice of violating the pat-down procedure by committing offensive and unlawful sexual touching of female co-workers and women in the general public."[2] (Tulare County eventually agreed to pay $2.2 million to settle the lawsuits.[3])

The threat of such a terrible news story couldn't have come at a worse time. Both the sheriff, Mike Boudreaux, and the district attorney, Tim Ward, were about to go before voters for the first time. Both men had been appointed to their posts—a common means by which outgoing politicians ensured that their favored candidates had a leg up in forthcoming elections. And no politician wanted to ride into his or her first election with a violent sex scandal at the forefront of voters' minds.

In the middle of all this, on the morning of Tuesday, April 8, 2014, Tulare County officials summoned the media to a press conference. With great fanfare, they announced the county was filing nine murder charges against Jose Martinez for six killings in Tulare, two in Kern County, and one in Santa Barbara County: the murders of David Bedolla, Silvestre Ayon, Raul Gonzalez, Domingo Perez, Santiago Perez, Jose Alvarado, Juan Moreno, Joaquin Barragan, and Gonzalo Urquieta.

Tulare County district attorney Tim Ward opened his remarks with the assertion that law enforcement officials in the three counties "[stood] united under the principle that no victim of crime shall be forgotten, and justice shall not be delayed." Added Sheriff Boudreaux, "We hope that by solving these crimes there can be closure for families, who in many cases have been waiting years for answers."

The press conference rubbed some people the wrong way, including the editorial board of the *Visalia Times-Delta*. The following day's editorial page featured a stinging headline— "News Serves Candidates, Not Public"—and accused the district attorney and the sheriff of "commandeering this announcement for political reasons."[4]

The newspaper noted that the "timing and urgency of the press conference was somewhat surprising," given that Martinez had been arrested ten months earlier and wasn't set to be sent from Alabama to California to face justice for several months more. In fact, the paper accused the sheriff and district attorney of using the news for political gain.

Why, the editorial asked, had Boudreaux and Ward included a press packet with their own biographies—a packet that looked suspiciously like campaign material—as part of a handout to reporters during the news conference? Furthermore, the paper took officials to task for not even bothering to include any family members of Martinez's victims in their news conference. The newspapers didn't take note of it, but Rodney Klassen, the lead investigator in the case, hadn't even been invited to the news conference. He'd found out about it the way the public did—by reading about it in the paper.

The press conference made the front pages the next day.

Boudreaux said he was perplexed by the criticism. "The one thing that was not on my mind was politics," he said. His department had been pursuing Martinez for years, and now "the case had finally come together and the DA was finally filing charges, and it seemed appropriate to notify the public."

The sheriff added that he found it "funny that local politics played a bigger story [in the newspaper] than the actual serial maniac."[5]

Amid the sensational news and the graphics, maps of killings, and timelines, neither the district attorney nor the sheriff was ever forced to answer another question posed by the *Visalia Times-Delta* editorial: "Had local law enforcement ever connected Martinez to any of the murders committed in Tulare County" before Martinez had done police the favor of confessing to all of them?

Of course, the answer to that question was a resounding yes. But no one seemed interested in how a contract killer who had lived in Tulare County for decades and was widely known as "El Mano Negra" had had to go all the way to a tiny, underfunded police department in Alabama to get himself caught.

A few months later, Sheriff Boudreaux won his election by a landslide, and District Attorney Ward was also easily elected.

After the media lost interest in the case, the sheriff's department was still left with an important question: How many more bodies had Martinez left in lonely fields in Tulare County—and whose might they be?

On September 3, 2014, after a two-week journey across the country in the custody of the US Marshals Service, Martinez arrived at the federal building in Fresno and was transported to the Tulare County jail.

The next day, Detective Christal Derington showed up. Martinez had told her that he had left more bodies buried at a ranch in Richgrove. And she wanted to know exactly where.

"I make you a deal," he told her. "You can have the three bodies, but I want a signed document from you that I will get one contact visit per week and that I can have my own iPod, so I can hear music, and my family can bring me street food."[6]

Martinez had had this arrangement in Alabama. Eager to keep his confessions flowing, officials there had allowed him Burger

King meals brought by his family, as well as almost unlimited cigarette breaks in the grass outside the jail. California officials, whose jails ran on much stricter rules, were flabbergasted when they came out to talk to Martinez and witnessed how he was being treated. Now that he was back in Tulare County's jail, the special treatment had stopped. Derington told him she couldn't control custody arrangements inside the jail.

"No deal, no bodies," Martinez responded.

Next it was Klassen's turn. He had met Martinez twice in the past— once when Martinez tried to get his white Suburban back and once when one of Martinez's close friends was murdered and Martinez was upset about it. Klassen felt like they had a rapport. Maybe he could get Martinez to reveal the location of the bodies.

They talked for hours, first in the jail and later in the office, but Martinez was adamant: he would not help them by going out to the ranch and showing them where he had buried the bodies. Instead, he drew a crude map.

Klassen tried to reason with Martinez, to appeal to his sense of decency to give closure to the families of his victims. No luck.

Meanwhile, as he and Martinez talked, Klassen's cell phone was buzzing with texts from his bosses, who were listening outside the room. They wanted the location of those bodies, and they wanted it now. The department had budget problems, like almost all departments in California in 2014, in the aftermath of the Great Recession, and officers were on standby—being paid overtime—waiting to head out to dig. Get him to tell you where the bodies are, Klassen said the texts said. Get a new case.... This conversation is getting expensive.

Klassen too got nowhere, either because Martinez, yet again, had outsmarted the department or perhaps—as Klassen sometimes thinks—because sheriff's officials, worried about overtime expenses, would not let him conduct the interrogation the way he wanted.

*   *   *

Three weeks later, on the morning of September 24, Klassen, Derington, and another detective arrived at the farm near Rich-grove where Martinez said he had buried more bodies.

The third detective—he had grown up on a farm—climbed into a Bobcat excavator and began to dig. Klassen listened to the roar of the engine, inhaled the smell of the turning earth, and hoped they would find something soon.

Klassen did not have explicit permission from his bosses to be out there.

Practically the whole department, including some top brass and a cadaver-smelling dog on loan from the Los Angeles County coroner, had been there the day before. They'd had copies of Martinez's map—he was still refusing to help them by coming himself—and they had dug and dug.

But they had found no remains.

The top brass had been furious. They thought Martinez was obviously lying to them. He was wasting their time. Not to mention generating all that extra expense of bringing people from Fresno and Los Angeles and inconveniencing a farmer. Just so they could look ridiculous. They called off the search.

Klassen and Derington weren't so sure. Martinez was undoubt-edly a vicious murderer—and a manipulative one. But he hadn't lied to them yet about murders he had committed—at least as far as they knew. If he said there were bodies out here, there probably were.

So they'd come back out to dig some more. Klassen hadn't told his bosses. He figured he knew what the answer would be, and it would be better to ask for forgiveness, preferably in possession of long-interred remains, than to seek permission that might not be granted. Derington, however, had told her chain of command. Rather quickly, word of what they were doing reached Klassen's sergeant, who, Klassen said, was livid.

They weren't going to find anything, he told Klassen. And he wouldn't have them further inconveniencing a farmer for nothing.

"I'm sorry," Klassen said. "I want to make sure we didn't leave the bodies."

But the search was called off. Being a homicide detective in Tulare County was frustrating. "We had a high homicide rate," Klassen said. "We'd go from scene to scene. We'd triage. We were running from homicide to homicide" and not solving them, he said, "unless we got real lucky" because everyone was spread so thin.

What's more, it sometimes felt to Klassen that murder was a lower priority than the theft of tractors or water or other agricultural crimes. He recalled being at one murder scene and watching with dismay as five detectives were pulled off. A farmer's tractor had been stolen, and he had called the sheriff on his cell phone to complain about it.

Klassen was sympathetic to farmers. He had grown up on a farm, he said, "but don't put a property crime above the death of a person."

And now, they had an opportunity to close more cases. It didn't get easier than this. Martinez was a monster, no doubt. But he was a monster with a photographic memory, and he was giving them a chance to clear old cases, to provide closure to families, some of whom had been waiting years to find out what had happened to their missing loved ones. Dejected, Klassen went back to the office.

When asked about this conflict at a later date, Sheriff Boudreaux said anyone who thought cost was an issue in the Martinez case was mistaken.

"When it came to that guy, when we started learning the full extent of what we had, I said, you guys, use whatever you need," the sheriff said. "No restrictions on flights. No restrictions on anything. I don't care what we have to do."[7]

Martinez, meanwhile, had come to his own decision about those bodies. He wasn't going to give anyone any more information about them. They were his bargaining chip.

He was well aware that after he was adjudicated in California, Florida planned to grab him next, to prosecute him for the 2006 double murder there. He knew, too, that his chances of beating the rap on that weren't great: not only did Detective Watts have DNA, but Martinez had confessed.

But Martinez had no interest in spending the rest of his life in a Florida jail. Those bodies—and a few others—were, he figured, his ticket out of Florida and back to California. His plan was elegant and macabre: he would give out details on those murders when it suited him and force officials to bring him back to California to plead guilty to those murders.

He revealed the whole scheme to a homicide detective from Riverside County in Southern California, James Dickey, who had come up to try to talk to him about the three people he said he had killed in retaliation for his sister's murder. Dickey got nowhere on learning where Martinez had buried those bodies either. But Martinez told him that could change—depending on how things in Florida went.

"I'm going to go to Florida," he told Dickey. "If I don't like Florida, I'm going to write you back and tell you I'm ready to talk."[8]

Detectives believed him. They believed there were at least six more bodies out there, buried somewhere in California, six more families waiting and wondering what had happened to their loved ones. But what could they do?

Once they gave up trying to get Martinez to reveal where he had buried additional bodies, Tulare officials busied themselves with a different task: trying to convince the families of Martinez's victims to come into open court and testify against him.

In late October 2015, Martinez pled guilty to nine murders and one count of attempted murder in Tulare County Superior Court. His sentencing hearing—in which family members of the victims could talk about how the loss of their loved ones had affected them—was set for November.

Some victims' family members flatly refused to appear. They were too scared. Or too heartbroken. Or both. Other victims' families did not have to be asked twice.

"I'm old, but I haven't forgotten," Cecilia Camacho said. Mostly she wanted to lay eyes on Martinez, to look into the face of the man who had killed her husband and stolen her son's father. Yes, she told detectives, she would happily come to court and tell her story.

Juan Moreno's daughter, Asenneth, didn't hesitate either. Her father was the one who was killed when a deal over black-market fruit went bad. After her father's murder in 2009, when she was eleven, the family had fallen apart. First, they'd been unable to pay the electric and water bills, and the power had been turned off. Then they had lost their home to fore-closure. And then Asenneth had become pregnant at sixteen. After fighting with her mother over the pregnancy—her mother wanted her to go to college, make a life for herself, and then have children—she had moved to stay with relatives in Minnesota, a faraway, freezing place stripped of any reminders of the violence at home or of her father, whom she missed terribly.

But when the Tulare County Victims/Witness Assistance Division called her, she told them to buy her a plane ticket. She was coming in part to clear her father's name. He hadn't been involved in drugs. She was sure of it, and she needed the community to know it. She also had unanswered questions. What had her father done to get mixed up with a man like Martinez? Would she ever get answers?

She flew into Fresno with her baby daughter on her lap. The trip was emotional for her before she ever got near the courtroom. She saw her mother for the first time in more than a year the day before the sentencing hearing. As she watched her mother meet her baby, feelings welled up in her. All the things that had happened in their lives because of her father's murder. She probably wouldn't have gotten pregnant so young. She never would have been estranged from her mother.

The next morning, her mother picked her up. All the things they weren't saying filled the car with heavy silence. But they were together again.

Martinez asked his family not to come to court. He was worried for their safety. And he didn't want to put them through the ordeal of witnessing all the suffering he had caused.

Sometimes victims' statements can carry weight with judges, influencing them one way or another in sentencing. Not in this case. In exchange for Martinez's cooperation, prosecutors had agreed not to seek the death penalty. But no one—not even Martinez—was arguing that he deserved less than a life sentence.

Still, on November 2, 2015, the family members of Martinez's victims finally got to face him in court. The testimony of the victims was for the official record, to lay down in the annals of law what Martinez had done and the impact of his crimes. After a brief instruction to the media that no family member's face should be photographed or broadcast, the judge invited the three who had agreed to speak to approach the microphone.

The first to speak was the daughter of Santiago Perez, the husband of the woman with long dark hair, murdered by Martinez in his bed. "I just wanted to say that you hurt my family so deeply," she said, adding that her father was "a kind, gentle, hardworking, humble man."

Asenneth Moreno went next. "I shouldn't be sitting here today," she said. "I should be at home with my father."

Last came Cecilia Camacho. It was fitting. She was the wife of his first murder-for-hire victim. She had been living with the horror of what he had done the longest.

"Since that date, we haven't been happy," she said. "I've always, I've always had that in my mind." She added that, in a strange twist of fate, her husband had been buried exactly thirty-five years earlier, on November 2, 1980.

And she had a request for the court. She desperately needed help with an immigration issue. She had become a US citizen in the 1980s, but her oldest child, David Bedolla's son, had not. Instead, he had been deported. He was living in Tijuana, far from family, and she was desperate to get him home. Was there nothing the court could do? Help him get papers? Help her get money to help him?

No one in the courtroom responded to her pleas. They were not there to help her, only to take her statement to help punish Martinez. Martinez was sentenced to multiple life terms without the possibility of parole.

Cecilia Camacho had tried to look Martinez in the eye the entire time he was in the courtroom. "But he never lifted his eyes," she said. "He didn't have the courage to look at me."

When the hearing was over, Cecilia Camacho walked out of the courthouse and into the sun. She felt strange. Awful. Like her head was going to explode.

Her husband brought her home. He was very emotional. He had cried in court hearing her testimony. "I never heard the full story of what happened," he told her. He knew her first husband had been murdered. He knew how she had suffered, how she grieved for the tragedy that had befallen her son. But until that day, he had not understood how the bullets had flown past her head and her husband had lain dying in her arms.

When they got back to their house, she retreated to her bed and told herself she had finally gotten what she wanted. "The only thing I asked God—before I die, I want to know who it was. And I got to see that day. It was like a knot that was finally untied."

In a funny bit of timing, around the time of Martinez's California sentencing, as jailers prepared to send him to Florida to stand trial there, Tulare County officials began holding meetings in Earlimart to gather residents' feedback, part of an official county process to update the general plan for the area.

In one sense, this represented huge progress. In the early 1970s, officials had proposed starving communities like Earlimart of services so they would "enter a process of long term, natural decline as residents departed." It hadn't worked out. Earlimart's population had doubled in the intervening years. Now officials wanted to hear residents' ideas for making the town better. The residents' requests—even through the dry, bureaucratic language of the county documents—were a study in deprivation and frustration.[9]

Up the road from Earlimart, Visalia, the Tulare County seat, fielded a minor-league baseball team, an opera, and a symphony. To the east, Exeter, which was only a little bigger than Earlimart, was known for its public art, its gorgeous murals commemorating the valley's agricultural heritage, and was celebrating the opening of its newest French bistro, owned by a chef who hailed from the French Alps and had trained in London.

In Earlimart, the residents packing the veterans hall told county officials they "worried for their safety" and were "very concerned with the rise in shootings and drug-related violence." The three-hundred-page document officials eventually produced about Earlimart underscored other ways the town was, as county planners put it, "severely disadvantaged." Roads weren't maintained. Many streets didn't have sidewalks. There weren't enough streetlights and what streetlights there were had burned-out bulbs. There weren't enough places for children to play. A promised park was behind schedule.

But residents' number one concern was public safety. The sheriff's department, some complained, sometimes took so long to respond to calls that "criminals feel unstoppable in Earlimart."

Sheriff Boudreaux wasn't involved in the community plan update. But he said he was deeply sympathetic to the community's concerns.[10] He had been born and raised in Tulare County. He had followed his father into the sheriff's department and was proud that it was relatively free from the kinds of scandal and corruption that plagued some other valley departments. Since his election, Boudreaux said, he had made it a point to visit farmworker communities often, sometimes handing out gifts accompanied by deputies dressed in holiday costumes to delight children and show them that law enforcement cared. But, he insisted, there was only so much he could do.

"We're trying to put as many cops on the street as we can," he said. But he had a huge, sprawling county to patrol, and although every year he requested a bigger budget, he did not always get the funds he thought he needed. It felt, sometimes, like an uphill battle to convince people they could trust law enforcement and tell what they knew about crimes in their communities.

"Here's what scares me," he said. "What else is out there? This guy went under the radar, right under our noses, for so long."

PART FIVE

The Death Penalty

2018–2019

Every beginning has an ending and it seems like mine has come. Now I have to carry my guilt and the damage I have caused....It's very well known that next to me, the devil was a saint.

—Certified court transcription of "El Mano Negra," a song about the exploits of Jose Martinez

Chapter Thirty-Three

M artinez's mother, brother, and sister sat in his mother's house one Sunday afternoon in the late summer of 2018.

The front room was spotlessly clean and sparsely decorated, with two sofas, a kitchen table, and a television. Grapes, omnipresent in valley farmworker homes during the season, sat in a bowl. Family photos of children, grandchildren, and great-grandchildren smiled down from shelves and the walls. Loreto had come to the Central Valley more than half a century earlier. She had picked America's food. Her family had fought in America's wars, and now many of them were living the American dream. Loreto had come from poverty, but many of the people in her family photos were teachers, nurses, and court and law enforcement professionals. On weekends, they all gathered for baby showers and birthdays, hardened criminals from decades past mixing easily with a younger generation that could not imagine the world they came from.

And then there was Loreto's beloved oldest son, sitting in a Florida jail awaiting a trial in which, if convicted, his penalty could be death.

At Martinez's request, Loreto and other members of the family had agreed to talk to me, but they didn't seem happy about it. In my less than perfect Spanish, I was asking all kinds of questions about their lives, their feelings, what they had and hadn't known. They responded with short, polite answers and long silences. Martinez's double life as a murderer was not something they had an easy explanation for and definitely not something they wanted to hash out with a stranger.

This had always been, as one relative would later explain, a family with "a lot of secrets." They were a self-described "crime family," which necessitated keeping secrets from the authorities. And they also kept secrets from each other in the way that all families do—things not discussed, things evaded.[1]

But no one had any inkling that one of those secrets involved multiple contract killings.

"He was a nice person," Martinez's brother Antonio kept repeating. "A nice person. Never aggressive. A nice person."

"With us he was very noble," said Martinez's oldest sister, telling story after story of things her brother had done for her. Many of those stories spoke to their hardscrabble childhood, none more than the story she told of the time her brother saved her from being sold to the circus.

The children were then living in Mexico. The little kids didn't go to school yet, but Jose and his oldest sister used to walk together down Calle Arteaga, each wearing blue bottoms—pants for Jose, a skirt for Carmen—and white shirts with collars that the nanny starched until they were stiff.

The shirts were no fun. But the walk to school was pleasant enough. Perched high in the Sierra Madre, Cosalá was colorful compared to the dusty beige flatness of the Central Valley; the streets were paved with cobblestones that had first been laid during the time of the Spanish conquistadors in the 1500s, and the houses were painted in bright pinks, yellows, and turquoises. Many of the nicest ones were rumored to be haunted by spirits.

The children had to pass through the center of town, with its church and plaza, to get to the school on the other side. One morning, they saw a troupe setting up a show on the plaza.

"How much for your sister?" one woman asked.

It took Jose a second to understand. His older sister was his constant companion. She bossed him around, laughed at his jokes, and never backed down from a fight. He forgot that other people saw her differently because she was a dwarf. They wanted to buy her and put her in their traveling show.

"Run," he screamed to his sister, pulling her by the hand as they flew through the square.

The oldest sister finished her story and began to weep. The family stared at each other. They had run out of words. Martinez's mother shed a few tears, quietly, like someone who didn't let herself cry very often. One of the few times she smiled that afternoon was when Martinez happened to call from jail. Then her face lit up with joy, and her eyes danced as she talked to him.

Outside the Martinez family's home, something ominous was stirring in the streets and the fields.

Above all, there was fear. Donald Trump was president. He'd campaigned in Tulare County, and big growers—including a well-known pistachio farmer and big players in fruit and cattle—had feted him at a fund-raiser where the cost of one-on-one time with the candidate was $25,000. Shortly thereafter, Trump had courted agricultural interests in the valley by declaring that the state, suffering through its driest four-year period on record, didn't really have a water problem. "It's so ridiculous where they're taking the water and shoving it out to sea," Trump told a crowd in Fresno.[2] Growers, who had long railed against water restrictions imposed to protect endangered species, were delighted.

In farmworker communities, where many were undocumented, Trump's ascension brought nothing but dread. The president talked of building a wall, of sealing the border, of deporting as many immigrants as he could. And to go along with his rhetoric—which felt violent and insulting—agents from Immigration and Customs Enforcement (ICE) seemed to make a show of stepping up sweeps and raids. People were afraid to leave their homes, afraid to send their children to school. In the valley, farmers reported that laborers were so fearful of being deported that they weren't showing up for work. Parents left instructions for their children on what to do if one day they failed to come home.

Then came the knock on the door of Santos Hilario Garcia and Marcelina Garcia Profesto. The couple, who lived with their six children not far from the Martinez family in Delano, were at home on Tuesday afternoon, March 13, 2018, when ICE agents showed up on their doorstep. The agents were seeking someone else, but Marcelina and Santos didn't wait to find out. Afraid of being deported, they got in their car and drove away. ICE agents gave chase, and the Garcias—terrified, driving erratically—crashed their SUV into a utility pole. Both died at the scene.

Four hundred people turned out for the funeral at Our Lady of Guadalupe Church in Delano, the parish church of Cesar Chavez. Among them was United Farm Workers president Arturo Rodriguez. "Marcelina and Santos were not criminals," he told the *Bakersfield Californian.* "They were hard workers who only wanted to provide for their family."[3]

The paper reported that many of the people at the service felt like "they could be next." "A tragedy like this could happen to anyone," Aurelia Talavera told the paper. "They did what they did because of fear."

But many of the young people in the Central Valley, the American-born children of these terrified farmworkers, had a different reaction: they began to mobilize.

Around the time the Garcias died, the University of California (UC) at Santa Cruz announced a groundbreaking new program. It was dubbed the "Central Valley Freedom Summer," in homage to the Freedom Summer that had sent college students to fight for civil rights in the South. Twenty-five UC Santa Cruz and UC Merced students who had grown up in the valley signed up to go back home for the summer to organize their communities to push for change.

Among the participants was a young woman from Richgrove, the same small town southeast of Earlimart where Martinez had lived with his mother and extended family.

Rosanai Paniagua, the daughter of farmworkers, had graduated from high school and then gone to UC Santa Cruz, a secluded campus tucked between the Pacific Ocean and a misty grove of redwoods. Her first year at college had been hard, a double whammy of culture shock and difficult academic demands. She'd felt lonely as one of the few kids of color from the Central Valley among a student body that felt very white and very rich. She'd also felt underprepared for her classes, in part, she said, because she had never been pushed at school in Richgrove.

But eventually she had settled into college, made friends, and grown accustomed to life in a mellow California beach town. And as she did, she came to see the place where she was from with fresh eyes.

Why did farmworkers have to work so hard for so little money? Why didn't her town have a park? Or sidewalks or streetlights? Why was it just accepted that in some towns in Tulare County, you couldn't even drink the tap water in your home? Why did her community have substandard schools? Why were prisons one of the only growth industries? Why did her mother come home from a day in the fields so covered in pesticide dust that she had to change her clothes before she would even let her own children hug her?

"Now I think, why did she even have pesticides on her clothes?" Paniagua said. "I grew up thinking it was normal."[4]

Like many people growing up in these small towns— Richgrove, Earlimart, Delano—Paniagua had also learned to live with a level of violence unthinkable in most of America. She recalled that one of her neighbors had been shot and another held up at gunpoint. No one seemed to think that was extreme or unusual.

At first, as she learned more about the history of her town and others like it—the environmental catastrophes, the lack of services—she felt angry but powerless.

"What could I do? Go to my teachers and scream at them? What is that going to do?"

She studied the history of social movements in the valley with a professor who pushed Paniagua to think critically about where she was from.

"There's people at a table making these decisions," she said. She began to envision the possibility that she, too, might sit at that table one day. That people could make different decisions, if they were persuaded by reason or pressure.

At the end of the Freedom Summer program, another student, Jose Orellana, from Delano, founded an organization, Loud for Tomorrow, dedicated to helping high school students in the area become advocates for their communities. Working with him was a woman named Valerie Gorospe, a professional organizer from the Center for Race, Poverty & the Environment, a Delano-based nonprofit. Gorospe was also the daughter of Teresa De Anda, the Earlimart woman who had organized the town's women to combat pesticide accidents. De Anda had died in 2014—the cause was cancer, which some in the family worried had been caused by pesticide exposure.

Recently, Paniagua had made a decision that would have shocked her only a few years earlier, when she wanted nothing more than to escape the valley. When she finished at UC Santa Cruz, she would return and work for Loud for Tomorrow. She just might start with the school system, to encourage more kids to go to college and to fight for improvements so they would be properly prepared when they get there.

She was part of a small movement. Melissa Morales, the teacher from Earlimart whose father had helped build the swimming pool in response to the violence of the 1980s, was still working in the town's schools. In 2016, she became a principal. She was, by all accounts, a gifted educator. A colleague suggested that her talents could take her far. "You're good," he told her, but for her career to truly blossom, he told her, "you have to leave here for a bigger school district."

"I'm sorry," she responded. "But there's nowhere else for me to go."

And now, she was delighted to see, other young people were following in her footsteps. She hired one former student from her elementary school as a teacher in 2017, another in 2018, and one more in 2019.

Morales had, of course, heard about Martinez's arrest. She had been shocked—he'd always been so polite when she waited on him at the grocery store. But, as always, Morales chose to focus on the positive, on the young people coming back to make the future better. Earlimart, she said, "is in my heart. The person that I am, my happiness…it stems from my community and my school and I want to give back to that."

There were other signs of change in the valley. The anger over Trump's election had spawned dozens of local activist groups, many run by women who had never been politically involved. Congressman Devin Nunes, one of Trump's most reliable supporters, was reelected to represent most of Tulare County, but TJ Cox, who beat the Republican incumbent by fewer than one thousand votes, was elected to represent a district that included

Earlimart.[5] In 2019, Cox held a ceremony to recognize Latino leaders, and among the honorees was Gorospe, the daughter of Teresa De Anda.

Also in 2019, California governor Gavin Newsom signed a new law that aimed to finally bring safe drinking water to small communities in California that didn't have it.[6] Tulare County's poor farmworker communities were ground zero for the problem—more than fifty water systems in the county were out of compliance with state standards.[7] "The idea that we're living in a state with a million people that don't have access to clean, safe, affordable drinking water is a disgrace," the governor said. A few months later, Representative TJ Cox moved to add federal funds to the effort.[8]

And then there was McDonalds. In most places in America, the opening of a new McDonalds might not even be noticed, let alone rejoiced over as a symbol of community advancement. But when the Golden Arches were erected in a strip mall at the north end of Earlimart, the grand opening befitted a new amusement park or a church.[9]

A short time after that, the town of eighty-five hundred people celebrated another long-hoped-for milestone: it got a new park.

Progress? Yes. But also a reminder of how few resources places like Earlimart have—and how far these little towns have to go.

Then another grisly crime story with a Tulare County angle broke. In April 2018, California authorities announced they had arrested the so-called Golden State Killer, a former police officer who had prowled neighborhoods from Sacramento to Orange County in the 1970s and 1980s, raping and killing. His victims—some of them, police said, in Tulare County—were mostly white women. The media went predictably bonkers. Twenty-eight hundred stories mentioned the murderer between 2016 and mid-2019. During the same period, there were fewer than fifty about Jose Martinez, who had, with convincing evidence, claimed to have killed three times as many people.[10]

For some detectives and victims in the Martinez orbit, the Golden State Killer served as yet another reminder of why some lives—and some deaths—mattered more than others. To a remarkable degree, the response to Martinez's confessions had mirrored the response to his crimes: few seemed to care that much.

There wasn't even much of an effort to close all the murders for which he claimed responsibility. After Martinez began confessing, Tim McWhorter, the Alabama detective, dutifully reached out to places where Martinez said he had left bodies, trying to interest detectives in combing through their cold cases. He didn't get a lot of takers, he recalled. One officer in Seattle just laughed at him and said, "Yeah, we've had twenty-five murders in the last six months."[11]

Martinez's confession landed as police departments in the United States were in the middle of an epidemic of unsolved killings. In the last decade, according to research compiled by the *Washington Post*, *BuzzFeed News*, and others, half of all murders failed to lead to an arrest.[12]

But that grim statistic tells only part of the story. In poor communities and communities of color, the solve rate is even worse. The *Washington Post*, crunching numbers from fifty cities, found that an arrest was made 63 percent of the time when the victim was white but only 48 percent of the time when the victim was Latino. (The rate was even lower—46 percent—when the victim was black.) The *Post* looked at urban departments, but there is reason to believe that in rural areas, where Martinez did the vast majority of his killing, the rate can be even lower.

In Kern County, the closure rate for murders from 2010 to 2018 was just 37 percent.[13] This didn't surprise Kavin Brewer, the Kern County homicide detective who worked the Martinez cases. There were weekends, he said, when he picked up three murders one after another. That meant he had to rush, sleepless and hopped up on coffee, from crime scene to crime scene. There was no way to talk to all the witnesses or thoroughly study the scene, let alone do all the other work necessary to close cases.

In 2019, there was one person working to help police close additional Martinez homicides: Martinez himself. Sitting in jail awaiting trial in central Florida, he wrote letter after letter.

Many were to his family, and those were full of loving advice and good wishes for birthdays, anniversaries, and new babies. Others were to homicide detectives around the country, particularly in California. Those letters were often just as polite, but in lieu of loving sentiments, they contained matter-of-fact descriptions of brutal violence he had committed and gotten away with. His goal was not necessarily justice. He was putting into action his plan to get back to California—and to succeed, he had to get charged with more murders.

He wrote to Klassen and confessed to a murder he had earlier denied committing—of a utility worker in the little farm town of Teviston. "I told you that it wasn't me, and you believed me," Martinez wrote. "Well, you want to know the truth? It was me."[14]

Martinez wrote to Brewer too, confessing to two more murders from the 1980s in Kern County. But he hadn't had any response. They didn't have time for cold cases—even with a suspect all but begging to confess. They had too many hot ones.

Martinez's family members, meanwhile, were grappling with their own questions about crime and accountability. Specifically, they were trying to decide how much about their own lives—their family history, their criminal enterprises—to reveal to Martinez's Florida attorneys.

Prosecutors in Tulare County have historically been proponents of the death penalty, and yet they did not seek it for

Martinez. Part of the reason was that without his cooperation, they had little evidence against him, and they wanted closure for the victims. But another reason may have been Florida.

Thanks to Tony Watts and his sharp eye for the Mountain Dew can, Florida actually had DNA evidence, which would make a conviction easier without Martinez's cooperation, should he choose to fight the charges. And prosecutors there seemed almost gleeful about seeking the ultimate punishment. "If we're not seeking the death penalty, you have to question whether it's worth the money," then chief assistant state attorney Ric Ridgeway said about the case.[15]

To save his life, Martinez's Florida attorneys wanted his family to fly out and testify about who he was, where he had come from, and how his background had shaped his life.

Martinez was going on trial. But in a way, so was Earlimart—and the way it and towns like it had always been treated by people in power.

Chapter Thirty-Four

On a Saturday afternoon in June 2019, Martinez called me from his Florida jail cell with a question: "What is a sociopath?"

His death penalty trial was set to start the following Monday, June 10, in Ocala, a sleepy city in the flat middle of central Florida. His lawyers had introduced a motion to prevent prosecutors from uttering the word "sociopath."

Hearing Martinez described that way, his lawyers argued, might prejudice the jury. A judge ultimately ruled to keep the word out of the trial, but through it all no one had explained to Martinez what it meant. When I told him it referred someone who had no conscience and lived outside the rules of society, he responded, "Huh," as if he wasn't quite sure what to make of that.

Ocala, which touts itself as the "horse capital of the world," looks and feels like a typical southern town, circa 1950: two-story buildings, charming but listless in the heat, cluster around a classic town square. Right off the square, the brand-new courthouse—all gleaming glass and modern lines—hulks over the edge of town like a spaceship that has crashed in from the future. During Martinez's trial, the courthouse was full of SWAT team officers, stationed there to make sure Martinez's drug-world associates didn't try to bust him out—or worse, to kill him and others too.

Under Florida law, Martinez's trial would proceed in two phases. First, a jury would determine whether he was guilty of murdering Javier Huerta and Gustavo Olivares-Rivas, the two men left in the truck at the edge of the swamp in 2006. If he was found guilty, then, after hearing more testimony from both the prosecution and the defense, the same jury would decide whether his punishment should be death or life in prison.

After a few days of testimony, it took the jury less than thirty minutes to find Martinez guilty. The verdict came down on the afternoon of June 13, Martinez's fifty-seventh birthday. He took it in stride. "This is like dust on my clothes," he said by phone a few hours later. "I knew it was going to happen."

The penalty phase started the following week. Many in the courtroom were sure the outcome would be a death sentence. Martinez was a self-confessed contract killer—and a Mexican American man facing an almost all-white jury drawn from conservative central Florida. President Donald Trump launched his reelection campaign in nearby Orlando, in the middle of the trial, with a fiery speech denouncing immigration.[1]

The next day, Amy Berndt, a career prosecutor with years of experience in the Marion County District Attorney's Office, made the state's case for executing Martinez, pacing in front of the jury and holding her finger up like a gun as she acted out how Martinez had killed again and again and again.

"You're going to see what he did," she promised the jury, as Martinez sat between his lawyers at a table a few feet away, wearing a soft-gray charcoal suit. He watched impassively, as if not that interested in what she had to say.[2]

Berndt wasn't allowed to tell the jury about every murder to which Martinez had confessed. Only the ones of which he had been convicted. But that was still plenty—she didn't even have time to go through all of them in her opening statement.

When she began telling of the murder of Santiago Perez, how he had been shot in his bed while he slept and how Martinez had pursued romance with his wife, a few members of the jury—who were starting to look numb from the catalogue of death—perked up enough to look visibly shocked.

If the death penalty wasn't appropriate for someone like Martinez, who sometimes laughed as he described the damage his bullets had done, then who was it right for?

As the prosecution laid out its case, current and retired detectives from around the country were in rental cars, streaming north from the Orlando airport to testify about their dealings with Martinez and his murders.

From Tulare County, Christal Derington, Mario Martin, Cesar Fernandez, and Bari Molyneux had all flown in. Of the four, only Molyneux still worked for the Tulare County Sheriff's Department. Kern County homicide detective Kavin Brewer had also come. A Trump fan, he was dismayed that he hadn't been able to go watch the president's speech, which had begun just as his plane landed.

The detectives and their tales of murder flew by in a grisly, awful blur. Art Knight from Santa Barbara, one of the first officers on scene at Silvestre Ayon's shooting, had total recall for the type of tractor Ayon had been riding (a David Brown 770) but couldn't remember Silvestre's name without being prompted. A retired crime scene investigator from Tulare County, testifying about another victim via Skype, was instructed—outside the presence of the jury—not to say a word about "cranial maggots" when he talked about the murder for fear it could unduly prejudice the jury.

One of the first witnesses for the prosecution was not a police officer. It was Cecilia Camacho, wife of Martinez's first victim, David Bedolla. The state of Florida had flown her across the country to tell her story, yet again, in a courtroom in front of the man who had killed her husband. Prosecutors wanted her because the detective who had investigated that murder, Ralph Diaz, had died in 2015. His longtime partner, Jay Salazar, had died a few months later.

Martinez's lawyers objected to having Camacho on the stand. She wasn't a police officer, they pointed out; she was a grieving widow. As the lawyers argued their points, Cecilia sat on a bench against the window outside the courtroom. She wore an olive-colored pantsuit with little white flowers on it. Silver hoops glinted in her ears, her hair was in a bun, and her face was expressionless. A translator sat on one side of her, and her husband sat on the other, his face conveying all the anguish and worry that hers did not.

Finally, Judge Anthony Tatti allowed her to testify. The bailiff called her in, and Cecilia stood up and stepped carefully through the courtroom's double doors. She did not look at Martinez as she walked up to the witness stand. Her husband followed her, then took a seat in the back row of the spectators' benches.

Prosecutors brought out a sepia-tinted black-and-white photograph of a young man with vivid eyes and a handsome face and asked her to identify him.

It was David Bedolla, she answered, in a voice so controlled it hurt to hear. Without emotion, she told the story of her husband's death. After he was shot, he had "whimpered three times and that was the end."

Martinez watched her testimony with what appeared to be detached interest.

Defense attorneys had no questions. Cecilia had flown across the country for less than fifteen minutes of testimony. She and her husband walked slowly out of the courtroom like two people carrying a big burden. They didn't look at the jury or at Martinez.

Prosecutors' pièce de résistance was hours and hours of taped interviews featuring Martinez confessing about murders to many of the detectives who had flown in. On the tapes, Martinez talked with chilling cheer, sometimes even laughing as he made references to zip ties, or bullets to the head, or the intricate ruses he used to lure people into his cars and then to their deaths. The footage was horrifying, despite the sometimes poor quality of antiquated police department audiovisual equipment.

When the last tape came to its scratchy end, the prosecution rested. It was time for Martinez's lawyers to make the case that the jury should spare his life. Not that anyone thought it would do much good. After that display of remorselessness, most people in the courtroom thought Martinez's defense seemed destined to be little more than a formality. What on earth could his lawyers possibly say?

Many of the people sitting on death row in the United States are there, in part, because they had bad lawyers. Lawyers who didn't mount a defense or didn't even bother to make an opening statement to the jury. Lawyers who slept through parts of the trial.[3]

Throughout his long tenure as a killer for hire, Martinez had been lucky. Police had made many mistakes. Failing for years to test the cigarette butt in Florida. Failing to heed the pattern of evidence that kept leading them to his homes. Failing to charge him with murder even when he was the prime suspect.

Now, when he seemed headed for death row, Martinez got lucky again.

His case was assigned to John Spivey, a trial lawyer experienced in capital cases working for a public defender's office that was prepared to spend money on experts and trips to California to interview witnesses. (In fact, the office would spend $578,823.16 on Martinez's defense.[4]) Spivey, a graduate of the University of Arkansas School of Law, had begun his career in the public defender's office in 1991. Even as a young, inexperienced lawyer, he had shown a certain brashness and willingness to advocate furiously on behalf of his clients—even if it earned him mild ridicule in the local newspaper. In one of his first cases, he had tried to get a drunk driver off by arguing that the man wasn't drunk at all but had been bitten by a snake. Why had no snake been found in his car when he was pulled over for drunk driving? Spivey's answer: police had unfortunately then tossed the exculpatory reptile from the car. The ploy, if that's what it was, hadn't worked. The man had been convicted of drunk driving.[5] Spivey had gone on to a successful career as a private defense attorney. By the time he came to represent Martinez, he still had spunk and passion, but now he also had experience as one of the best trial lawyers in central Florida. Along with Spivey, Martinez had three other lawyers and a team that included a trauma expert, a neurologist, a neuropsychiatrist, several psychologists, and a substance abuse expert.

Medical experts—in hours of mind-numbing testimony that sent at least one of the armed guards in the courtroom into a deep and peaceful slumber—made the point that Martinez's brain was irreparably damaged. A trauma expert, Dr. Yenys Castillo, told the jury she had spent twenty-seven hours interviewing Martinez and his family, including his mother, four of his sisters, his former wives, and several of his children. It had been difficult, she told the jury. They had resisted talking to her, cancelled appointments, and given her platitudes and lies, but eventually, she said, she had prevailed. The portrait she came away with would be nothing short of Dickensian, if Charles Dickens had written about farmworkers living in the Central Valley and making frequent visits to rural Mexico.

Then it was time to call the most important witnesses. And they had no expert credentials at all.

On the third Monday of the trial, shortly before the jury was brought into the courtroom, a bailiff handed Martinez a pile of tissues. His family was outside the courtroom. Siblings, children, nieces, and nephews had made the trip from California, and his oldest daughter and her family had come from Alabama. They were there to plead for mercy and to make the case that, as horrifying as his murderous reign had been, he had redeeming qualities and a childhood harrowing enough to warrant consideration.

Martinez's seventeen-year-old granddaughter went first, walking into the courtroom dressed demurely in a fine gray jacket and a white shirt over a skirt. Tears streamed from her eyes, and she sobbed even harder when she made eye contact with her grandfather.

Her testimony was brief: she identified her grandfather, waved at him, wept and wept, and told the jury he would do anything to make her laugh. Her sisters gave similar testimony, talking of his love, of the way he taught them to make grilled cheese sandwiches and took them swimming. As each girl left the courtroom, they waved or blew kisses at their grandfather, who tried to muster a smile. This cold-blooded killer who had so nonchalantly confessed to murder after murder without a twinge of remorse looked stricken—as he never had in front of his victims' families.

His own children came next, two of his daughters and one of his sons. His oldest daughter, from Alabama, sobbed as she took the stand. Since her father's confession she had unequivocally supported him, talking to him on weekly video chats, writing him letters, and not only praying for him but encouraging other members of her church to do so as well. She had deliberately not learned details about the lives he had taken. She wanted to think of him only as her loving father, to remember only the joy he brought to her life.

Through her tears, she told the jury that Martinez was "a great father." He took her to Disneyland and always tried to make her laugh. When he had come to visit her in Alabama, he would wake up early and make breakfast for the whole family. He cleaned. He cooked. He took care of the children. When one of her girls was elected class president, he had a cake made. "I can't imagine not having him," she said.

Martinez's other daughter, a student at California State University at Bakersfield, took the stand, sobbing so hard she could barely take her oath. Her father was always there when she needed him. When she was little, it was lunch at Denny's and constant fun. When she was older, his help was more significant. When she was nineteen, she told the court, she became pregnant and was told her baby had a chromosomal disorder. Her doctor recommended an abortion. Her first call was to her father. She told him she didn't want an abortion. She wanted to put it "in God's hands." When the doctor told her she had to spend the rest of her pregnancy on bed rest, her father drove fifty miles each morning from Richgrove to Bakersfield to spend the day taking care of her and making her laugh while her husband was at work.

And when the baby died in utero, her father took her to Denny's for lunch and then back to the hospital to induce labor to deliver the stillborn baby. Then, in accordance with her wishes, he helped organize a beautiful funeral.

Some of Martinez's other children testified, as did some of his siblings and nieces. They all said a version of the same thing: He is the one who is always there for us. He is the one who takes care of us. He is the one who takes us to the hospital, and who makes us laugh, and who comes up with the money for the emergency expenses.

It was a tender portrait—and a surprising one, given everything the jury had been told about Martinez over the previous few weeks—but it didn't move the courtroom any closer to the central moral question facing the jury: Did anything in Martinez's life explain how this person, who was so kind to his family, so determined to bring them joy, could have become such a monstrous, remorseless killer? And even if something might explain it, how could it possibly be enough to spare him punishment for all the lives he had taken?

Then Martinez's middle sister was called into the courtroom by the bailiff. She was a formidable-looking woman: tall, with a composed expression and intelligent eyes that swept across the room as she walked, taking in her older brother at the defense table and the members of the jury, sitting in judgment on the other side of the room. She set her shoulders as she headed toward the witness box, looking nervous but steely, like a marine heading into battle. She had overcome her family's criminal past to get an education and a job as an interpreter. And now, she was going to reveal it all—the abuse, the secrets, the trauma—to try to save her brother.

Martinez's lawyer began to talk the sister, who was about four years younger than her brother, through the childhood they had shared. In a clear, expressionless voice, she evoked the despair and powerlessness of growing up poor and Mexican American in Earlimart in a family laced with criminality and racked with physical and sexual violence. Her stepfather's Earlimart ranch, sitting windswept and baking in the heat amid the ocean of grape fields, was suddenly conjured in the Florida courtroom.

Going further back in time, she painted a picture of the siblings, young, hungry, and with only each other to rely on in the violent isolation of the town of Cosalá in the Sierra Madre of Sinaloa. "It was a very rough life," she said. In Cosalá, they lived in a house made of mud bricks, with no running water and no electricity. It was, she told the jury, "a very criminal drug town. Major drug cartels. Lots of drugs, killing, kidnapping." Their grandmother was sometimes cruel to them. There wasn't enough to eat. And when the children acted out or tried to steal food, they were beaten.

Martinez's lawyer asked who received the worst abuse.

"My brother," she answered. "He would protect us."

And then, all at once, like a dam breaking, her face crumpled, and she began to cry. The composure that had enveloped her up until that point made this all the more shocking.

"Excuse me," she said.

The jury waited, transfixed. When she had collected herself, Martinez's sister continued.

She told about how her brother would steal food for them in Mexico and climb trees to shake down mangos for them to eat. And about how, once the children came back to California, her parents had split up and her mother had married Pedro Fernandez. They had moved to his ranch, and she had watched her brother get pushed into the drug business, distributing drugs to various dealers even though he wasn't even old enough to have a driver's license.

And then—crying again—she told of how she had been assaulted and molested by the ranch hands. She had tried to kill herself. Her brother Antonio had seen the marks and, as the siblings did when they were in trouble, gone straight to Jose for a solution.

Her brother put a stop to the molestations. She wasn't sure how. "Those men left the ranch."

She related how Martinez had rescued her once again, a few years later, when she had fallen into a relationship with an abusive man. He came and took her to safety.

And she told how devastated and depressed Martinez had been when he found out that their older half sister had been raped and murdered and he had been unable to save her.

"He's been more than a brother," she said. "I'm alive because of him. He took beatings for us. He fed us. He saved me from killing myself, from feeling useless."

If he were to get the death penalty, she said, "it would destroy me."

The courtroom was silent as she walked out.

The jury began deliberations the next afternoon and came back two hours later with a verdict.

No death penalty.

Behind Martinez in the courtroom's gallery, his oldest daughter began to weep with joy. The verdict was the will of God, she said, adding that she was "sorry to every single person my dad has caused suffering. I'm sorry on his behalf. I hope they can find peace."

Judge Anthony Tatti sentenced Martinez to two life terms in Florida, on top of his life terms in California and the fifty-year sentence he had received in Alabama. The judge offered Martinez the chance to say something. Martinez declined to say a word.

Chapter Thirty-Five

I came home to California and wrote a news story about Martinez's trial. After it ran, as always happened when I published anything about his case, a heartbreaking query landed in my inbox. The specifics varied, but the gist was always the same: Someone they loved had been murdered or gone missing in the Central Valley. The authorities didn't seem to care. Could I help them find out what had happened to their loved one, find some semblance of justice or peace?

I never could.

The local media in Tulare County, as I had come to expect, took little notice of the shocking outcome in the trial of the county's homegrown contract killer. I couldn't find a story about it in any of the valley's newspapers, which, like local papers across the country, had shrunk to skeleton staffs.[1] One of the deadliest killers in American history, a man who had terrorized farmworker communities for decades, had avoided execution, and no one seemed to care.

The detectives who had spent years chasing Jose Martinez were dismayed and outraged by the Florida jury's decision to spare his life—but not surprised that no one took note. "Maybe he'll be lucky and run into one of the relatives of the victims" in prison, mused one detective.

Detective Kavin Brewer was so shocked that the jury had shown mercy for this killer that he was moved to a rare burst of sarcasm. "Dang, if he would have killed forty"—just a few more bodies—"he would have gotten a toaster oven."

Brewer was close to retirement but still working too hard. It was shaping up to be another violent summer in the San Joaquin Valley. Among those killed, one afternoon in July 2019, was one of Martinez's close associates. He was gunned down in broad daylight in a rural area on the border between Delano and Earlimart.

As dismal as the public murder statistics were, Brewer feared the real numbers were even worse. It sometimes seemed like every time a farmer plowed a fallow field, another body turned up. Some of them could not be identified. Few had been reported missing. So many were farmworkers far from home or, lately, undocumented men drafted to work in illegal marijuana-growing operations in the nearby forests. When they disappeared, no one even knew where to look.

Cecilia Camacho had left Florida by the time the jury voted to spare Martinez's life. Her family was shocked, but Cecilia, as usual, was stoic. Whatever the verdict was, it wasn't going to bring her dead husband back.

In a bid to bring Martinez to justice, she had relived the worst day of her life in courtrooms in Florida and California. She had hoped that authorities, perhaps grateful for her courage when so few were willing to come forward or perhaps in recognition of the terrible wrong done to her family, might have given her some assistance. At one point, they had said something about a fund to compensate victims—such money would come in handy. She still desperately needed help bringing her oldest child, David Bedolla's son, who had been deported, home to California.

Still, she did not regret her decision to bear public witness to the violence and the injustices that Martinez had done to her. Seeing him in court and making a formal record of his crimes had given her "a little closure"—a feeling that her story and her pain mattered.

After she had walked out of that courtroom into the steaming Florida heat, her second husband at her side, the couple had taken a few days to enjoy themselves, sitting by the pool and going out to dinner. It was the first trip they had ever taken together without children or other family obligations. It was a bizarre sort of vacation, to be sure, but it left them feeling lighter, more connected with each other, more deeply in love.

Now Cecilia was back in the valley with her family. She had retired from picking oranges. Her diabetes and her arthritis bothered her, but she had a husband who doted on her, three daughters who lived nearby, and grandchildren she adored.

Like Rosanai Paniagua from Richgrove, Melissa Morales from Earlimart, and all the former students Morales had hired as teachers, Cecilia's daughters were part of a generation that had the potential to transform the valley: children of farmworkers getting an education and then coming home to make their communities better, more just. Cecilia's oldest daughter, Fidelia, taught in a local elementary school, trying to ensure that young people had more opportunity than their parents. In the school where she taught, 95 percent of the students lived in poverty. Cecilia's two other daughters were in college. One aspired to a career in agriculture.

That terrified young woman was still inside Cecilia, the one who had dodged an assassin's bullets and then hurtled through a vineyard in the predawn darkness, who had cradled her dying husband, held back her tears, and wondered whether she would be able to feed her son. But so was the woman who had stood her ground against senseless violence, suspicious police, and deep injustice, who had become an American and made sure her daughters achieved the American dream. Despite it all, Cecilia's days were full of the joys of a life well lived.

Acknowledgments

I am indebted, above all, to the people—named and unnamed—who trusted me with their stories. Families whose loved ones were murdered told me of the toll it took and shared memories even when it was painful. Detectives took time away from their busy jobs to go over details from crimes that were years or decades in the past. Members of the Martinez family shared their stories, even when their natural inclination was toward privacy. In Earlimart and Richgrove, people patiently put up with my questions about their towns.

This book was born out of an article for *BuzzFeed News*. Editor Ben Smith supported that reporting with unbelievable resources and incisive editorial suggestions. Mark Schoofs, my former boss on the BuzzFeed News Investigations Desk, originally agreed to let me write "a quick feature" about the Martinez case and then sent me back for more reporting again and again. Heidi Blake gave crucial support at times when I needed it most. Ariel Kaminer, who now runs BuzzFeed News Investigations, has magical powers that make my prose sharper than it has any right to be and is an unfailingly brilliant and generous editor and friend. My colleague Ken Bensinger read this book and the original story and offered key reporting advice and sharp editorial suggestions on both. Jeremy Singer-Vine patiently talked me through crime and census data sets, then cheerfully did it again when it became sadly apparent I hadn't grasped it the first time. Thanks also to my wonderful colleagues Melissa Segura, Kendall Taggart, Aram Roston, Mat Honan, Caroline O'Donovan, and Chris Hamby.

I first heard of the Martinez case when I was an editor and reporter at the *Los Angeles Times*, and many of my former colleagues at that wonderful newspaper contributed generously to the process of reporting and writing this book. Jack Leonard and Joel Rubin provided key background on policing in California. Diana Marcum and Mark Arax shared their wealth of knowledge about the San Joaquin Valley. Jill Leovy was a resource on murder, writing, and lots of topics in between. Shelby Grad, the paper's metro editor, was an indefatigable voice of encouragement and also delivered some important straight talk. Julie Marquis, my former editor, read an early version of the manuscript and offered an incisive critique, then followed it up with a fantastic pep talk as I stood in the rain in a parking lot in central Florida. Miriam Pawel, who hired me at the *Los Angeles Times* and has since written several books on California history and the United Farm Workers, was so generous with her time, knowledge, and editing chops that the only way I can ever repay her is to pay it forward.

Several friends also read part or all of the manuscript. I'm grateful to Reyna Grande for her close read and tough questions. To Laura Wides-Munoz for the same. Thanks, also, to Julie Sze, Suju Vijayan, Ofelia Cuevas, Harriet Ryan, Anna Gorman, Lara Bazelon, Leticia Garza, Susie Neilson, Hugo Lindgren, Hans Tobeason, and Sam Nicholson. Deep gratitude goes to Courtney Everts Mykytyn, who spent countless hours listening to me talk about this project, and who put me up in her beautiful home on reporting trips to Los Angeles. Courtney was killed in an accident as this book was being finished, in a tremendous loss for me and for the many, many people whose lives she touched.

At Hachette, Krishan Trotman guided this project with brilliance and enthusiasm, offering structural suggestions that were so simple and so inspired that I remain in a state of awe. Carrie

Napolitano manages to make every paragraph she touches better. Michael Clark shepherded this book, and me, through the production process with patience, unbelievable cheer, and a keen eye. Jen Kelland is a copy editor extraordinaire, and Robin Bilardello and Marie Mundaca made it look beautiful. And as always, thanks to my agent, the calm and wise Katherine Flynn.

My biggest thanks to my family. My mother brought dinner on many a hectic Monday night so I could sneak in some more work. My wonderful mother-in-law and father-in-law helped make travel possible and picked up several chapters' worth of carpool duty. And most of all, thanks to my husband, Michael, who read drafts, listened to me babble, and makes it all possible.

A Note on Sources

The Devil's Harvest is an attempt to situate a true crime narrative within the larger social, cultural, and historical context of its setting, the southern part of California's Central Valley from the 1970s to the present.

The story of Jose Martinez's murders and the impact those crimes had on his victims' families, the police officers who chased him, and his own family is drawn almost entirely from my interviews, conducted in person and over the telephone between 2016 and 2019, and from court records, trial transcripts, and other primary source documents obtained through public records requests.

I sought out everyone I could find who was involved in this story, including witnesses, relatives of victims, every living law enforcement official who had substantial dealings with Martinez, and members of Martinez's family. Some were happy to tell their stories; others refused. Some who talked were happy to do so on the record, with their names attached, and some would speak only on background. Many members of Martinez's large extended family asked not to be identified by name in this book, a request I granted to protect their privacy or because they feared association with his crimes could put them at risk or complicate their lives. To better understand the history and context of this crime story, I also interviewed numerous people in the communities of Earlimart and Richgrove about life in those towns and how it has changed from the time Martinez was a child to the present day.

To conduct these interviews, I flew to Alabama and Florida and made numerous trips to Tulare and Kern Counties. In almost all cases, these in-person interviews were the beginning of a relationship that led to dozens of follow-up phone and text conversations.

Jose Martinez himself has attempted to provide a complete accounting not only of most of his crimes but of his entire life story—with one crucial exception: he flatly refused to talk about who hired him, either with me or with police. I met with Martinez once in person in the Marion County jail in Florida and spoke to him numerous times on the telephone. I also sent him questions via letter, which he answered in letters of his own. He also arranged for me to review his handwritten autobiography. Starting in June 2013, Martinez also gave a number of lengthy confessions to officers across the country. Many of those conversations were recorded, and I have obtained tapes and transcripts.

Many of the events in this account took place decades ago, and memories fade. Whenever possible, I have sought to corroborate the recollections of interview subjects with police reports about the incidents in question and, when they existed, with contemporaneous newspaper accounts. I have also attempted, as with any reporting project, to check people's stories against each other and the documentary record. In cases where there are discrepancies among accounts, I have tried to determine which seems most accurate and to indicate the discrepancies in the text or in the notes that appear at the end of this book.

In California, where Martinez committed the bulk of the murders for which he has been convicted, unredacted police reports are generally exempt from public disclosure. But Martinez also committed murders in Florida, and at the request of prosecutors there, California officials sent along thousands of pages of their investigative files, which became part of the official case record in that state. Because Florida has among the most open public records laws in the United States, I was able to obtain California's reports via the Florida State Attorney's Office. Perhaps because they were never intended to become public, many of these reports are remarkably vibrant. Some are scrawled in longhand, and some are so descriptive that they detail not just whom detectives interviewed on any given day but what they ate for lunch afterward (and if they were on the road, how much they billed the county for the meal).

Still, despite my best efforts, a few of the events recounted in this book are based on a single source with no definitive corroboration. For example, Martinez claims to have committed several murders around the United States for which he has never been charged. In three cases, I was able to identify unsolved murders that hew closely to Martinez's recollection of places, dates, and patterns. But that correlation is by no means proof that Martinez committed the crimes.

In addition to interviews and documents related directly or indirectly to Martinez's case, this book also draws on extensive archival research on the history of Kern and Tulare Counties, the farmworker movement led by Cesar Chavez, and the town of Earlimart. I relied on materials stored in the History Room at the Tulare County Library in Visalia and on tapes and interviews of the Farmworker Documentation Project, now housed at the library of the University of California, San Diego. I also read hundreds of articles from the *Tulare Advance Register* and the *Visalia Times-Delta* from the 1960s, 1970s, and 1980s, an invaluable resource and a sad reminder of how vibrant local newspapers used to be and how much they have been diminished in so many parts of California and the United States.

Unless otherwise indicated in the text or notes, all the quotes in the book are from my interviews, from my notes from trial testimony that I witnessed firsthand, or from my review of official police interviews or transcripts. In most cases where there is dialogue between two people that I did not witness and that is not recorded in an official record, that dialogue is drawn from one person's memory but has been corroborated with contemporaneous notes or with the other person in the conversation. Important exceptions to this rule are the conversations Martinez said he had with his victims before he murdered them. On this, we have only his word.

Notes

INTRODUCTION

1. The geography of the interior of California can be tricky even for natives. The Central Valley stretches almost the length of the state, 450 miles from Shasta County and the Cascade Mountains and Trinity Alps in the north to the Tehachapi Mountains in the south. The Sierra Nevada forms the eastern border, and the coastal range, the western. The northern part of the Central Valley, from Sacramento to Shasta, is called the Sacramento Valley, while the southern part is referred to as the San Joaquin Valley. Further confusing matters, some refer to the southern part of the San Joaquin Valley as the Tulare Basin.

2. According to the United States Geological Survey, the Central Valley produces one-quarter of the nation's food, including 40 percent of the nation's fruits and nuts. More than 250 different crops are grown in the valley, with an estimated value of $17 billion a year.

3. "Income Inequality and the Safety Net in California," Report from the Public Policy Institute of California, May 2016.

4. For a sense of some of the valley's biggest growers, see Mark Arax and Rick Wartzman, *The King of California: J. G. Boswell and the Making of a Secret American Empire* (New York: PublicAffairs, 2003); Mark Arax, "A Kingdom from Dust," *California Sunday Magazine,* February 2018, https://www.california sunday.com/issues/2018-02-04. The details about en suite bathrooms and infinity pools come from the author's review of real estate listings.

5. Jonathan London et al., "The Struggle for Water Justice in California's San Joaquin Valley: A Focus on Disadvantaged Unincorporated Communities," UC Davis Center for Regional Change, February 2018.

6. The correct Spanish would be *La Mano Negra*, but Martinez preferred *El Mano Negra*. He also writes his name without accent marks.

7. All quotes from Cecilia Camacho are from the author's interviews with her. The only exceptions are her statements in court, which are drawn from transcripts of the proceedings or the author's courtroom notes. Whenever possible, her memories of events from 1980 and 1981 have been corroborated with contemporaneous reports from the Tulare County Sheriff's Department.

CHAPTER ONE

1. Martinez's account of his early life is drawn primarily from his own writings and from discussions with the author. Certain aspects of his family history—such as life on his stepfather's ranch and drug smuggling that took place there—were also the subject of newspaper reports from the 1970s and of court testimony in various cases reviewed or witnessed by the author. Family members also offered their own accounts in discussions with the author. Quotations from the 1980s, unless otherwise indicated as being sourced elsewhere, are drawn from Martinez's recollections.

2. This is all according to Martinez. His first wife was not interviewed.

3. Any number of accounts have chronicled the disputes between then governor Ronald Reagan and farmworkers. Even half a century later, the subject came up during journalist Jose Gaspar's interviews on the fiftieth anniversary of the grape strike. Jose Gaspar, "50 Years Later, Delano Grape Strike Changed Labor History," *KBAK Bakersfield*, September 21, 2015.

4. The "Dust Bowl" migration is another area of history that has been written about by numerous sources. One account is University of Washington professor James N. Gregory's *American Exodus: The Dust Bowl Migration and Okie Culture in California* (New York: Oxford University Press, 1989).

5. Hal Moore, "Mexican Connection: The Key Link for Heroin," *San Diego Union Tribune*, March 14, 1976.

6. The Martinez children's time in Cosalá was described by Martinez in his memoir and in conversations with the author. His siblings also discussed their time in Cosalá in sworn court testimony in Florida. For background

on the history of the drug business in Sinaloa and Durango, I am indebted to numerous newspaper accounts, as well as the work of Benjamin Smith, a professor of Latin American history at the University of Warwick, and his equally generous colleague Nathaniel Morris.

7. The life and work of Chavez, Huerta, and the UFW have been well documented in any number of sources. I am particularly indebted to John Gregory Dunne, *Delano: The Story of the California Grape Strike* (New York: Farrar, Straus & Giroux, 1967), as well as two books by Miriam Pawel, *The Crusades of Cesar Chavez* (New York: Bloomsbury Press, 2014), and *The Union of Their Dreams* (New York: Bloomsbury Press, 2009). I am even more indebted to Pawel herself, who was generous with her knowledge and time.

8. This violence was covered in newspapers across the country. It was also documented in photographs, many of which are available for view on the website of the Farmworker Movement Documentation Project, compiled by LeRoy Chatfield and housed at the library of the University of California, San Diego (https://libraries.ucsd.edu/farmworkermovement).

9. *Tulare Advance Register*, September 1, 1980, 1.

CHAPTER TWO

1. This account of the murder is drawn from the recollections of Cecilia Camacho, from the Tulare County Sheriff's Department's reports on the crime, and from Martinez's official confessions and his recollections.

2. This encounter was related by Cecilia Camacho in an interview in 2018 and also recounted in police notes of their interviews with the Good Samaritans on the day of the shooting.

3. The most famous of the guest-worker programs is the Bracero Program, which was intended to fill labor shortages during World War II. Other programs include the H-2A program, which has recently surged in popularity among growers in California.

4. US Department of Homeland Security, Immigration Statistics, Table 39, https://www.dhs.gov/immigration-statistics/yearbook/2017/table39.

5. Carey McWilliams, *California: The Great Exception* (New York: Current Books, 1949), 150.

6. Cited in ibid., 151.
7. Douglas S. Massey and Karin A. Press, "Unintended Consequences of US Immigration Policy," *Population and Development Review* 38, no. 1 (2012): 1–29.
8. *Tulare Advance Register*, September 1, 1980, 10.

CHAPTER THREE

1. Martinez's siblings discussed this in testimony during their brother's murder trial, *State of Florida v. Jose Martinez*, June 2019, and also in one case in interviews with the author.
2. *State of Florida v. Jose Martinez*, author's notes of trial testimony, June 2019.
3. *State of Florida v. Jose Martinez*, author's notes of trial testimony from Martinez's sister, June 26, 2019.
4. Ralph Diaz could not give his account of this investigation. He died in 2015 after a long and celebrated career. His family declined to talk about him. Many of his former colleagues from Tulare County and around the state did share their recollections. Diaz was also the subject of numerous newspaper articles, including his obituary.
5. The *Tulare Advance Register* (February 23, 1973, 1) reported that the department had just 9 Mexican American officers among a staff of 182. Sheriff Bob Wiley, a proponent of hiring more Mexican American officers, spoke out about his intention to do so.
6. This conversation is as recalled by Cecilia Camacho. Colleagues of Ralph Diaz also recall him telling them in general terms about initially hearing suspicions about Cecilia, but those suspicions were not documented in his police reports, or if they were, they were removed before the reports were released to the author.

CHAPTER FIVE

1. Victor Geraci, *Salud: The Rise of Santa Barbara's Wine Industry* (Reno: University of Nevada Press, 2004).

2. Jean Charles Sarri, interview with the author.

3. From witness accounts of the party, contained in Santa Barbara Sheriff's Department, Case Number 4-82-01101.

4. "Trial Ordered for Two," *Tulare Advance Register*, May 1, 1981, 6.

5. I am grateful to many retired law enforcement officers, from both local and federal agencies, who talked to me about drug smuggling in the valley in the 1970s and 1980s.

6. "Haven't We Outgrown the Old Style Politics?," *Tulare Advance Register*, May 28, 1986, 12.

7. The rise of the Guadalajara Cartel is reported in rich detail in Elaine Shannon's *Desperados: Latin Drug Lords, U.S. Lawmen, and the War America Can't Win* (New York: Viking, 1988). The book also details the kidnapping and murder of DEA agent Enrique "Kiki" Camarena, who was murdered in Mexico in 1985. Before he was transferred to Mexico, Camarena was assigned to the DEA's Fresno office, where he worked with a number of the officers who arrested Pedro Fernandez and who would go on to chase Martinez. Among them was Detective Ralph Diaz.

8. This portrait of Martinez as family oriented is drawn from interviews with family members and from the sworn testimony of several family members in *State of Florida v. Jose Martinez* in June 2019.

9. The photographer and historian Richard Steven Street chronicled Huron in an essay and photographic project, "Knife Fight City: The Poorest Town in California," *Peace Review* 12, no. 2 (2000).

CHAPTER SIX

1. These thoughts were recorded in Martinez's unpublished memoir.

2. From Martinez's unpublished memoir.

3. Art Knight trial testimony in *State of Florida v. Jose Martinez*, June 19, 2019.

4. Karen White, "Last of Detective Trio Retires," *Santa Maria Times*, June 17, 2002.

CHAPTER SEVEN

1. This account of the murder is drawn from Martinez's autobiography and corroborated by police reports from Santa Barbara County, Case Number 4-82-01101, and from interviews and trial testimony from detectives. The quotes from Denny's are as Martinez recalled them in his memoir.

2. Tulare County General Plan update 1971, cited in Michelle Wilde Anderson, "Cities Inside Out: Race, Poverty, and Exclusion at the Urban Fringe," *UCLA Law Review* 55, no. 1095 (2008): footnote 182.

3. Mark Arax, *The Dreamt Land: Chasing Water and Dust Across California* (New York: Knopf, 2019), 224.

4. The San Joaquin Valley newspapers in the early 1890s were full of the exploits of the "Dalton gang," brothers who robbed a train in Alila and then proceeded to have a court case full of twists and turns. See, for example, a wire story, "The Reward for the Dalton Gang Will Be Paid," which ran in the *Daily Delta*, October 8, 1892, 1.

5. Santa Barbara County Sheriff's Department, Case Number 4-82-01101.

CHAPTER EIGHT

1. Miriam Pawel, *The Crusades of Cesar Chavez* (New York: Bloomsbury Press, 2014), 141.

2. The Sierra Vista Labor Camp was an ongoing saga in the newspapers in the early 1980s. See Julie Fernandez, "New Hearing Asked for Delano Boxcars," *Tulare Advance Register*, February 25, 1982, 4, and David Watson, "Tear It Down," *Tulare Advance Register*, August 3, 1983, 1.

3. Martinez's account of Raul Gonzalez's murder is drawn from his unpublished memoir and from transcripts of his confessions; it is corroborated by contemporaneous police reports from 1982. The conversation between Martinez and Gonzalez is as remembered by Martinez.

CHAPTER NINE

1. This account of the interaction between Diaz and Martinez is drawn entirely from Martinez's recollections in his unpublished memoir and interviews with the author. There were no notes about it in the Tulare County Sheriff's Department case file on the Raul Gonzalez murder, although some detectives who worked with Diaz had vague recollections of hearing about it.
2. "Two Held in Man's Slaying," *Tulare Advance Register*, October 20, 1982, 5.
3. Santa Barbara County Sheriff's Department, Case Number 4-82-01101.
4. David Watson, "Murder in Earlimart Becoming Routine," *Tulare Advance Register*, November 10, 1982, 1.
5. Ibid.

CHAPTER TEN

1. John Gregory Dunne, *Delano: The Story of the California Grape Strike* (New York: Farrar, Straus & Giroux, 1967), 86.
2. "An Examination of Violence in the Farm Labor Dispute," California Assembly Select Committee on Farm Labor Violence, October 2, 1972.
3. "UFW Pickets Battle Deputies," *United Press International*, August 8, 1973.
4. This account of the Santa Barbara detectives' foray into Tulare County was drawn from their police reports from the 1980s and from the author's interviews with Detective Bruce Correll.
5. Carolyn van Schaik, "A Peaceful March to Protest Violence," *Tulare Advance Register*, December 4, 1982, 1.
6. The account of how the Earlimart Youth Foundation came together to build a pool and other facilities is drawn from interviews and from numerous articles in the *Tulare Advance Register*, including Logen Molen, "Earlimart Voters OK Pool, Gym," *Tulare Advance Register*, February 26, 1986, 1, and Felicia Cousart, "Earlimart Schools Await the Verdict," *Tulare Advance Register*, March 13, 1985, 3.
7. Story drawn from the author's interviews with Melissa Morales.

CHAPTER ELEVEN

1. All the conversations in this chapter between Martinez and the man he said he kidnapped are as recollected by Martinez in his unpublished memoir.
2. Jenifer Warren, "Mysterious Cancer Clusters Leave Anxiety in 3 Towns," *Los Angeles Times*, July 12, 1992, 1.
3. Associated Press, "McFarland Cancer Bill Is Vetoed," *Tulare Advance Register*, October 1, 1988, 1.
4. This is according to Martinez, in his unpublished memoir.
5. This section is based on Cecilia Camacho's interview with the author.

CHAPTER TWELVE

1. The events in this chapter are based on the recollections of Jose Martinez as related in his memoir and in interviews with the author and, when possible, corroborated by interviews with other members of his family. All quotes are as recollected by Martinez.
2. Twin Falls Sheriff's Office, Case Number 9070, reviewed by the author. The author obtained open unsolved murder cases from Twin Falls from the early 1980s that appeared to match Martinez's dates and patterns. This case fit.
3. Testimony in *State of Florida v. Jose Martinez*, penalty phase of trial, June 2019.
4. The split between Martinez and his wife is as recalled in Martinez's memoir, corroborated in part by the recollections and trial testimony of other family members. Martinez's wife was not interviewed by the author.
5. Family members testified at trial in the *State of Florida v. Jose Martinez*, June 2019, about going with Martinez to retrieve his daughter.

CHAPTER THIRTEEN

1. Santa Barbara County Sheriff's Department, Case Number 4-82-01101.
2. Bruce Correll, interview with the author.
3. The story of this period in Martinez's life—during which, he reported, he spent a great deal of time in Yuma—is based on his recollections as recounted in his memoir and in interviews with the author. Other members of the Martinez family recall him spending time in Yuma but could not corroborate all the details of his recollections.
4. This conversation is based on Martinez's recollections. The woman, who became Martinez's second wife, was not interviewed by the author.
5. The story of this episode in Martinez's life is also based solely on his recollections.

CHAPTER FOURTEEN

1. Nancy Morse, "Man to Stand Trial for 1982 SY Murder," *Santa Maria Times*, May 7, 1991, 1.
2. The Santa Barbara detectives' visit to Pelican Bay is recounted in their police reports. Correll also shared his recollections of this visit with the author. All quotes are either recounted in the police reports or as remembered by Correll.

CHAPTER FIFTEEN

1. Nancy Morse, "Action on Murder Case Held Up," *Santa Maria Times*, September 5, 1991, 1.
2. Ibid.
3. Karen Holz, "Suspect Must Stand Trial in 82 Slaying," *Santa Maria Times*, April 2, 1992, 1.
4. Ibid.

CHAPTER SEVENTEEN

1. This account of the murder of Domingo Perez is drawn from Martinez's memoir and from his interviews with the author and his taped confessions to police officers.

2. These details are drawn from Tulare County Sheriff's Department, Case Numbers 95-5552 and 95-7963, the missing persons and murder cases involving Domingo Perez.

3. Quoted in Gustavo Arrellano, "Prop 187 Forced a Generation to Put Fear Aside and Fight," *Los Angeles Times*, October 29, 2019, 1.

4. "Crime Trends in California," Public Policy Institute of California, October 2018, https://www.ppic.org/publication/crime-trends-in-california, and "Crime Rates in Urban and Rural California," California Department of Justice, Division of Criminal Justice Information Services, December 1997.

5. Jana Ballinger, "Sheriff Candidates Debate Police-Minority Relations," *Tulare Advance Register*, May 9, 1994, A1.

6. Associated Press, September 3, 1991.

7. Cary J. Rudman and John Berthelsen, "An Analysis of the California Department of Corrections' Planning Process: Strategies to Reduce the Cost of Incarcerating State Prisoners." California State Assembly Office of Research, 1991, via Ruth Wilson Gilmore, *Golden Gulag: Prisons, Surplus, Crisis, and Opposition In Globalizing California* (Berkeley: University of California Press, 2007).

8. Ruth Wilson Gilmore, *Golden Gulag: Prisons, Surplus, Crisis and Opposition in Globalizing California* (Berkeley: University of California Press, 2007), 129.

CHAPTER EIGHTEEN

1. The account of Martinez's time in Alaska is based upon his recollections in his memoir and interviews with the author.

2. Martinez's second wife was not interviewed for this book.

CHAPTER NINETEEN

1. From "In Her Own Words: Remembering Teresa De Anda, Pesticide Activist," compiled from an oral history interview by Tracy Perkins, assistant professor of sociology, Howard University.
2. Ibid.
3. Amee Thompson, "Residents Sickened by Pesticides Unable to Meet with Supervisors," *Tulare Advance Register*, December 9, 1999, 1.
4. Miriam Pawel, *The Crusades of Cesar Chavez* (New York: Bloomsbury Press, 2014), 457–459.
5. Ibid., 471.
6. From "In Her Own Words."
7. Ibid.
8. Amee M. Thompson, "Residents Angry About How Situation Was Handled," *Visalia Times-Delta*, December 9, 1999, 1.
9. From Martinez's account of this murder, in statements to police and in interviews with the author.
10. The woman with the long dark hair was not interviewed for this book.

CHAPTER TWENTY

1. The children's statements to police are included in Tulare County Sheriff's Department, Case Number 00-2564.
2. Ibid.
3. This version of events comes from Martinez's unpublished memoir.
4. Tulare County Sheriff's Department, Case Number 00-2564.
5. *The People v. Kenneth Ray Neal*, in the California Supreme Court, opinion number S106440, July 14, 2003.
6. Ibid.
7. Superior Court transcripts cited in *The People v. Kenneth Ray Neal*, in the California Court of Appeal, Fifth District, case number F036055, April 2, 2002 (unpublished opinion).

8. Maura Dolan, "Police Are Rebuked on Miranda," *Los Angeles Times*, July 15, 2003, 1.

9. Amee Thompson, "Earlimart Residents to Meet with Supervisors," *Tulare Advance Register*, February 15, 2000, 1.

10. Staff reports, *Tulare Advance Register*, May 31, 2000.

11. Staff reports, *Tulare Advance Register*, September 22, 2000.

12. Melissa Morales, interview with the author.

13. From Martinez's unpublished memoir and interviews with the author.

14. Martinez's children with his second wife testified to this at trial in *State of Florida v. Jose Martinez*.

15. US Department of Justice, Central Valley High Intensity Drug Trafficking Area Report, 2007.

16. Ray Winter, "New Factories in the Field," *Boom California*, March 21, 2012.

17. Martinez, in letters to the author, insists that his family members exaggerated his drug use during their trial testimony in *State of Florida v. Jose Martinez* in a bid to get the jury to spare his life.

18. The story of De Anda's work in Arvin was told in "In Her Own Words: Remembering Teresa De Anda, Pesticide Activist," compiled from an oral history interview by Tracy Perkins, assistant professor of sociology, Howard University.

19. Ann Simmons, "Plaintiffs Win Damages in Pesticide Suit," *Los Angeles Times*, November 25, 2005, online.

CHAPTER TWENTY-ONE

1. The account of the murder is as recalled by Martinez in interviews with the author, from his memoir, and from transcripts of his interviews with police. It is corroborated, where possible, by interviews with detectives from the Marion County Sheriff's Office in Marion County, Florida, and by Marion County Sheriff's Office, Case Number 06054530. All quotations between Martinez and his victims are as recalled by Martinez.

2. This account of the investigation is based on interviews with former Marion County Sheriff's detective T. J. Watts and Marion County Sheriff's Office, Case Number 06054530.

3. Martinez's first arrest was in Tulare County in December 1974, when he

was twelve years old. A 2015 California probation report shows that he was convicted more than a dozen times as an adult, including several times after California's DNA-collection law went into effect. "Report and Recommendation of the Probation Officer," October 27, 2015, in *People of the State of California v. Jose Manuel Martinez*, Case Number VCF297873.

CHAPTER TWENTY-TWO

1. David Castellon, "Gang Wars," *Visalia Times-Delta*, March 3, 2007, 1.
2. Jon Swaine and Oliver Laughland, "The County of America's Deadliest Police," *Guardian*, December 1, 2015.
3. Murder Accountability Project data for Kern County Sheriff's Department, 2009–2018, based on the FBI's Supplementary Homicide Report.
4. Kavin Brewer recounted his dealings with Martinez and his victims and the story of his own career in interviews with the author.
5. This is Martinez's recollection of his interactions with his parole officer. The officer, through her attorney and her employer, declined to comment on any aspect of the case, including whether she believed Martinez's recollections were accurate. All dialogue is as recalled by Martinez.
6. Testimony from family members in *State of Florida v. Jose Martinez*, June 2019.
7. Kai Ryssdal, "Stockton: America's Foreclosure Capital," National Public Radio, July 25, 2008; J. N. Sbranti, "Valley Counties Ranked 234 in the Nation for Foreclosures," *Modesto Bee*, March 13, 2008.
8. This account is based on Martinez's recollections of his conversations with his parole agent.

CHAPTER TWENTY-THREE

1. This account of the murder is based on Martinez's recollections in his memoir, in interviews with the author, and in transcripts of his confessions to police. It is corroborated, to a great extent, by police reports.

2. The account of the police investigation of Barragan's death is drawn from Tulare County Sheriff's Report #09-00012309 and from interviews with numerous members of the Tulare County Sheriff's Department.

3. Detective Cesar Fernandez declined interview requests for this book. This account is drawn from his police reports of the incident, which were obtained by the author.

4. This account of the arrest is based on Martinez's recollections, corroborated by Tulare County Sheriff's Department reports.

CHAPTER TWENTY-FOUR

1. Michael Doyle, "Where's Recession Really Bad? California's San Joaquin Valley," McClatchy Newspapers, June 17, 2009.

2. Diana Marcum, "Wars Take a Heavy Toll on One California School," *Los Angeles Times*, July 31, 2010, 1.

3. The account of the police investigation was drawn from the Tulare County Sheriff's Department, Case Number 11-00001708, as well as from transcripts of police interviews with Martinez and from Martinez's recollections in his memoir and in interviews with the author.

4. From Tulare County Sheriff's Department, Case Number 11-00001708.

5. Detective Bari Molyneux declined to be interviewed for this book.

6. Kern County Superior Court, Case Number DF010807A. Filed May 30, 2012, and dismissed on October 15, 2012.

7. Anne Burleson, "Days Later, McFarland PD Explains Chase, Shooting," *Bakersfield Californian*, July 27, 2012.

8. "Former McFarland Police Sergeant Pleads No Contest in ID Theft Case," *Bakersfield Now*, April 20, 2016.

9. Laurence Du Sault and Katey Rusch, "'Second Chance PD': One California Town's History of Hiring Cops with Troubled Pasts," *Sacramento Bee*, November 11, 2019, https://www.sacbee.com/news/investigations/article237090084.html.

10. Matt Hamilton, "Bakersfield Detective Pleads Guilty to Bribery, Drug Possession," *Los Angeles Times*, June 1, 2016. Online.

11. Joe Moore, "Kern Deputies Accept Plea Deals in Drug, Corruption Investigation," *Valley Public Radio*, May 9, 2017.

12. Marion County Sheriff's Office, Case Number 06054530.

13. Watts in interviews with the author and pursuant to the author's observations of Watts.

CHAPTER TWENTY-FIVE

1. Martinez's daughter, interview with the author.

2. The account of the murder is as recalled by Jose Martinez in interviews and from his memoir, and from interviews with Lawrence County Sheriff's detectives.

CHAPTER TWENTY-SIX

1. The account of the investigation of Ruiz's murder is based on the author's interviews with Detective Tim McWhorter and other members of the Lawrence County Sheriff's Department, as well as a review of some reports from the Lawrence County Sheriff's Office.

CHAPTER TWENTY-SEVEN

1. Martinez's account of his arrest in Earlimart in 2013 is based on his interviews with the author, his memoir, and a review of subsequent transcripts of his interviews with detectives. All quotes are as recalled by Martinez, corroborated when possible with members of the Tulare County Sheriff's Department.

2. Christal Derington gave some limited interviews to the author about the Martinez case in 2017 while working for the Tulare County Sheriff's Department but has declined additional requests to talk about the case.

3. This account is based on a review of Marion County Sheriff's Office, Case Number 06054530, and the author's interviews with Watts.

CHAPTER TWENTY-EIGHT

1. This account is based on the author's interviews (conducted separately) with McWhorter, Burke, and Watts and corroborated by Marion County Sheriff's Office, Case Number 06054530, and a review of some reports from the Lawrence County [Alabama] Sheriff's Office.

2. The source for this exchange is the author's interviews with Burke and McWhorter.

CHAPTER TWENTY-NINE

1. All quotes in this section are derived from a tape and transcript of the interview between Sergeant Christal Derington and Jose Martinez, conducted on June 5, 2013, in Moulton, Alabama, and reviewed by the author. The transcript was filed in *State of Florida v. Jose Martinez*, Case Number 2013-CF-1870; the tape was obtained by the author.

CHAPTER THIRTY

1. Austin L. Miller, "MCSO: 2006 Double Slaying Solved: Suspect Admits Killing More Than 30," *Ocala Star Banner*, June 12, 2013.

2. This conversation is as recalled by Martinez in interviews with the author. All quotes are as recalled by Martinez.

3. This interaction is based on the author's review of an audiotape of the police interview, as well as the author's interview with Detective Rodney Klassen.

4. All quotes in this section are derived from a tape and transcript of the interview between Sergeant Christal Derington, Lieutenant Scott Logue, and Jose Martinez, conducted on June 19, 2013, in Mouton, Alabama. The transcript was filed in *State of Florida v. Jose Martinez*, Case Number 2013-CF-1870; the tape was obtained by

the author. In addition, the author interviewed Scott Logue about the exchange.

CHAPTER THIRTY-ONE

1. Author's interview with Cecilia Camacho.

2. Diana Marcum, Scott Gold, and Melissa Gerber, "Arrest Brings a Tale of a String of Slayings," *Los Angeles Times*, April 10, 2014, 1.

3. According to a Nexis search, the *Visalia Times-Delta* didn't write a story about Jose Martinez and his murders until Tulare officials held their own news conference in the spring of 2014—nine months after Martinez began confessing.

CHAPTER THIRTY-TWO

1. Lewis Griswold, "Former Tulare County Deputy Who Sexually Assaulted Female Drivers Gets Five Year Sentence," *Fresno Bee*, January 13, 2016.

2. *Alma M. v. William Nulick et al.*, civil complaint, Case Number 1:15-CV01386, filed September 10, 2015, in the Eastern District of California. Page 5 of the complaint indicates that the county was served with a claim for damages on March 4, 2014.

3. Lewis Griswold, "Five Women to Get $2.2 Million to Settle Sexual Assaults by Sheriff's Deputy," *Fresno Bee*, March 16, 2017.

4. "News Serves Candidates, Not Public," *Visalia Times Delta*, April 8, 2014, page 1.

5. Sheriff Mike Boudreaux, interview with the author.

6. As noted in previous chapters, Derington declined to speak in depth about this case. This account of their conversation is drawn from Martinez's recollections and also from the recollections of other Tulare County officers.

7. Boudreaux, interview with the author.

8. From the author's review of a tape of the interview between Martinez and James Dickey.

9. "Earlimart Community Plan Update 2017," from the Tulare County

Resource Management Agency, Economic Development and Planning Branch, adopted October 17, 2017, by the Tulare County Board of Supervisors.

10.   Boudreaux, interview with the author.

CHAPTER THIRTY-THREE

1.   Family members talked about their propensity for secrets during the penalty phase of Jose Martinez's Florida trial. *State of Florida v. Jose Martinez*, testimony during the week of June 23, 2019.

2.   "Trump Tells California There Is No Drought," Associated Press, May 28, 2016.

3.   Steven Mayer, "Couple Who Fled ICE Mourned at Delano Service," Bakersfield.com, April 2, 2018, https://www.bakersfield.com/news/couple -who-fled-ice-mourned-at-delano-service/article_f05fbb46-36ab-11e8-9 fa0-fbb557dbe5bc.html.

4.   Rosanai Paniagua, interview with the author.

5.   Miriam Pawel, "Inside the Fight to Turn Red California Blue," *New York Times*, November 7, 2018; Rory Appleton, "How Did TJ Cox Erase a 25-Point Primary Loss to Become the Valley's Next Congressman?," *Fresno Bee*, December 12, 2018.

6.   Kerry Klein, "Newsom Establishes Long-Term Safe and Affordable Drinking Water Fund," *Valley Public Radio*, July 25, 2019.

7.   Joshua Yeager, "Toxic Taps Abound in Rural Tulare County, Bond Brings No Relief," *Visalia Times-Delta*, November 13, 2018.

8.   Joshua Yeager, "Rep. T.J. Cox Says It's Time for Feds to 'Step Up' to Drinking Water Crisis, Announces $100M Bill," *Visalia Times-Delta*, December 3, 2019.

9.   "Earlimart McDonalds Grand Opening—Tulare County," posted to You-Tube by Tulare County Film Commission, May 17, 2016, https://www .youtube.com/watch?v=8wZGsoDTYKQ.

10.   These facts are according to Nexis searches run by the author.

11.   Tim McWhorter, interview with the author.

12.   "Murder with Impunity," a series by the *Washington Post*, published throughout 2018 and posted on the paper's website on January 7, 2019;

Sarah Ryley, Jeremy Singer-Vine, and Sean Campbell, "Shoot Someone in a Major U.S. City and Odds Are You'll Get Away with It," *Buzzfeed News*, January 24, 2019.

13. Murder Accountability Project data for Kern County Sheriff's Department, 2009–2018, based on the FBI's Supplementary Homicide Report.

14. Letter reviewed by the author.

15. Nicki Gorney, "Self-Confessed Cartel Hitman Jose Martinez Will Return to Florida," *Gainesville Sun*, November 11, 2015.

CHAPTER THIRTY-FOUR

1. Maggie Haberman, Annie Karni, and Michael D. Shear, "Trump, at Rally in Florida, Kicks Off His 2020 Re-election Bid," *New York Times*, June 18, 2019.

2. From the author's notes while observing the trial in *State of Florida v. Jose Martinez*, Case Number 2013-CF-1870.

3. There are numerous studies on this point. One such is from Brian Stull, "Good and Bad Lawyers Determine Who Lives and Who Dies," ACLU Capital Punishment Project, March 10, 2010.

4. According to John Spivey, via email with the author, December 2019.

5. Background on John Spivey came from interviews with the author and from news stories such as Jim Runnels, "Jury Doesn't Bite, Convicts DUI Suspect," *Orlando Sentinel*, November 16, 1991, 47.

CHAPTER THIRTY-FIVE

1. Nexis search by the author.

Bibliography

BOOKS

Arax, Mark. *The Dreamt Land: Chasing Water and Dust Across California.* New York: Knopf, 2019.

Arax, Mark, and Rick Wartzman. *The King of California: J. G. Boswell and the Making of a Secret American Empire.* New York: PublicAffairs, 2003.

Dunne, John Gregory. *Delano: The Story of the California Grape Strike.* New York: Farrar, Straus & Giroux, 1967.

Gilmore, Ruth Wilson. *Golden Gulag: Prisons, Surplus, Crisis, and Opposition in Globalizing California.* Berkeley: University of California Press, 2007.

Gregory, James N. *American Exodus: The Dust Bowl Migration and Okie Culture in California.* New York: Oxford University Press, 1989.

Grillo, Ioan. *El Narco: Inside Mexico's Criminal Insurgency.* New York: Bloomsbury, 2011.

Leovy, Jill. *Ghettoside.* New York: Spiegel and Grau, 2015.

Martinez, Jose Manuel. "Autobiography." Unpublished manuscript. Completed in 2018.

McWilliams, Carey. *California: The Great Exception.* New York: Current Books, 1949.

———. *Factories in the Field.* Boston: Little, Brown and Company, 1939.

Olmsted, Kathryn. *Right Out of California.* New York: New Press, 2015.

Pawel, Miriam. *The Crusades of Cesar Chavez.* New York: Bloomsbury Press, 2014.

———. *The Union of Their Dreams.* New York: Bloomsbury Press, 2009.

Shannon, Elaine. *Desperados.* New York: Viking, 1988.

Steinbeck, John. *The Grapes of Wrath.* New York: Penguin Classics, 1992.

ARTICLES, WEBSITES, AND COURT FILES

Anderson, Michelle Wilde. "Cities Inside Out: Race, Poverty, and Exclusion at the Urban Fringe." *UCLA Law Review* 55, no. 1095 (2008).

Farmworker Movement Documentation Project. "Cesar Chavez: The Farmworker Movement: 1962–1993." https://libraries.ucsd.edu/farmworkermovement.

Matthiessen, Peter. "Organizer." *New Yorker.* June 13, 1969.

People of the State of California v. Jose Manuel Martinez, VCF 297873.

State of Florida v. Jose Martinez, case number 2013-CF-1870.

Tulare Advance Register archives.

Visalia Times-Delta archives.

INTERVIEWS

The author interviewed more than one hundred people for this book. Select interviews are listed here, in order of appearance in the book.

Jose Martinez, interviewed numerous times between 2016 and 2019
Cecilia Camacho, 2018 and 2019
Loreto Fernandez, 2018
Jean Charles Sarri, 2019
Select siblings of Jose Martinez, 2018 and 2019
Select children of Jose Martinez, 2016 to 2019
Bruce Correll, 2018 and 2019
Melissa Morales, 2019
Scott Logue, 2017 to 2019
Kavin Brewer, 2017 to 2019
Valerie Gorospe, 2019
Asenneth Moreno, 2017 to 2019
Tony Watts, 2017 to 2019
Tim McWhorter, 2017 to 2019
Bill Burke, 2019
Christal Derington, 2017
Rodney Klassen, 2019
Mike Boudreaux, 2019
Rosanai Paniagua, 2019